HOW BRITAIN VOTES

Pergamon Titles of Related Interest

BAILEY, R.
The European Connection: Britain's Relationship with
The European Community

BENYON, J.
Scarman and After: Essays Reflecting on Lord Scarman's
Report, The Riots and Their Aftermath

CARTER, L.
Contemporary Constitutional Lawmaking: The Supreme
Court and the Art of Politics

DAVIS, E.
Changing Federal Budget

HART, J.
The Presidential Branch

MOSLEY, R. K.
Westminster Workshop: A Student's Guide to British
Government, 5th edition

HOW BRITAIN VOTES

Anthony Heath, Roger Jowell and **John Curtice**

with the assistance of **Julia Field** and **Clarissa Levine**

PERGAMON PRESS

Oxford · New York · Toronto · Sydney · Frankfurt

U.K.	Pergamon Press Ltd., Headington Hill Hall, Oxford OX3 0BW, England
U.S.A.	Pergamon Press Inc., Maxwell House, Fairview Park, Elmsford, New York 10523, U.S.A.
CANADA	Pergamon Press Canada Ltd., Suite 104, 150 Consumers Road, Willowdale, Ontario M2J 1P9, Canada
AUSTRALIA	Pergamon Press (Aust.) Pty. Ltd., P.O. Box 544, Potts Point, N.S.W. 2011, Australia
FEDERAL REPUBLIC OF GERMANY	Pergamon Press GmbH, Hammerweg 6, D-6242 Kronberg, Federal Republic of Germany
JAPAN	Pergamon Press Ltd., 8th Floor, Matsuoka Central Building, 1-7-1 Nishishinjuku, Shinjuku-ku, Tokyo 160, Japan
BRAZIL	Pergamon Editora Ltda., Rua Eça de Queiros, 346, CEP 04011, São Paulo, Brazil
PEOPLE'S REPUBLIC OF CHINA	Pergamon Press, Qianmen Hotel, Beijing, People's Republic of China

First edition 1985
Reprinted 1985 (twice)

Library of Congress Cataloging in Publication Data
Heath, A. F. (Anthony Francis)
How Britain Votes.
1. Elections — Great Britain. 2. Voting —
Great Britain. 3. Great Britain — Politics and
government — 1945– . I. Jowell, Roger.
II. Curtice, John. III. Title.
JN956.H39   1985   324.241'0858   85-12098

British Library Cataloguing in Publication Data
Heath, Anthony
How Britain Votes.
1. Great Britain. *Parliament* — Elections, 1983
2. Voting — Great Britain — History — 20th
century
I. Title   II. Jowell, Roger III. Curtice, John
324.941'0858   JN956
ISBN 0–08–031859–2 (Harcover)
ISBN 0–08–032647–1 (Flexicover)

Printed in Great Britain by Hazell Watson & Viney Ltd., Aylesbury.

To Eleanor, Marco, Oliver and Ruth

Contents

Tables and Diagrams

Tables labelled "N" appear in the notes following each chapter

Preface

This study of the 1983 British General Election has been a collaborative venture in a number of ways. First, the project has been located jointly within two institutions — the University of Oxford and Social and Community Planning Research (SCPR). In contrast with previous election studies in which 'political science' concerns have been distinguished and divorced from 'survey' concerns, we have in this case regarded them as inseparable and have, we believe, been richly rewarded by doing so. Second, this book has been a collaborative venture between a sociologist (Anthony Heath), a political scientist (John Curtice) and a social survey specialist (Roger Jowell). We have thus tried to draw upon the strengths of a variety of academic traditions and to break down some of the disciplinary barriers that we believe have impeded the development of social and political science in the past.

Third, the study has been funded collaboratively. The Economic and Social Research Council (ESRC), Pergamon Press and Jesus College, Oxford have each given us substantial support. We are especially grateful to Robert Maxwell at Pergamon Press whose timely and generous intervention enabled the ESRC to enter into a joint-funding arrangement. We are greatly indebted to him and to Michael Posner (then Chairman of the ESRC) for the support they gave to our initiative, and to Jesus College for its subsequent gesture in providing additional funds. As a result, despite initial doubts that a study of the 1983 election would be funded, we have been able to continue a series of studies that now spans the last seven general elections.

The series was started by David Butler and Donald Stokes in 1963 and continued by Ivor Crewe, Bo Sarlvik, James Alt and David Robertson at the University of Essex during the 1970s. It is the longest series of nationally representative academic social surveys in Britain and has produced distinguished contributions to political science not only from the original project directors but also from many other scholars, in this country and abroad, who have reanalysed the data. Our data set too has now been deposited in the ESRC Data Archive at the University of

Essex, so we expect and hope that others will use it to draw further conclusions and to challenge some of ours.

Our debts are many. First, while we are responsible for the contents of this book, the British General Election Study Team included Julia Field (SCPR) and Clarissa Levine (Department of Social and Administrative Studies). We cannot blame them for the interpretations we have put upon the data, but we must emphasise that they took an equal share in the execution of the project. We cannot thank them too much for their work and dedication.

Second, for their support or advice at various stages of the project, we would particularly like to thank Eric Batstone, Hugh Berrington, David Butler, Peter Clifford, Ivor Crewe, Frank Dobson, Jack Donaldson, John Goldthorpe, Chelly Halsey, Nevil Johnson, Denise Lievesley, Kenneth Macdonald, David McKie, David Miles, Geraint Parry, Clive Payne, John Ridge, David Robertson, Chris Rootes, Richard Topf, Jennifer Waterton and Hugo Young.

We are also indebted to a number of institutions. We are grateful to SCPR for its efficient conduct of the survey, for contributing its director's time on the project, and to the many people within that organisation whose advice and skills played so great a part in maintaining the project's momentum. We must thank Jesus College for administering the study, the Department of Social and Administrative Studies at the University of Oxford for providing a home and research support for the analysis of the data set, Nuffield College, Oxford for giving us access to its unrivalled library facilities, and the Department of Political Theory and Institutions at the University of Liverpool for enabling John Curtice to spend a large amount of time on the project after he moved there. And we must also thank the ESRC Data Archive at the University of Essex, and the previous election study teams, for making available the data sets of the earlier surveys in the series.

A project as large as this, initiated, as it turned out, only after the election was called but still committed to producing a book more quickly than its predecessors, inevitably makes heavy demands not only upon the directors but also their families. Their help, encouragement and tolerance throughout the last twenty months has been invaluable.

Finally, we are, as always, indebted to the army of interviewers and coders upon whose care and diligence we have once again relied so heavily. But above all we must thank our respondents for their time and cooperation. We hope that some of them will read and enjoy this book and feel that their participation in our research has helped to illuminate how Britain votes.

AFH
RMJ
JKC
March 1985

Chapter 1

The 1983 General Election

On the surface the British general election of 9th June 1983 was a rather ordinary, even dull, affair. In contrast with the 'surprise' outcomes in June 1970 and February 1974, when the polls and commentators had contrived to pick the wrong winners, this time everyone (or almost everyone) got it right. The Conservative party duly won the election handsomely and confirmed its hold on power. By the time of the next election in, say, 1987 the Conservative party will have reasserted its claim to be Britain's natural party of government, having held power for twenty-five of the forty-two postwar years.

But in other respects the 1983 election was a rather remarkable one. The formation of the Social Democratic Party, its Alliance with the Liberals, and their greatly increased share of the vote seemed to mark the end of the 'two-party politics' that had dominated the postwar period. The Alliance just failed to beat Labour into third place overall, but in individual constituencies it had many more second places than Labour. Labour had its worst result for fifty years and its prospects of regaining power looked slight.

This book is based primarily on a study of the 1983 election. It is, however, an attempt to look beneath the surface, to examine the most recent election in the context of previous elections, and to uncover the social and political origins of electoral change. Our principal source of material is a major survey of the electorate that we carried out immediately after the 1983 election, but we have supplemented this material by reanalysing the results of similar studies of the previous six general elections. (The technical details of these surveys are described in the appendices to this volume.) We have thus been able to investigate trends in electoral attitudes and behaviour and can make some judgements about the parties' electoral prospects. We do not pretend that there can be clear answers to the questions about the future of British politics, but by uncovering the sources of change we can better understand the possibilities.

The Election Result

As table 1.1 shows, the scale of the Conservative victory was dramatic. It secured half as many votes again as its nearest rival, the Labour party. This ratio of six Conservative votes to every four Labour votes cast was greater than that achieved by the governing party over the chief opposition party at any election since 1931. The resulting margin of 144 seats over all other parties in the House of Commons was larger than any achieved since the Labour victory of 1945. The result has properly been described as a landslide.

TABLE 1.1 1983 British General Election Result

	Votes	Percentage	Change in percentage since 1979	Seats
Conservative	13 012 316	42.4	−1.5	397
Labour	8 456 934	27.6	−9.4	209
Social Democratic Party/ Liberal Alliance	7 780 949	25.4	+11.6	23
Scottish National Party	331 975	1.1	−0.5	2
Plaid Cymru	125 309	0.4	−0.0	2
Others (Great Britain)	198 729	0.6	−0.5	0
Others (Northern Ireland)	764 925	2.5	+0.3	17
Turnout	30 671 137	72.7	−3.3	

Source: Craig (1984)

On the other hand, although the margin of victory was impressive, the total level of support won by the Conservatives was not particularly high. Only Bonar Law in 1922 (38 per cent) and Harold Wilson in October 1974 (39 per cent) have been asked to form majority governments this century with a lower share of the popular vote for their parties. Indeed, Margaret Thatcher's Conservatives won the 1983 election with a smaller proportion of the total vote than that achieved by Sir Alec Douglas Home's Conservatives when they lost power to Labour in 1964. In ten of the eighteen elections since the emergence of the present party structure in 1922, the Conservative party won a larger share of the vote than Mrs Thatcher's Conservatives managed in 1983.

Still, the Conservatives did more or less maintain the share of the vote that they had won in May 1979. In contrast the Labour party lost a quarter of its vote and suffered a larger fall in its share than any party had suffered since 1945 (when the

TABLE 1.2 Share of the Vote 1922–1983

	Conservative	Labour (percentages)	Liberal	Others
1922	38.5	29.7	18.9	12.9
1923	38.0	30.7	29.7	1.6
1924	46.8	33.3	17.8	2.1
1929	38.1	37.1	23.6	1.2
1931	55.0	30.8	6.5	7.7
1935	47.7	38.0	6.7	7.5
1945	36.2	48.0	9.0	6.8
1950	43.5	46.1	9.1	1.3
1951	48.0	48.8	2.6	0.6
1955	49.7	46.4	2.7	1.2
1959	49.3	43.9	5.9	0.9
1964	43.4	44.1	11.2	1.3
1966	41.9	48.1	8.5	1.5
1970	46.4	43.1	7.5	3.0
February 1974	37.9	37.2	19.3	5.6
October 1974	35.8	39.2	18.3	6.7
1979	43.9	37.0	13.8	5.3
1983	42.4	27.6	25.4	4.6

Sources: 1922–1979 Craig (1981); 1983 Butler and Kavanagh (1984)

Conservative party also lost a quarter of its vote). It achieved fewer votes per candidate than it had done since the party was formed in 1900. Its share of the overall vote was lower than it had been since 1918. Fewer Labour MPs were elected to the Commons than at any time since 1935.

The 1983 election was also remarkable for the challenge it posed to the long-standing and overwhelming dominance of the Conservative and Labour parties within British electoral politics. The newly-formed Alliance between the Liberal party and the Social Democratic Party, contesting its first general election, succeeded in winning the largest share of the vote achieved by a third party since 1923. Although the operation of the British electoral system meant that the number of seats won by the Alliance was very modest, it was still larger than any number accumulated by the Liberals alone since 1931. The Alliance fell short of achieving its declared aim of 'breaking the mould' of British politics, but it succeeded nonetheless in breaking the habits of many former Labour and Conservative voters.[1]

The 1983 election also came at the end of five years of (by British standards) rather remarkable political change. In late 1978 Mr Callaghan appeared to have every chance of winning the next election, but he delayed going to the country and, in the event, Labour went down to a heavy defeat. Within six months of the 1979 election however Labour had pulled ahead in the opinion polls and continued to increase its lead until the end of 1980, when its support reached 50 per cent. At that time the 1980s seemed likely to see a continuation of the pattern established during the 1960s and 1970s of fairly rapid alternations of political power between the Conservative and Labour parties.

But in the wake of its 1979 election defeat the perennial philosophical differences within the Labour party had begun to develop into deep conflicts.[2] These came to a head at a special conference in January 1981. The conference confirmed a decision made the previous autumn to alter the party's constitution: the party leadership was no longer to be elected solely by the parliamentary party but instead by an electoral college in which the trades unions were to have 40 per cent of the votes while the parliamentary party and the constituencies were each to have 30 per cent.

That decision was followed by the most serious split in British party politics since 1931. Although by that time a split in the party was probably inevitable, regardless of the outcome of the special conference, it was the constitutional change that determined the timing for three prominent Labour leaders (David Owen, William Rodgers and Shirley Williams — all recent ministers in James Callaghan's government) to resign from the party and, together with former Labour Deputy Leader Roy Jenkins, to set up the new Social Democratic Party.[3]

Even after the split, the Labour party remained in internal turmoil as Tony Benn challenged Dennis Healey for the Deputy Leadership under the new constitutional procedure. Moreover, with unemployment rising relentlessly, the Conservative government was also losing support and by the summer of 1981, the new Alliance had filled the vacuum. That autumn it achieved some spectacular by-election successes and took the lead in the opinion polls. It remained in front until the Argentinian occupation of the Falkland Islands on 31st March 1982.[4]

According to many commentators at the time, the Falklands occupation was designed by the Argentinian military government as a diversion from domestic political problems. Ironically it turned out that way instead for the British government. Whereas the previous autumn Margaret Thatcher had been the most unpopular Prime Minister in the (admittedly short) history of British political polling, by the end of the conflict in June she was seen as a triumphant and resolute national leader. At the same time the Conservative party had recovered its popularity to lead Labour by well over 10 percentage points — a position that proved to be unassailable in the year that remained until the 1983 election. The Alliance slipped into third place and never quite recovered its momentum.

So, within the short period from the beginning of 1981 to the middle of 1982 Britain had witnessed two apparently momentous political events. A new third party, or more properly a third force comprising two parties, had emerged as a serious contender for sharing power in Britain. And a major military adventure, not experienced since the Suez crisis nearly thirty years earlier, had transformed the Prime Minister's image from that of an unpopular, even unsuccessful, party leader into that of a national leader of considerable and apparently enduring stature.

Political Explanations

During the four years of Conservative tenure, then, each of the three major parties had for a time captured the support of the electorate. But to give a narrative of the events is not to explain them. The fact that the Alliance moved ahead in the opinion polls after the split with Labour and the formation of the Social Democratic Party does not, on its own, explain why the Alliance managed a larger share of the vote in 1983 than the Liberals had managed for sixty years. It is quite conceivable that the Liberals would have done well without any assistance from the SDP. After all, they had been increasing their share of the vote, albeit unsteadily, ever since their nadir of 2 per cent of the poll in 1951. Perhaps they would have capitalized on dissatisfaction with Labour's internal wrangling and with the Conservatives' unemployment policies even if the Labour party had stayed intact. And there were of course some Liberals who, perhaps for this very reason, had argued that the Social Democratic Party should have been 'strangled at birth' (the comment of Cyril Smith, Liberal MP for Rochdale).

Similarly, although the Conservatives slumped in the opinion polls after their victory in 1979, and recovered only after the Falklands war in 1982, we cannot conclude that the Conservative party would not have won without the Falklands victory. By the end of its term of office the Conservative government had other achievements to show, notably the control of inflation.[5] And while unemployment continued ever higher, it could certainly be argued that inflation, not unemployment, was the greater threat to potential Conservative voters. After all, Conservative unpopularity in the first few years of its term of office coincided with a particularly high rate of inflation. It may be, therefore, that high unemployment damages a Labour government's popularity with its supporters, but high inflation does more to damage a Conservative government.

There is plenty of evidence too from the history of opinion polling that government popularity tends to decline after winning office, reaches its trough mid-term, but then recovers as the election draws nearer. Diagram 1.3 shows this rather clearly with the 1955, 1959, 1966 and 1974 governments.

DIAGRAM 1.3 Party Popularity 1950–1983

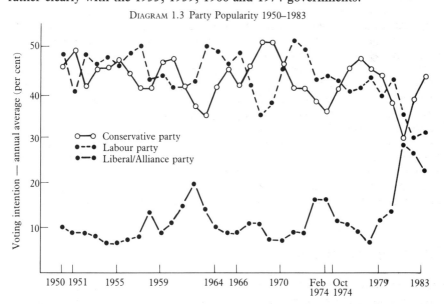

Source: Gallup Political Index Reports

A mid-term opinion poll (or by-election) gives the electorate a chance to comment on the government's handling of the nation's affairs. It is a chance for protest or applause. It does not necessarily have much to do with the next general election. Opinion polls ask people "If there were a general election tomorrow, which party would you support?" [if don't know] "Which would you be most inclined to vote for?" but we should be cautious in our interpretation of such hypothetical questions. If there really were a general election tomorrow, people would be likely to have given the question some thought; their answers are therefore likely to be a good measure of their voting intentions. But many people will not have any voting intentions mid-term, and we cannot measure what does not exist.

Our guess is that mid-term opinion polls measure how well people think the government is managing. However, as we shall show in the course of this book, it would be a dangerous over-simplification to imagine that a general election result is purely a verdict on the government's handling of the nation's affairs. There are deep ideological divisions that separate the Labour and Conservative parties, and when people vote in a general election they are not only saying whether the government has done a good job but also what kind of government they want. They are voting for competing philosophies not just selecting competing teams of managers.

These more enduring differences of belief seem to reassert themselves at general elections. The Conservative supporter who believes in free enterprise, private education and a property-owning democracy may enjoy the luxury of a mid-term protest, as with Shirley Williams' spectacular by-election victory for the Social Democratic Party in traditionally Conservative Crosby, but no-one should be surprised that the deeper ideological differences reasserted themselves in the 1983 general election.

On this account the major puzzle is why Labour failed to recover its popularity as the election drew nearer. (Indeed, its support actually fell further during the election campaign.) What had happened to the Labour supporters who believe in greater equality, the welfare state and government intervention to secure full employment? Constitutional wrangling can perhaps account for Labour's mid-term unpopularity. But it does not explain why Labour's potential supporters did not rally to the cause as the election approached and another five years of Conservative government with high rates of unemployment looked more and more probable.

Two rather different explanations have been suggested. First, it has been argued by some commentators that, although the electorate favoured Labour's policies on unemployment, their other policies such as those on nuclear disarmament were far too left wing for the electorate's tastes.[6] On this account Labour fought the election on the wrong policies. It failed to recover its share of the vote because it had moved too far to the left. Its policies were now out of line with the views of a large fraction of its previous supporters. So if Labour is to have any hope of winning in future, it was said, the party must reoccupy the centre ground.

An alternative view is that there was a 'credibility gap', a widespread doubt whether Labour could successfully implement its programme.[7] It was not policies but performance that was in question. In support of such a view commentators could point to the public disagreements between Labour leaders on defence policy in the course of the campaign itself. Internal dissension, it is said, undermined people's confidence in the Labour party as an effective government.

These sorts of question do not have simple or unequivocal answers. We can never be sure what would have happened if Argentina had not invaded, if the Social Democratic Party had not been formed, if the Labour leadership had not been divided. But our evidence is, we believe, interesting enough to report without over-interpretation or embellishment.

Sociological Explanations

In any case, our aim is not simply to provide political explanations of the 1983 election result. The series of election studies from 1964 to 1983 gives us an unrivalled opportunity to look at the changing social bases of British political parties. While social change, which takes place relatively slowly, cannot account for sudden political upheavals such as the nine point drop in Labour's share of the vote, it can nonetheless offer us important clues to the long-run prospects of the parties.

It is a standard assumption of political science that, to be viable in the long run, a party needs a definite social base. Such a base may be a religious or ethnic group, a geographical region, or a social class.[8] True, a party will obtain many of its votes from outside its social base, but unless it represents a distinct social group and advances its interests, a party is unlikely to acquire the activists, the funds and the organisation needed for long-run viability.

This is clearly of some significance for the Social Democratic and Liberal parties. The view of most previous commentators has been that the Liberal vote was essentially a protest vote, a vote of disaffection from the two established parties which represent Britain's two main social classes.[9] The implication is that the large Alliance vote in 1983 was the product of transient disagreements with Labour and Conservative and that many of these voters are likely to revert to their 'natural' parties representing their respective social classes.

Past research certainly suggests that the Liberal vote had little in the way of a distinctive social base and was much more transient than the Labour or Conservative vote. If we wish to ask about the future of British politics, a central question must therefore be how far this transient character of Liberal voting remains true of the Alliance. Is there an alternative social base which would permit the establishment of an enduring 'third force' in British politics? Without it, hopes of 'breaking the mould' are surely unrealistic.

The conventional picture of British society suggests a negative answer. Regional differences provide a basis for (statistically) minor parties such as Plaid Cymru, the Scottish National Party, and the Ulster Unionists, but the dominant social divisions in Britain are those of social class. Most commentators adopt a two-class model of class structure which neatly fits the two-party political system. There is, on this view, no room for a major third party.

We shall show, however, that the two-class model is grossly oversimplified. While Labour may fairly be described as the party of the working class, to say that the Conservatives are the party of the middle class is to misunderstand the nature both of Conservatism and of the middle class. There is, as we shall show, a section of the middle class that can be identified as a political base for the Alliance.

But while the two-class, two-party model has dominated British political science, most commentators have agreed that class, both as a social and a political force, has been steadily declining in Britain.[10] Rising levels of affluence and the break-up of traditional communities are held to have eroded class solidarity. Labour in particular, it is said, can no longer rely on working-class support in the way that it could a generation ago, and the new breed of affluent skilled manual workers in the South of England are believed to have swung decisively to the Conservatives. The spread of home-ownership in the working class exacerbates the trend. Such changes in the character of the working class are held to explain why a left-wing ideology can no longer win the working-class vote.

The withering away of class, if true, would have quite serious implications for the future of the political parties. It would suggest that a more volatile period was likely to follow in which no party could be sure of its share of the vote. However, the evidence that class has withered away is very thin. Indeed, it has largely been inferred from the political volatility of the last twenty years rather than the other way round. We are sceptical whether the social changes have been quite so far-reaching as most commentators have assumed, and we are accordingly sceptical of the more radical prognoses of the parties' futures.

Alternative Voting Theories

Before going on to examine the election itself and its possible implications, we ought to provide some signposts to the alternative theories of voting behaviour on which most political analysis in Britain has been based and to the theoretical perspective which we shall adopt ourselves.

The 1983 election not only produced an unusual result but also came at an unusual time in the study of electoral behaviour. Two theories with contradictory views of the voters' motivations were competing for support. Both theories provided persuasive explanations for long term trends in British political behaviour; both were based on convincing research evidence.

The first theory is based on a sociological explanation of electoral choice. It suggests that one's voting behaviour is influenced essentially by one's social characteristics. Thus, since political parties reflect class interests, they receive their support largely from their natural class constituency. More generally, the theory holds that different aspects of social structure — class, housing, union membership — constitute the bases of voting behaviour. True, the theory also admits that group membership alone is insufficient to explain voting patterns and that psychological factors, linked to group membership, play a major part. It is held that many voters form an attachment to a particular party which both reinforces their propensity to vote for it and is in turn reinforced by the act of voting. This attachment, or 'party identification', is developed in childhood and early adulthood when the voter first participates in politics. As a result it is deeply rooted in an individual's psyche.

The theory does not suggest that voting is determined solely by one's social and family history. But it does suggest that group membership and its consequences

— including the influence of parents, friends and workmates — has an adhesive quality which binds people to their parties. Voting is seen largely as a symbolic act whereby people express their allegiance to their social group. The manual worker, for example, votes Labour out of class solidarity because it is 'the party of the working class'.

In both Britain and the United States the first major nationwide studies of electoral behaviour were dominated by the concerns of this theory.[11] So in both countries the party identification theory of voting soon became academic orthodoxy. And it remains very influential. Social changes, and in particular a 'fragmentation' of the social classes and a decline in class solidarity, thus became the favoured explanations for Labour's loss of popularity over the years, as well as for the rise in centre party support and the increasing volatility of the electorate.

But this 'expressive' theory of voting (as we may call it) has recently been challenged by an alternative — the 'instrumental' theory. Whereas the orthodox expressive theory held that voters possess little detailed knowledge of the policies or programmes of the parties but form their attachments on the basis of generalised conceptions and transmitted family and group attachments, the instrumental theory suggests the opposite. It holds that voting is primarily an individual action, based not on group identity but on rational calculation. Emotional ties, habit and group loyalty do not come into it. Voting is a means by which the individual attempts to maximise his or her interests. The act of voting is therefore analogous to other consumer choices and involves deliberate comparisons between the competing qualities of the various packages on offer.

This theory, derived from economic models of human behaviour, has become increasingly influential in recent years.[12] It has been argued that the old orthodoxy was more appropriate in the past when social groups were more cohesive. But the suggested decline of class solidarity has now opened the way to instrumental voting. People will no longer vote for the Labour party, it is said, simply because it is the party of the working class, but must be persuaded by its policies and record. If the Conservative party offers policies that promise to help the affluent manual worker, then it will win votes accordingly, irrespective of class loyalty. It is this second theory of voting which blames Labour's defeat on Labour policies. Labour's policies have moved to the left and the rational voter switches to the Alliance whose policies now accord more closely with his or her own views.

We believe that this antithesis between expressive and instrumental theories of voting behaviour is a false one. We doubt if voters ever were quite so loyal and unthinking in their voting decisions as the old orthodoxy maintained. Manual workers did not vote for the Labour party out of blind allegiance to 'the party of the working class' but because its programme suited their interests. That is surely one of the major reasons for the rise of the Labour party before the war. Programmes and policies have always been important.

But it is equally evident that on its own the new orthodoxy of instrumental voting will not do either. If people voted purely on the basis of rational calculation about the benefits the rival parties would bring them, they would never vote at all.[13] The individual vote can make so little difference to the outcome of an election that the rational, instrumental elector would never waste his or her time and effort in going to the ballot box. We have to introduce an expressive or moral element to explain the act of voting itself.[14]

So we believe that it is quite unnecessary to decide for or against either theory. Any act of voting must involve both expressive and instrumental elements, and we very much doubt whether the balance between these two elements has changed much in the course of this century, let alone in the last twenty years that have marked the decline of Labour and the revival of the Liberals.

In place of this false antithesis we suggest that these are two, complementary aspects of political behaviour. On the one hand social class, housing, education and other aspects of social structure constitute the sources of group interests. These interests provide a potential for political action. On the other hand, the political parties may help to shape group values and foster an awareness of their interests. They can influence the extent to which the potentials are realized. It is the interaction between the social and the political that determines how people vote.

Accordingly, in this book we investigate both the social and the political sources of electoral change. We shall show that there has been no 'withering away of class' but that changes in the shape of the class structure have been important in altering potential support for each of the main parties. We shall also show that this is only half the story and that it is political change — what the parties stand for and how the voter perceives them — that provides the other half. The two are complementary sources, not rival theories, of electoral change.

Notes

[1] The magnitude of the Alliance's achievement in 1983 should not, however, be overstated. If one makes due allowance for the failure of the Liberal party to contest all the seats on the occasion of its previous best performance in February 1974, the 1983 vote only represented a 3½ per cent higher level of support than on that occasion.

[2] For a full analysis see Kogan and Kogan (1983).

[3] On the foundation of the Social Democratic Party see Bradley (1981) and Stephenson (1982).

[4] The precise course of Alliance support during this period has been the subject of some dispute. See Crewe (1982b), Worcester (1983) and Crewe (1983a).

[5] The year on year increase in the retail price index was 4 per cent in May 1983, the lowest figure since 1968.

[6] See, for example, Crewe (1983b).

[7] See, for example, Miller (1984).

[8] The classic analysis of the importance of social cleavages in determining the structure of party competition is Lipset and Rokkan (1967).

[9] See, for example, Lemieux (1977), Himmelweit et al (1981).

[10] See, for example, Sarlvik and Crewe (1983); Rose (1980); Franklin (1982).

[11] See Butler and Stokes (1974); Campbell et al (1964). For a comprehensive review of the history of the survey-based study of electoral behaviour in both countries see Miller (1983).

[12] The classic statement of the theory is Downs (1957). The most important application of this view to British electoral behaviour is Himmelweit et al (1981). See also Franklin (1983).

[13] See the discussion in Barry (1970).

[14] See, for example, Riker and Ordeshook (1968).

PART 1

SOCIAL CHANGE

Chapter 2

Class and Politics

"Class has long been pre-eminent among the factors used to explain party allegiance in Britain" (Butler and Stokes, 1974: 66). At its crudest, class can be seen as a contrast between the 'haves', who are in favour of preserving the status quo, and the 'have nots' who favour social change and the redistribution of income. The 'haves' are usually equated with white-collar, nonmanual workers and their families — the middle class; the 'have nots' are taken to be blue-collar, manual workers — the working class.

This highly simplistic two-class model of the class structure is often used in political analysis.[1] While it may have some value as a first rough approximation, we hold that it is wholly inadequate for studying the social bases of politics since it ignores important divisions which have little to do with the colour of a man's or woman's collar.

The limitations of the two-class model are widely recognised but unfortunately, when political scientists have wanted a more refined measure of class, they have turned to the highly unsatisfactory 'social grade' schema.[2] This is commonly used in market research and in opinion polling, but is very rarely used in academic research in other branches of social science. We believe that it gives a misleading view of the relation between class and politics. Indeed, many social scientists would argue that social grade has more to do with the concept of social status than it has with class, as these terms are usually defined in the technical literature.

The social grade scheme comes close to the layman's view of class as a hierarchy of social groups based on differences in income and life-style. Six social grades labelled A,B,C1,C2,D and E are usually distinguished.[3] Grade A is labelled the 'upper middle class' and consists of families where "the head of household is a successful business or professional man, senior civil servant, or has considerable private means . . . In country or suburban areas, 'A' grade households usually live in expensive flats or town houses in the better parts of town" (Monk, 1978:

13

9). Grade B is termed the middle class and its members are described as "quite well off" but "their style of life is generally respectable rather than luxurious". Grade C1 is termed the lower middle class and "is made up of the families of small tradespeople and nonmanual workers who carry out less important administrative, supervisory and clerical jobs". Grade C2 is the skilled working class, grade D the semi- and unskilled working class, and grade E consists of a residual category of "Old Age Pensioners, widows and their families, casual workers and those who, through sickness or unemployment, are dependent on social security schemes" (Monk 1978:12).

The focus on income and life-style is evident from these descriptions of the social grades. It may of course be entirely appropriate for market researchers who are professionally concerned with such things as consumer purchases. We would however question whether income and life-style are particularly relevant to politics. We do not believe that voting behaviour can usefully be equated with consumer choices, and indeed we suspect that serious errors have been made by adopting this approach to politics.[4] The focus on life-style has led political scientists to believe that rising standards of living would erode the class basis of politics, and as we shall show in chapter 3 this view is almost wholly without merit.

The assumption which lies behind the use of social grade, with its emphasis on life-style and standard of living, is that people will vote for the party that does most to raise their standard of living. Now there may be a little truth in this, but it is a limited and one-sided view of politics. An important distinction must be made between those objectives like economic prosperity on which there is broad consensus and those such as nationalisation or income redistribution on which there is fundamental dissensus.[5] Economic prosperity is certainly not irrelevant to how people vote, but a view of politics which concentrates on prosperity to the exclusion of all else is a myopic one indeed. In the 1950s many commentators believed that there had been an 'end of ideology' and that management of the economy was the key to political success. The events of the 1960s proved them wrong, and they are still wrong today. As we shall show, it is the questions over which there are fundamental ideological differences, not the consensus ones of economic management, which provide the major basis of political allegiance. What we need is a conception of social class that reveals the social roots of dissensus. The social grade conception with its emphasis on life-style obscures them.

The conception of class which we shall use focusses not on income levels *per se* but on economic interests.[6] Broadly speaking, wage labourers have different interests from those of the self-employed or from those of salaried managers and professionals. Their incomes may overlap, but the conditions under which they earn that income differ quite markedly. We shall show that these employment conditions are more fundamental determinants of values and political allegiance than is life-style. It is the competitive position of different groups in the labour market which provides the basis for their differing values and political principles.

For example, manual wage-labourers have relatively little security of employment and relatively poor fringe benefits such as sick pay and pension schemes. They have little control over their own working conditions and little discretion, being subject to managerial authority, over what they do at work. They also have relatively poor chances (despite some social mobility) of gaining promotion to the better paid and secure managerial positions. As a result manual wage-earners cannot be sure to improve their lot through *individual* action. Instead they must look to *collective* action, either through trades unions or political parties. They have a shared interest, in other words, in collective bargaining over wages and working conditions and in government intervention to reduce the risks of unemployment and redundancy. While there is bound to be much variation in the extent to which these conditions apply, in general we would expect manual wage-earners to be more receptive to socialist or interventionist values than other groups of workers.

The salaried manager or official represents one contrast to the manual wage-earner. The salaried official has a relatively well-paid and secure job in bureaucratic employment. Even if only at the bottom of the bureaucracy, the official may reasonably hope to climb to the more lucrative and powerful positions higher up, and at more or less every level the official will enjoy the advantages of staff pension schemes, incremental salary scales and the like. Most importantly, he or she has a vested interest in the preservation of the social order that gives rise to this advantaged position.

A second important contrast is with the self-employed. This is a group which cuts right across the conventional manual/nonmanual distinction. The self-employed include skilled artisans as well as shop-keepers and farmers. They may have very different incomes, but what they share is the fact of being 'independents' who are directly exposed to market forces without the cushioning of bureaucratic employment or trade union membership. They have an interest in creating conditions favourable to private enterprise and individual success. They will be particularly receptive to individualistic and 'free enterprise' values.

The self-employed constitute the most serious challenge to the use of social grade for political analysis. Their existence is wholly ignored by the social grade schema and, since their life-styles differ greatly, they will be dispersed across the social grades from A to D. But as we shall show they are very distinctive and homogeneous in their political values and behaviour.

At the very least, then, a three-fold schema which distinguishes the manual wage-earner, the salaried official and the self-employed is required. Two further distinctions are also useful. First, we distinguish routine nonmanual work from the salaried managers and professionals. Routine nonmanual work as a clerk, typist, receptionist and salesworker may have some of the advantages of bureaucratic employment and for some, younger employees it is the first step on a ladder which leads up to management. In many other respects however it is poorly-paid wage labour; it is subject to managerial authority and constitutes a kind of white-collar labour force. We shall treat it as a separate class, marginal to the 'salariat' proper.

Second, we distinguish foremen and technicians from the working class proper. Again these workers are somewhat marginal in their position. The foreman, for example, is differentiated from rank and file manual employees by his (or more rarely her) limited exercise of authority which gives a modicum of managerial involvement. Nonetheless, foremen lack full membership of the managerial bureaucracy, and their interests are therefore somewhat ambiguous. They will have been recruited from ordinary manual jobs but have in a sense stepped outside the ordinary manual world by accepting the promotion.

We therefore distinguish between the following five classes:

1 *The salariat*. This consist of managers and adminstrators, supervisors of nonmanual workers, professionals and semi-professionals. These are all occupations which afford a secure basis of employment, typically affording a high income. They either involve the exercise of authority over subordinates or, in the case of semi-professionals, involve a fair degree of discretion and autonomy.

2 *Routine nonmanual*. This consists of workers such as clerks, sales-workers and secretaries. These are subordinate positions with relatively low levels of income and constitute a kind of white-collar labour force.

3 *The petty bourgeoisie*. This consists of farmers, small proprietors and own-account manual workers. As we have said, what they share is the fact of being 'independents' who are directly exposed to market forces and con-straints. They also of course have direct ownership of their own capital, although in many cases this will be very small in quantity.

4 *Foremen and technicians*. This is a kind of blue-collar elite, its members being set apart from the mass of wage labour by their supervisory functions or greater amount of discretion and autonomy. Because of the small numbers in each we shall sometimes be forced to combine classes 2, 3 and 4. We will then term them the intermediate classes.

5 *The working class*. This consists of the rank and file manual employees in industry and agriculture. In some cases, take-home pay may be quite high, particularly if overtime is worked, but the jobs are relatively insecure and are subject to the authority of others. Within the working class we do not distin-guish between skilled and semi-skilled work since, as we shall see below, this distinction is of little political importance.

TABLE 2.1 Class and Earnings

	Relative earnings: base — working-class men	
	Men	Women
Salariat	170	119
Routine nonmanual	102	72
Petty bourgeoisie	96	72
Foremen and technicians	121	77
Working class	100	66

An important feature of this scheme is that it is not neatly hierarchical. Table 2.1 shows the differences in hourly earnings between the five classes.[7] While the salariat is clearly advantaged in comparison with the others, it should be clear that the differences between classes 2,3,4 and 5 are not ones of income. Rather they are differences in what might be termed 'market situation' and employment condit-ions. It is these differences, not those of income, which determine the interests of the different classes, their potential for political action and their sympathies for rival political ideologies.

Class and Values

While it is the distinctive pattern of interests which lies at the heart of our class schema, these interests will be translated into political action only if they are recognised by the members of the different classes themselves. People will vote according to their own principles and their own perceptions of self or class interest, not according to political scientists' assertions about their 'real' interests.

Our thesis, however, is that the five classes we have distinguished will be associated with values which to some extent express, and which have their roots in, these differing interests. We are not advancing the proposition that people vote merely according to self or class interest. Rather we maintain that different positions in the division of labour will be fertile soil for distinct social and political values. These values may be inculcated in part by the political parties themselves; a Labour party which defines public ownership of the means of production as an essential step for working class advancement may thereby help to foster the spread of that principle in the working class. But the relation between interests and values will not be random or arbitrary. The petty bourgeoisie for example will be a great deal more receptive to free enterprise principles than will the working class. Whatever the mechanisms involved, our thesis is that different values and principles will flourish in the different classes and will provide the basis of political allegiance. Values thus provide the crucial link between class interests and political behaviour.

In the 1983 British General Election Study we asked respondents their views on a wide range of social and political questions. These covered among other things the economy, the welfare state, trade unions, defence and civil liberties. The questions on which the classes differed most sharply were:[8]

(1) "whether some of the industries that are now nationalised should become private companies" (Q37),
(2) "whether income and wealth should be redistributed towards ordinary working people" (Q34b),
(3) "whether the government should spend more money to create jobs" (Q30d),
(4) "whether the government should introduce stricter laws to regulate the activities of trade unions" (Q40a),
(5) "whether the government should get rid of private education in Britain" (Q35a).

The class differences on these five questions are shown in table 2.2.[9]

The most striking feature of this table is that, in every case, it is the petty bourgeoisie which is most likely to take up what would normally be thought of as the 'free enterprise' or 'right-wing' option. Despite its members' low income, and despite the fact that it contains many manual workers, the petty bourgeoisie is the class most committed to private industry and private education and the most opposed to income redistribution or job creation. This is powerful testimony to the congruence between market situation and political ideology.

Of course, we must remember that individualistic values may have led people to set up business on their own account in the first place. It may thus be that

TABLE 2.2 Class and Values

	Percentage agreeing with "right-wing" alternative				
	Nationalisation	Income redistribution	Job creation	TU legislation	Private education
Salariat (N = 1021)	50	49	27	64	76
Routine nonmanual (N = 923)	37	33	17	61	66
Petty bourgeoisie (N = 300)	60	60	32	71	77
Foremen and technicians (N = 277)	40	41	20	55	71
Working class (N = 1270)	24	25	10	46	53

'natural Conservatives' are disproportionately recruited into the petty bourgeoisie. We do not wish to advance a naive structural determinism. Values may influence occupational choice as well as the other way round. It is the *congruence* between the two which is evident in the data.

Another feature of table 2.2 is the similarity in the attitudes of routine white-collar workers and of the foremen and technicians. Although they stand on different sides of the conventional manual/nonmanual divide, they are almost indistinguishable in their attitudes.

However, while table 2.2 shows definite class differences in values, it would be quite wrong to think of society as polarised. Thus a majority of all classes favoured the 'left-wing' proposal of job creation and a majority of all classes opposed the 'left-wing' proposal of abolishing private schools. On both these questions there is broad consensus despite the class differences. Even on public ownership of industry polarisation was muted. Although there were big class differences in support for privatisation, the majority of the working class favoured the *status quo* rather than further nationalisation. Only on redistribution was a majority of the working class in favour but a majority of the salariat and petty bourgeoisie opposed.

Britain does not, therefore, exhibit diametrically opposite class beliefs. Rather, we should think of these questions as representing points along an ideological continuum.[10] At one extreme we have the minority who favour further extensions of public ownership and the abolition of private education. There are few such people in any class, although they are least uncommon in the working class and most uncommon in the petty bourgeoisie. Next, there is rather more support for government intervention to reduce income and wealth inequalities, presumably through policies of progressive taxation (although we did not put this specifically to our respondents). And there is more support still for government intervention in the economy, presumably through deficit financing, to create jobs and restore full employment. Even in the petty bourgeoisie the majority are in favour of this form of government intervention, although it is in the petty bourgeoisie that we are most likely to find people, again only a small minority, who are opposed to all these forms of government intervention.

We are thus measuring differing degrees of support for government intervention and for free enterprise. The majority of people lie towards the centre of this continuum rather than polarised at the extremes, but it nonetheless represents the major, class-based, source of dissensus and, as we shall show in chapter 8, these class values are the major source of political allegiance.

We have not included the question on trade union legislation on this ideological continuum since it cross-cuts the other questions to some extent.[11] It was not uncommon for respondents to adopt a socialist position favouring public ownership but at the same time to wish to see legal curbs on trade unions. Of course, it is also true that union membership itself cross-cuts class. Only a minority of the working class are themselves union members, and substantial members of the salariat are trade unionists.[12]

Class and Party in 1983

Support for the Conservative and Labour parties follows very similar lines to those of the class values described in table 2.2. Table 2.3 shows the pattern.[13]

TABLE 2.3 Class and Vote in 1983: the Political Distinctiveness of the Classes

	Conservative	Labour	Alliance	Others	
Salariat	54	14	31	1	100% (N = 867)
Routine nonmanual	46	25	27	2	100% (N = 749)
Petty bourgeoisie	71	12	17	0	100% (N = 245)
Foremen and technicians	48	26	25	1	100% (N = 220)
Working class	30	49	20	1	100% (N = 992)

As before we see that it is the petty bourgeoisie which is the most Conservative class, and indeed by far the most united class in its politics. As we have said already, this plays havoc with the conventional manual/nonmanual division and with the more detailed social grade schema. Thus our definition of the petty bourgeoisie groups together such superficially disparate groups as farmers (90 per cent of whom voted Conservative), small proprietors (70 per cent of whom voted Conservative) and self-employed manual workers (of whom 68 per cent voted Conservative).

The second striking feature of table 2.3 is the contrast between the foremen and the working class. Among the foremen there is a big Conservative lead, bigger indeed than the Labour lead in the working class. The Labour party is certainly not the party of the blue-collar elite.

However, when we exclude the self-employed artisans and the foremen from the working class proper, we are left with a class that is somewhat more united politically than is often supposed. Even in 1983, a particularly bad election for Labour, half of working-class voters still cast their votes for the Labour party. Support for the Conservative party in the salariat was scarcely greater.

The differences between skilled and semi-skilled workers also disappear once we adopt a stricter definition of the working class. Many commentators have suggested that skilled manual workers are much more Conservative than the semi- and unskilled workers, but this is an artefact of the social grade schema.[14] Some skilled manual workers are foremen or self-employed. When these are excluded, the majority who remain prove to be rather more prone to vote Labour, not less, than the rest of the working class. 51 per cent of the skilled workers voted Labour compared with 48 per cent of the semi- and unskilled. Skill level is indeed associated with income differences, but it is not associated in the same way with political differences. Self-employment or a supervisory position, not income or skills, make for Conservatism.

Table 2.3 also shows that the Alliance has more of a class base than is usually recognised. Butler and Stokes concluded from their review of the evidence, based on social grade, that "In marked contrast to the intimate ties between class and Conservative and Labour support, support for the Liberals was remarkably unrelated to class self-image and to occupational grade. The Liberals indeed constitute a standing challenge to any over-simple account of class and party" (Butler and Stokes 1974: 79). Butler and Kavanagh's analysis of the 1983 election results, using the social grade schema, reaches the same verdict.[15]

We would certainly agree that any over-simple account must be avoided. Table 2.3 however shows a quite definite relation between Alliance voting and class (on our definition of class). Like the Conservative party, the Alliance is quite clearly less popular in the working class and stronger in the salariat. But it is equally clear that its support does not run parallel to that of the Conservative party for its lowest popularity occurs in the Conservative stronghold of the petty bourgeoisie. The Alliance's class appeal is of a different character from the Conservatives', and as we shall see in chapter 5 its strength is in a different segment of the salariat too. But in 1983 it was not *the* party of any one class in the way that the Conservatives were so overwhelmingly *the* party of the petty bourgeoisie or Labour, less overwhelmingly, *the* party of the working class.

So far, we have been considering the 'political distinctiveness' of the classes, the petty bourgeoisie proving to be easily the most distinctive. However, another perspective is to consider the 'class distinctiveness' of the parties. This provides a rather different view of the class/party relation. This is done in table 2.4.

TABLE 2.4 Class and Vote in 1983: the Class Distinctiveness of the Parties

	Conservative	Labour	Alliance	Others
Salariat	34	14	35	24
Routine nonmanual	25	21	26	37
Petty bourgeoisie	12	3	5	2
Foremen and technicians	8	6	7	5
Working class	21	55	26	32
	100%	99%	99%	100%
N =	1388	881	762	41

Table 2.4 shows that the class composition of the Conservative and the Alliance vote is remarkably similar. The petty bourgeoisie makes up only a tiny proportion of the electorate, and so the Conservatives must draw the bulk of their support from elsewhere. They may be *the* party of the bourgeoisie, but they are not a 'bourgeois' party. Their vote is in fact drawn almost as evenly from across the classes as is the Alliance vote. On this criterion the Conservatives and the Alliance have almost equal claims to be called classless parties.

In comparison Labour is much more obviously a working-class party, even on our rather strict definition of class. Over half its votes come from this one class alone, and much of the remainder of its vote comes from the two 'marginal' classes of routine white-collar and supervisory blue-collar workers. It is still a party of the subordinate.

Class and Gender

In constructing a class schema one has to decide not only how to classify occupations but also whose occupation should be classified. In social research married women are commonly classified according to their husbands' occupations irrespective of whether or not they are currently in paid employment themselves.[16] The practice follows a traditional conception of the division of labour within the family. It is assumed that the husband is the primary source of income and that in consequence the class situation of other members of the family is dictated by the husband's, or 'head of household's', occupation. Strictly speaking, young people living in their parents' homes should also be classified according to the head of household's occupation.

Recent work on the relative importance of their own and their husbands' occupations upon political behaviour suggests however that married women's own workplace experience should not be ignored.[17] In this book therefore we have decided to treat men and women alike. Thus we treat people who are currently 'economically active' or retired on the basis of their own occupation.[18] We do so whether they are male or female, married or single. People who are not economically active, or who describe themselves as engaged in housework rather than as retired, we classify according to their spouse's occupation (if of course they have a spouse engaged in paid work). Again, we apply this rule equally to men and to women.[19].

Our procedure will not meet with universal assent, but we have checked carefully to see if it affects our substantive findings. Since the distribution of men and women in the labour market is very different, the procedure necessarily affects the numbers allocated to each class. Women are greatly overrepresented in routine nonmanual work and in the lower levels of the working class. They are grossly underrepresented in the more advantaged positions of the salariat or the blue-collar elite. This is shown in table 2.5, which allocates people on the basis of their present occupation (or most recent one if they are retired).

Some of the women in routine white-collar work will of course be married to manual workers, so if we follow the 'head of household procedure' and allocate these married women to their husbands' class, we would obtain a rather larger estimate of the size of the working class. We obtain a rather larger estimate of the size of the salariat too, if we follow this procedure since many women in white-collar jobs have professional and managerial husbands. The end result, then, would be to get a rather more polarised picture of the shape of the class structure. It becomes more of an 'hour glass' with large bowls at top and bottom and a thin stem joining them.

TABLE 2.5 Men and Women's Occupations

	Men	Women
Salariat	30	23
Routine nonmanual	11	46
Petty bourgeoisie	10	4
Foremen and technicians	11	2
Working class	38	25
	100%	100%
N =	1743	1265

Sample: economically active and retired women and men

However, while the choice of procedure affects the estimates of class *size*, it has virtually none on our conclusions about class *differences*. We get almost identical measures of the political distinctiveness of the classes from the two methods.[20] Our conclusions are in that sense robust ones. More interestingly, we find that there are no major differences in the voting behaviour of men and women within a class.

Table 2.6 shows how men and women voted in 1983. The one notable difference is in the working class where women are rather more likely than men to vote for the Alliance. But in general it is the absence of a gender difference which is striking. The relation between class and voting may be modest, but it is extraordinarily uniform.

Perhaps even more surprisingly we find that there are few differences between single and married women either.[21] This is particularly striking when we remember that a single woman in the salariat is likely to be earning a great deal less than her married male colleague, to have a lower standard of living and probably live in a less desirable part of town than her married female counterpart. If income determined one's politics and ideology, single women should be radicals. There was little evidence in our data that they were, at least in their voting behaviour, any more radical than their male colleagues.

Notes

[1] The first substantial attack on the use of the two-class model in political science, and to a lesser extent on the use of social grade, only came with the publication of Robertson (1984).
[2] The classic works on social class in British politics have all followed this broad practice. See Benney et al (1956), Bonham (1954), Butler and Stokes (1974), Sarlvik and Crewe (1983).
[3] The precise practice of previous election studies has differed somewhat from that of the Market Research Society scheme. In particular, grade C1 was split into two, while grade E was not utilised. For further details see Kahan et al (1966). For full details of the Market Research Society scheme see Monk (1978).

TABLE 2.6 Class, Gender and Vote

		Conservative	Labour	Alliance	Others		
Salariat	Women	54	14	30	2	100%	(N = 423)
	Men	54	14	31	1	100%	(N = 444)
Routine nonmanual	Women	45	26	27	2	100%	(N = 581)
	Men	48	23	27	2	100%	(N = 168)
Petty bourgeoisie	Women	72	11	17	0	100%	(N = 100)
	Men	70	13	16	1	100%	(N = 144)
Foremen and technicians	Women	48	30	21	0	99%	(N = 66)
	Men	48	24	26	1	99%	(N = 155)
Working class	Women	29	46	24	1	100%	(N = 457)
	Men	30	51	17	2	100%	(N = 535)
All	Women	44	28	27	1	100%	(N = 1647)
	Men	46	30	24	1	101%	(N = 1446)

[4] See, for example, Abrams et al (1960), Butler and Rose (1960), Crewe (1973). A sophisticated critique of the thesis was offered by Goldthorpe et al (1968).

[5] We are here following Butler and Stokes' distinction between valence and position issues. We find their terminology rather obscure and hence prefer the terms consensus and dissensus issues. See Butler and Stokes (1974: 292).

[6] In what follows we draw extensively on Goldthorpe's Weberian analysis of social class. See Goldthorpe (1980, 1982). Marxist writers have also emphasised differences of interest other than those between manual and nonmanual workers. See in particular Wright (1979), Carchedi (1977). The essential difference between the Weberian and Marxist approaches to class is that the former is concerned with differences of interest arising from position in the labour market, the latter with differences arising from position in the productive process.

Goldthorpe's scheme has seven classes. We have simply combined his top two classes, I and II, to form the salariat. (Goldthorpe himself terms it the service class). And we have combined his two bottom classes, VI and VII, to form the working class. We should note that Goldthorpe's scheme is based on the 1970 classification of occupations and was not designed with women's occupations in mind. Goldthorpe has constructed a new, eleven-fold version, based on the improved 1980 classification of occupations and this is better suited to the analysis of women's jobs. However, we have had to use the 1970 version as this permits comparability with the earlier election studies. For details of the classification of occupations see Office of Population Censuses and Surveys (1970, 1980).

Details of the construction of the seven-fold schema can be ascertained from Goldthorpe (1980) in conjunction with Goldthorpe and Hope (1974). Alternatively, the details of this schema and of the eleven-fold schema can be acquired from either John Goldthorpe at Nuffield College, Oxford or Anthony Heath at Jesus College, Oxford.

[7] The source for table 2.1 is the General Household Survey 1979. It is based on an approximation to the Goldthorpe class schema using socio-economic groups.

[8] The attitude questions on which we compared voters were Q23a, Q23b, Q27a, Q27b, Q27c, Q30b, Q30d, Q34b, Q35a to Q35e, Q37, Q40a to Q40d, Q42b, Q42c, Q42e, Q43b. These were all questions which asked what the government (or Britain) should do. We excluded questions Q26a, Q26b, Q30c and Q30e which have a different character, being more evaluative than prescriptive. We should note that these evaluative questions correlate very highly with vote, just as do the questions (which we have also excluded) on the government's handling of unemployment, strikes, and so on. The essential thing is to compare like with like, hence our restriction to prescriptive questions.

[9] The 'right-wing' alternatives are taken to be agreement with privatisation, disagreement with redistribution and job creation, agreement with stricter trade union legislation and disagreement with the abolition of private education.

[10] An acceptable Guttman scale can be constructed from the four questions Q35a, Q37, Q34b and Q30d. The coefficient of reproducibility was .94 and the coefficient of scalability .74.

[11] Inclusion of the trade union question in the Guttman scale analysis reduced the coefficients below the acceptable level. In a general factor analysis of all the attitude questions listed above, attitudes to trade unions had a high loading on the main interventionist-free enterprise factor but also, unlike the other class values,

had a high loading on the second, civil liberties factor. For further details see chapter 5.

[12] Indeed, in our survey the proportions of the salariat who were currently members of a trade union (29 per cent) almost matched the proportion of the working class who were (34 per cent).

[13] Those who reported not voting are excluded from this table and from all the other tables in this book analysing vote. We have little to add to the admirable study of nonvoting by Crewe, Alt and Fox (1977).

[14] See for example Butler and Kavanagh (1984: 291). Table 2.7N shows the relation between social grade and vote in our data set. As can be seen Grade C2 proves to be more Conservative than Grade D. In constructing table 2.7N we have followed the procedures used by Crewe and his colleagues for constructing social grade. We are grateful to them for supplying the look-up table. To maintain comparability with Crewe's work we have allocated respondents to grades on the basis of head of household's occupation. Table 2.7N should therefore be compared with table 2.8N.

TABLE 2.7N Social Grade and Vote

Social grade	Conservative	Labour	Alliance	Others		
Grade A	69	7	23	1	100%	(N = 160)
Grade B	55	13	31	1	100%	(N = 764)
Grade C1	54	20	24	2	100%	(N = 595)
Grade C2	38	39	22	1	100%	(N = 930)
Grade D	30	47	22	1	100%	(N = 609)

[15] See Butler and Kavanagh (1984, table 13.2).

[16] For a defence of this position see Goldthorpe (1983). For alternative views see Garnsey (1978), Erikson (1984), Britten and Heath (1983), Heath and Britten (1984).

[17] Some material from earlier election studies is reported in Heath and Britten (1984). We shall be analysing this further in a later publication.

[18] Our definition of 'economically active' follows that used in the 1981 Census. See Office of Population Censuses and Surveys (1981: 24-25). It includes the unemployed, whose class is determined by their previous occupation.

[19] In constructing our class schema for previous election surveys we have not always been able to adhere strictly to this rule. In each case we used the best available approximation to it. We should also note that a small proportion (4 per cent) of the sample did not belong to any class on this procedure. Of these people who lacked a class position 46 per cent voted Conservative, 29 per cent Labour, 24 per cent Alliance and 1 per cent other. These figures are very close to the overall percentages in our sample and suggest that this category of 'classless' respondents lacks any distinctive political character.

[20] The political distinctiveness of the classes, using the head of household procedure, is shown in table 2.8N.

TABLE 2.8N Head of Household's Class and Vote

Head of household's class	Conservative	Labour	Alliance	Others	
Salariat	54	14	31	1	100% (N = 923)
Routine nonmanual	49	24	25	2	100% (N = 495)
Petty bourgeoisie	69	13	17	1	100% (N = 291)
Foremen and technicians	45	28	26	1	100% (N = 266)
Working class	30	48	21	1	100% (N = 1089)

[21] The vote of single women is shown in table 2.9N.

TABLE 2.9N Single Women's Vote

Class position	Conservative	Labour	Alliance	Others	
Salariat	57	14	24	4	99% (N = 61)
Routine nonmanual	44	26	26	4	100% (N = 96)
Petty bourgeoisie	—	—	—	—	— (N = 3)
Foremen and technicians	—	—	—	—	— (N = 1)
Working class	26	51	21	2	100% (N = 35)

Chapter 3

The Decline of Class Voting?

It has been widely argued that the class basis of politics has weakened in recent years, that Britain has experienced a period of 'class dealignment' and that class has lost the pre-eminence it once had in the explanation of political allegiance.[1] The source of the change, most commentators have argued, lies in the changing character of the classes themselves. Classes are no longer, it is claimed, the cohesive social formations that they once were. Rising standards of living, the spread of home-ownership, the decline of traditional heavy industries and their local communities, the emergence of new industries such as electronics in the affluent south, and increased social mobility out of the working class are all held to have reduced class solidarity, particularly that of the working class. Internal divisions within the classes are assumed to have become more marked, leading some commentators to coin the phrase 'the fragmentary class structure' while others have talked of a 'loosening' of the social structure.[2]

If true, these arguments have important implications for the future of our major political parties, and particularly for the Labour party. The claim is that the classes have changed in character, and the implication is that the parties can no longer rely on appeals to traditional class interests as they once did. The class basis of politics has changed, so it is argued, and the parties must change too or see their fortunes decline. Labour in particular must change if it is to regain power.

These arguments have a remarkable resemblance to the ones put forward after Labour lost a third successive election in 1959. Then, as now, commentators began to argue that the class basis of Labour's support was inevitably waning. In a famous booklet called *Must Labour Lose?* Abrams, Rose and Hinden analysed the causes of Labour's decline. They attributed Labour's defeat in 1959 to its out-dated class appeal, to the electoral handicap of nationalisation, and to the weakness and disunity of Labour leadership. The analysis has a surprisingly contemporary ring. But the prime mover they believed to be the changing character of the working class itself. Thus Hinden wrote:

"The majority of workers are no longer condemned to a constant struggle for a minimum of security. Some still are, but strong trade unions and full employment have revolutionised the position of most. Large groups of manual workers have higher earnings than white-collar workers or than sections of the middle class. They are cushioned by the provisions of the welfare state; their children have educational opportunities beyond the dreams of their parents. They now have opportunities for leisure, for the enjoyment of most of the good things of life. They are no longer a down-trodden section of the community; they are well able to assert their own rights and often do so in no uncertain terms" (Abrams et al 1960: 105).

Is it any wonder, Hinden went on to ask, that we should be reaching the limit of the old class appeal? "The old working-class ethos is being eroded by prosperity and the increasing fluidity of our society. People now know that they can improve their lot by their own efforts. And as they succeed, they change their values and cease to identify themselves with the class from which they sprang" (Abrams et al 1960: 106).

The analysis of Labour's decline in the 1950s is thus extraordinarily similar to that of the 1970s and 1980s. Then, as now, the class basis of politics was believed to be withering away. Labour had to change or lose. But Labour promptly won the next two elections in 1964 and 1966 and the level of class voting in those two elections was as high, if not higher, than it had ever been before. The commentators had confused the decline of Labour in the 1950s with the decline of class. They failed to distinguish political sources of change from social sources. They brought forward no evidence that the old working class ethos actually had been eroded by affluence.

Contemporary accounts of the decline of class are no more plausible than those of the 1950s. The commentators have once again confused a decline in *overall* support for Labour with a decline in its *relative* class support. In this chapter we shall show that Labour remained a class party in 1983; it was simply a less successful class party than before.

The History of Class Voting

Table 3.1 shows the pattern of class voting over the postwar period as a whole. Owing to the shortcomings of the earlier surveys we are unfortunately restricted to the manual/nonmanual dichotomy for the earlier part of the period.[3] Later in this chapter we shall be using the five-class schema described in chapter 2 to look at the trends from 1964 onwards, but the data of table 3.1 are nonetheless illuminating.

Throughout the 1950s and 1960s around two-thirds of both classes voted for their 'natural' class party. Despite the alleged erosion of working class solidarity in the 1950s, class voting remained at least as high in 1966 as it had been in 1945. True, there was something of a dip in working-class support for Labour in 1959, but its immediate recovery in 1964 suggests that the 1959 result had far more to do with changing politics than with the alleged change in the character of the working class.

TABLE 3.1 The History of Class Voting

	1945		1950		1951		1955		1959		1964	
	Non-manual	Manual	Non-manual	Manual	Non-manual	Manual	Non-manual	Manual	Non-manual	Manual	Non-manual	Manual
Conservative	63	29	68	32	75	34	70	32	67	30	62	28
Liberal	9	9	9	9	3	3	6	6	12	13	16	8
Labour	28	62	23	59	22	63	23	62	21	57	22	64
	100%	100%	100%	100%	100%	100%	99%	100%	100%	100%	100%	100%
Nonmanual Conservatives and manual Labour as % of all voters	62		62		67		65		61		63	
Odds ratio	4.8		5.5		6.3		5.9		6.1		6.4	

	1966		1970		Feb 1974		Oct 1974		1979		1983	
	Non-manual	Manual	Non-manual	Manual	Non-manual	Manual	Non-manual	Manual	Non-manual	Manual	Non-manual	Manual
Conservative	60	25	64	33	53	24	51	24	60	35	55	35
Liberal	14	6	11	9	25	19	24	20	17	15	28	22
Labour	26	69	25	58	22	57	25	57	23	50	17	42
	100%	100%	100%	100%	100%	100%	100%	100%	100%	100%	100%	99%
Nonmanual Conservatives and manual Labour as % of all voters	66		60		55		54		55		47	
Odds ratio	6.4		4.5		5.7		4.8		3.7		3.9	

Since 1966, however, there has been a much more striking decline in class voting (defining the level of class voting as the number of nonmanual Conservative plus manual Labour voters as a proportion of all voters). By 1983 less than half the voters were supporting their natural class party. This calculation assumes that the Liberal and Social Democratic parties were not class parties — a debatable assumption as we saw in chapter 2. If we include the Alliance as a nonmanual party along with the Conservatives, the decline in class voting becomes rather less marked, though still present.[4]

Even so, the proportion of each class that votes for its natural class party is a misleading measure of class voting. As in 1959 we run the risk of confusing a decline in Labour's electoral fortunes with a change in the class basis of voting. After all, if a class party like Labour does badly at the polls, it is almost true by definition that a smaller proportion of the working class will have turned out to support their natural party. Given the large size of the working class, this in turn is likely to mean that the overall level of class voting will have fallen too. We are, therefore, simply redescribing Labour's misfortunes rather than explaining them. We are simply measuring how well the Labour party (or the Conservative party) has fared at the polls. The measure does not necessarily tell us anything very interesting about the class basis of politics.

When commentators talk about the declining class basis of politics they have a more subtle but illuminating concept in mind than just a fall in working-class support for Labour.[5] It is an increase in *cross-class* voting that is usually taken to constitute 'class dealignment'. If Labour (or for that matter the Conservatives) begins to draw relatively more support from the opposing class than from its natural supporters, then we are indeed seeing a more interesting change in the class/party relation, one with more far-reaching implications.

Commentators were impressed by the fact that cross-class voting did seem to have increased in 1970. As table 3.1 shows, Labour support dropped sharply among manual workers in 1970 but held up among the nonmanual. In other words, its relative support in the two classes had changed and the character of the party seemed to have changed too. So while the overall proportion of the electorate voting for its natural class party can be thought of as a measure of *absolute* class voting, what we are really interested in is a measure of *relative* class voting. It is the latter which would tell us whether the class basis of voting has changed.

The most appropriate measure of *relative* class voting is the odds ratio. For example, the odds of a nonmanual worker voting Conservative rather than Labour in 1945 were just over two to one while the corresponding odds for a manual worker were (roughly) one to two. The ratio of these odds works out at rather more than four to one.[6] An odds ratio of 1:1 would indicate that there was no class basis to voting at all, that the relative strengths of the two parties were the same in both classes. Correspondingly the larger the odds ratio, the stronger the class basis of voting. The great advantage of the odds ratio is that it clearly distinguishes relative from absolute strength. Thus the Conservatives might get twice as many votes as Labour, but providing they did so in both classes equally, the odds ratio would still be 1:1.[7]

The pattern of odds ratios over time is shown in table 3.1. (The ones shown relate to Conservative and Labour voting by manual and nonmanual workers; odds ratios could also be calculated for Labour and Liberal, or for Conservative

TABLE 3.2 Class and Vote 1964–1983

	Salariat	Routine nonmanual	Petty bourgeoisie	Foremen and technicians	Working class	Odds ratio
1964						
Conservative	61	54	74	40	23	
Labour	20	31	12	44	70	
Liberal	18	14	13	15	7	9.3
Other	1	1	1	1	0	
	100%(N=268)	100%(N=256)	100%(N=106)	100%(N=134)	100%(N=674)	
1966						
Conservative	58	48	66	34	23	
Labour	25	42	19	61	72	
Liberal	16	9	13	5	5	7.3
Other	1	1	2	0	0	
	100%(N=280)	100%(N=266)	100%(N=102)	100%(N=127)	100%(N=670)	
1970						
Conservative	60	49	66	35	32	
Labour	29	42	18	58	60	
Liberal	9	8	11	5	6	3.9
Other	2	1	5	2	2	
	100%(N=227)	100%(N=166)	100%(N=75)	100%(N=82)	100%(N=379)	

Feb 1974						
Conservative	52	40	66	37	22	
Labour	23	35	18	38	59	
Liberal	23	24	14	24	15	6.1
Other	2	1	2	1	4	
	100%(N=439)	100%(N=390)	100%(N=174)	100%(N=134)	100%(N=769)	
Oct 1974						
Conservative	47	38	69	33	20	
Labour	27	37	13	43	63	
Liberal	23	22	15	22	12	5.5
Other	3	3	3	2	5	
	100%(N=361)	100%(N=344)	100%(N=104)	100%(N=109)	100%(N=579)	
1979						
Conservative	59	48	76	40	30	
Labour	22	36	13	44	55	
Liberal	17	15	10	13	13	4.9
Other	2	1	1	3	2	
	100%(N=403)	100%(N=280)	100%(N=123)	100%(N=153)	100%(N=477)	
1983						
Conservative	54	46	71	48	30	
Labour	14	25	12	26	49	
Liberal & SDP	31	27	17	25	20	6.3
Other	1	2	0	1	1	
	100%(N=867)	100%(N=749)	100%(N=245)	100%(N=220)	100%(N=992)	

and Liberal, voting.) The movements are somewhat different from those in the absolute level of class voting. For example, the absolute level fell in February 1974 when the Liberals increased their share of the vote, but the relative level rose. Indeed relative class support for the Labour and Conservative parties was as high in February 1974 as it had been in 1950. True, it was markedly lower in 1979, but it is worth noting that the increased support for the Alliance resulted in a further drop in the absolute, but not in the relative, level of class voting in 1983.

In general the period from 1945 to 1974 shows no consistent trend. There are certainly ups and downs, but we would see these as having more to do with changing political events — the nature of the parties' programmes, their success in office, and so on — than with any underlying evolution of the classes. The mistake of recent commentators is that they have taken 1964 as their baseline.[8] As we now see this was a rather unfortunate choice since it marked a peak in relative class voting (as measured by the odds ratio).[9] The adoption of a longer time perspective clearly calls into question claims about any secular trend towards class dealignment.[10]

This still leaves the question of the apparent drop in relative class voting in 1979 and 1983. That too could be no more than a temporary fluctuation as a result of specific political events, but our own view is that it is in fact almost wholly spurious, an artefact of the inadequate manual/nonmanual dichotomy.

The point is a simple one. The manual/nonmanual dichotomy ignores the important differences in the political interests of the three intermediate classes and runs the risk of confusing class dealignment with changing class sizes. For example, self-employed manual workers are much less likely to vote Labour than the working class proper. But they have also been increasing in number in recent years whereas the working class has been contracting. The internal composition of the manual category as a whole has thus changed, and its declining relative propensity to vote Labour will be, at least in part, a consequence of this change in composition.

Ideally, we would use the five-fold class schema to explore class voting over the whole period, but the deficiencies in the earlier data mean that we can do this only for the period 1964-1983. We must remember that the baseline of 1964 may be a misleading one: we are starting our time-series from the high point of class voting.

Relative Class Voting 1964-1983

Table 3.2 shows the pattern of class voting over the 1964-1983 period using the five-fold class schema. With this more complicated schema there is a large number of odds ratios that can in principle be computed. The one reported in the table is the ratio of Conservative and Labour odds in the salariat and working class.

Table 3.2 confirms in a more rigorous way that 1970 was an exceptional election. Cross-class voting in the salariat and working class was undoubtedly higher than in the 1960s. The 29 per cent of the salariat who voted Labour and the 32 per cent of the working class who voted Conservative in 1970 are the 'record highs' for cross-class voting in this period. But one exceptional election hardly amounts to class dealignment and is an extremely dubious basis upon which to build theories of social change.

On the other hand, table 3.2 does not confirm a decline in relative class voting in 1979 and 1983. True, Labour fared worse in the working class in 1983 than it had done in previous elections, but it also fared worse in every other class as well. Labour's decline was general, not class-specific.

Over the 1964 to 1983 period as a whole the dominant impression is one of 'trendless fluctuation' rather than steady dealignment. 1964 represents the high point of relative class voting, but as we have already seen represents an unfortunate baseline.[11] 1970 represents the low point, but can scarcely be said to have ushered in a period of continued dealignment. Faced with these short-run fluctuations the political scientist does better to search for political sources of the parties' success and failure than to blame long-run changes in the character of the classes.

These conclusions are confirmed by the use of the more rigorous statistical technique of log-linear modelling. This technique analyses the full set of odds ratios and enables us to test alternative models.[12] Taking the seven elections from 1964 to 1983 together, log-linear modelling confirms, as might be expected, that there have been statistically significant changes both in the fortunes of the parties and in the sizes of the classes. These two sorts of change are by far the most important components of the differences between the elections.

Some small variations in the relationship between class and party remain, however. The model which assumes a *constant* set of class/party odds ratios over time does not fit the data wholly satisfactorily.[13] But the deviations which remain have more of the character of 'trendless fluctuations' than steady dealignment. Perhaps most interestingly the assumption of constant odds ratios gives a rather good fit in 1983. In other words the level of class voting in 1983 (in the relative sense of class voting) was about average for the 1964-1983 period as a whole. In this one respect 1983 was not an exceptional election at all. As table 3.2 indicated 1964 and 1970 were the exceptional ones. And if these two elections are excluded from the analysis, the assumption of constant odds ratios turns out to give a perfectly acceptable fit.[14]

Changing Class Sizes

In focussing on class dealignment political scientists have concentrated on minor rearrangements of the furniture while failing to notice a major change in the structure of the house. Table 3.3 presents the class distribution of the electorate as measured by the election surveys of 1964 and 1983. It shows that Britain has been transformed from a blue-collar society into a white-collar one. Whereas in 1964 the working class was nearly three times the size of the salariat, constituting nearly half of the electorate, in 1983 the two classes were of almost the same size.[15] True, under our strict definition the working class is much smaller than it is if defined more broadly as manual workers. But in table 3.3 we use the *same* definitions for both 1964 and 1983. The scale of the change over time is therefore real enough. It is not an artefact of our class schema.

TABLE 3.3 Class Composition of the Electorate: 1964 and 1983

	1964	1983
Salariat	18	27
Routine nonmanual	18	24
Petty bourgeoisie	7	8
Foremen and technicians	10	7
Working class	47	34
	100%	100%
N =	1475	3790

The impact of these changes upon the electoral fortunes of the parties has probably been far greater than that of any class dealignment which may or may not have occurred. There is little evidence that class differences have withered away or that the classes have changed their character, but there can be no question that the *shape* of the class structure has been gradually changing throughout the postwar period.

The implications of the two claims are very different. If class dealignment has occurred, the implication is that the political parties should stop appealing to voters' class interests. If classes have become fragmented and lack the distinctiveness they once had, class issues will be less potent sources of votes.

But if, on the other hand, as we suggest the class structure has simply changed shape, the implication is that class interests persist. Parties must therefore continue to appeal to them, since they remain the fundamentals of electoral choice. For a party to abandon class appeals is to run the risk of losing the class votes that it still has (and in Labour's case a majority of its votes still come from the working class). According to this view Labour faces a particular dilemma. Its class base is shrinking, but it dare not abandon it for it has nowhere better to seek votes. Equally, all is not rosy for the Conservative party since, although the salariat is expanding, it has to compete with two other parties, the Liberal and Social Democratic parties, which are also relatively strong in the salariat.

The impact of these changes in class structure on the fortunes of the parties can be demonstrated by means of a simple simulation. Assume that the parties retained the same level of support within each class that they had in 1964. Since we can measure (as in table 3.3) how the classes changed in size over the period 1964-1983, we can estimate the extent to which these changes alone would have affected the parties' fortunes. (We are of course restricted to the analysis of 1964-1983 because of the absence of comparable data before 1964). The calculation tells us how the parties would hypothetically have fared if the only source of change had been the expansion and contraction of classes described in Table 3.3.[16]

On these assumptions the Conservative share of the vote would have increased by five and a half per cent. Labour's share would have fallen by seven per cent and the Liberal/Alliance share would have increased by one and a half per cent. Structural change alone, therefore, would have brought about a major decline in Labour's vote, but it does little to account for the rise of the Liberal/Social Democratic Party Alliance.

These results can be put in perspective if we compare them with the actual changes in party strength over this period. Thus the Labour share of the vote actually fell from 44 per cent to 28 per cent; structural change can thus account for nearly half this decline. The Liberal share rose from 11 per cent to 25 per cent, structural change therefore telling us little about the reasons for its rise. And the Conservative share remained roughly constant, falling just one point to 42 per cent, whereas on our assumptions it might have been expected to increase to 49 per cent. In this sense, therefore, there has been a shortfall in the Conservative share of the vote as well as in Labour's. To put it another way, the Conservative party was over six points down on its expected share of the vote in 1983, the Labour party was over nine points down, and the Alliance was twelve points up, having gained at *both* the other parties' expense.

Having controlled for the changes in the class structure, then, we get a rather more equivocal picture of Labour failure and Conservative success over the years. It turns out that the two parties have both done badly. In explaining electoral change over this period, therefore, we have to explain why the Conservatives did not do better, not just why Labour did so badly.

We must treat the precise estimates of the Labour and Conservative shortfalls with a measure of caution. As we have already pointed out, 1964 is an unsatisfactory baseline from which to start. And we must also remember that part (perhaps as much as five percentage points) of the Liberal gain due quite simply to the increased number of Liberal candidates.[17] In 1964 the Liberal vote was artificially low since there were many constituencies in which no Liberal candidate stood and hence no possibility of recording Liberal votes. However, even when we make allowance for these problems, our conclusions remain essentially intact: structural change explains a large part of Labour's decline, it explains little of the Alliance rise, and it suggests that the Conservatives should have don better than they actually did in 1983.

Perhaps even more interestingly we find that the 1979 result, when the Conservative vote increased to 44 per cent, the Liberal vote to 14 per cent and the Labour vote fell to 37 per cent, was rather close to what might have been expected given the expansion and contraction of the different classes. At the time Labour's result in 1979 was regarded as something of a disaster while the Conservative's was seen as a triumpth. Perhaps those interpretations should now be reappraised.[18]

Changing Class Values

Our main argument, then, is that the class basis of politics, if not the strongest it has ever been, nonetheless shows no good evidence of secular decline. Relative class voting certainly fluctuates but there is little evidence of any underlying downward trend. But it is also clear that the two main parties have both fared worse at the polls than a purely sociological theory of politics would have pre-dicted. In our view this decline has not been due to any 'loosening' or 'fragmenta-tion' of the classes but to political changes which have nothing at all to do with class. We shall in later chapters try to show what these political changes may have been.

To some, our argument may seem to fly in the face of common sense. Surely the claims advanced by writers like Abrams, Rose and Hinden in the 1950s — that economic progress had ameliorated the economic position of the working class and that affluence had brought middle-class living standards within the reach of a greater proportion of the population — have some truth in them.

Of course they do. It would be absurd to claim otherwise. But the political implications of economic progress have not been well understood.[19] *Absolute* living standards have certainly increased for many of the population, but conflicts of interest are as much, or more, about *relativities* as they are about absolutes. The cake may grow in size, but rising expectations will mean that conflicts over the size of the shares will continue unabated.[20]

In this context what is important is that, although average real incomes have increased, income relativities have diminished only slightly. Similarly, while there have been great increases in educational provision in sixth forms and univer-sities, class inequalities in access have remained unchanged. Absolute rates of upward social mobility have increased, but relative class chances have stayed the same.[21]

A powerful case, then, can be made out that objective class relativities have shown little sign of change despite the undoubted economic and social progress of the 1950s and 1960s. But this is only one side of the story. Commentators who talk of the withering away of class have been as concerned with subjective class aware-ness as with objective inequalities. It is the 'consciousness of class' and the 'sense of political solidarity' described by commentators such as Bonham in the 1950s which is held to have withered, not just the economic differences.

This emphasis on the *subjective* awareness of class interests is clearly impor-tant. However much political scientists may instruct the classes in their 'objective interests', these will be translated into political action only if there is some subjec-tive grasp of them as well. A class theory of politics must assume class differences in attitudes and values as well as in objective conditions.

However, there is no evidence that subjective class awareness has declined any more than the objective inequalities have done. The evidence is unfortunately scanty, but there is a good time series on one of the key class values described in chapter 2. We showed that responses to a number of questions on the role of government intervention in the economy were strongly associated with class. Of these, questions on nationalisation have been asked throughout the series of election studies (except 1970) and we can thus test whether subjective class differ-ences, at least with respect to this one question, have declined.[22]

Since we are concerned with relativities, table 3.4 presents odds ratios. The odds in question are those of preferring privatisation to nationalisation, and we have compared these odds in the salariat and working classes respectively. As in the case of voting there are many other odds ratios that could in principle be calculated, but log-linear modelling (which takes the full set into account) confirms the story of table 3.4.

TABLE 3.4 Changing Attitudes Towards Nationalisation 1964–1983

	1964	1966	Feb 1974	1979	1983
Salariat/working class odds ratio	2.9:1	2.5:1	2.1:1	3.6:1	4.5:1

The details of table 3.4 are rather different from those of table 3.2, which gives the comparable figures for voting. Thus, whereas relative class voting 'peaked' in 1964, relative class values appear to peak in 1983. There is no one-to-one relation between class values and class voting (although only a 'sociological determinist' would expect a one-to-one relation). However, the overall picture is again one of trendless fluctuation. We would not wish to argue that there has been a trend towards subjective class polarisation, although that would be as plausible a claim as the rival thesis of class dealignment.

It would be unwise to draw conclusions about trends in class consciousness from a single time series. A serious study of changing class consciousness would need a better set of questions tapping different aspects of class awareness and class values. All table 3.4 can do is place a large question mark against the claims that there has been any long-run decline in the subjective distinctiveness of the classes. Most such claims about the decline of class have been based on the intellectual equivalent of gossip and hearsay. Commentators have either assumed, without any evidence, that increases in absolute standards of living will erode class relativities, or they have inferred a withering away of class itself from the absolute decline in class voting. But this is to be guilty of a naive sociological determinism. Labour's decline, and the Alliance rise, have as much to do with political as with social sources of change.

Our conclusion, therefore, is that class differences, whether with respect to objective inequalities, subjective values or support for the political parties, remained at much the same level throughout the postwar period. Whether for better or worse, Britain is still divided by class. On the other hand the shape of the class structure has changed, with important electoral implications particularly for Labour. Its class base is clearly shrinking, and may be expected to continue to do so with the de-industrialisation of Britain. But this can account only for part of Labour's decline at the polls, and for virtually none of the Liberals' rise. Labour has changed form being a rather successful class party in 1964 to being an unsuccessful on in 1983. The Liberals, also a class party, have gained at both Labour and Conservative expense. To explain their modest success, we must look to political explanations, not social ones. The withering away of class is not the answer.

Notes

[1] This argument was first put forward by Butler and Stokes in the second edition of *Political Change in Britain* (1974: 206-208). A very detailed study of dealignment generally was made by Crewe, Sarlvik and Alt (1977). This dealt

with the broader concept of partisan dealignment, that is the decline in the electorate's attachment to the Conservative and Labour parties. While we have grave doubts about the phenomenon of *class* dealignment, we do not dissent from Crewe et al's account of *partisan* dealignment. Indeed their work on this represents one of the major contributions of the British Election Studies. See also Crewe (1974), Crewe (1982b), Sarlvik and Crewe (1983), Crewe (1984), Franklin (1982), Franklin (1984), Franklin and Mughan (1978), Kelley et al (1982), Rose (1980), Francis and Payne (1977).

[2] The phrase 'fragmentary class structure' comes from Roberts et al (1977). Butler and Kavanagh (1984: 8) talk of a loosening of the class structure. Robertson (1984) gives a somewhat similar analysis, and from a Marxist perspective so does Hobsbawm (1981).

[3] Figures for 1945-1955 are taken from Alford (1963), table b-1, and are based on quota samples conducted by the British Institute of Public Opinion. Those for 1959-1979 are taken from Sarlvik and Crewe (1983, table 3.5), and are based on representative probability samples conducted by Butler and Stokes and the British Election Study team at the University of Essex. The 1983 results are based on our probability sample (for details see Appendix I).

There are some important limitations to the series before 1964. The 1955 and 1959 figures are based on respondents' recall of how they voted some years earlier. (A second sample of 1955 recall vote conducted later than the one quoted here gives an odds ratio of 6.4.) The 1945-1951 figures were derived by Alford from Table 18 in Bonham (1954). Alford excludes a small number of voters who did not fit into Bonham's manual/nonmanual categorisation. In the original version Bonham did not distinguish between those voting for the Liberal party, other parties, or abstaining. Alford also excluded all of these voters from his table. We have assumed that the Liberal share of the vote (9 per cent in 1945 and 1950, and 2.6 per cent in 1951) was the same in both classes and was drawn in the proportion 2:1 from Conservative and Labour amongst nonmanual voters and 1:2 amongst manual voters. An alternative tabulation of BIPO data for this period is given in Rose (1976: 20). It suggests that our assumptions are reasonably satisfactory. Our procedure has little effect on the odds ratios. In the original Bonham data these are 4.7, 5.7 and 6.3 respectively for 1945, 1950 and 1951. Finally, the 1955 figures exclude those voting for other parties (who are included with the Liberals from 1959 onwards). We are grateful to Peter Cozens for his help on these problems.

[4] If we include the Liberal and Social Democratic parties as middle-class parties, the percentage of voters voting for their natural class parties becomes 71 in 1966 falling to 62 in 1983.

[5] This is apparent in Butler ans Stokes' original presentation of the class dealignment thesis (Butler ans Stokes 1974: 203-205). See also Crewe (1981) where Crewe refers to a higher swing to the Conservative between 1974 and 1979 amongst the working class than amongst those in professional and managerial occupations. However, the distinction between absolute and relative class voting was not made explicit by these writers.

[6] Thus the odds ratio for 1945 is $(63/28)/(29/62) = 4.8$.

[7] The usual method of measuring relative class alignment has been the Alford index (Alford, 1963). To calculate this for Labour we simply subtract the percentage of the middle class supporting Labour from the percentage of the working

class supporting Labour. Thus, in 1945 62 per cent of manual workers voted Labour compared with 28 per cent of nonmanual, giving a score of 34 points on the Alford index. Unfortunately, the Alford index is inappropriate as a measure of relative class alignment since it confuses relative with overall support. Suppose, for example, that Labour support among manual voters fell to 33 per cent while support among nonmanual fell to zero. On the Alford index this would give a score of 33 points, less than in 1945, but surely we would want to say that such a situation where Labour drew all its votes from the working class represented a much higher degree of class alignment than in 1945. The crucial point is that a decline in overall support for Labour may lead to a fall in the Alford index even if there is no change in relative class support for Labour.

[8] The choice has, of course, arisen simply because 1964 was the first election at which a nationwide academic survey of voting behaviour was undertaken and not for any theoretical or substantive reason.

[9] A defence for the choice of 1964 might be made by referring to Butler and Stokes' (1974) cohort analysis of class alignment. They showed that the class alignment was weakest amongst those who entered the electorate before 1918, was strongest among those entering in 1945 and became gradually weaker among those entering thereafter. Thus, although a process of class dealignment might have started after 1945, it would not have been manifest in the electorate as a whole because the class/party relationship among those entering the electorate after 1945, although weaker than among those who entered in 1945, was still stronger than among those who entered before 1945 and who were leaving the electorate through death. See Butler and Stokes (1974: 203-205). However, the lack of a consistent strengthening of the class alignment between 1945 and 1964 indicates that the 1964 figure probably reflects short-term factors rather than the process of generational change.

[10] The sceptical reader may be wondering if the limitations in the pre-1964 data limit the reliability of our conclusions. However, the BIPO data for the 1945-1964 period quoted in Rose (1976), in which the 'upper middle class' and 'very poor' are separated from the 'middle class' and 'working class' but in which the definitions are pursued identically across all elections, also show fluctuations rather than a steady trend during this period. The odds ratios for Conservative and Labour voting amongst the middle and working classes were 1945 4.5; 1950 6.0; 1951 3.9; 1955 5.1; 1959 6.4; 1964 4.7. Although these figures suggest that 1964 was not unusual in the strength of its class/party alignment, the same series also fails to show dealignment thereafter with an odds ratio of 5.4 in 1966.

[11] The evidence of the previous section on this point receives further backing if Butler and Stokes' respondents' recall in 1964 of their 1959 vote is analysed according to our five-fold scheme. This analysis shows that the salariat/working-class odds ratio for Conservative and Labour voting was 7.5 in 1959.

[12] The most authoritative account of log-linear modelling is given in Bishop et al (1975). For an accessible introduction see Gilbert (1981).

[13] This is shown by the results of the following log-linear analysis: (We are very grateful to Kenneth Macdonald who wrote the computer programme for our log-linear analyses.)

C represents class (five-fold schema), E represents election (seven elections 1964-1983), V represents vote (three categories — Conservative, Labour, Liberal and others).

TABLE 3.5N Log-Linear Analysis of 1964–1983

		G^2	df	p<
1	Grand total	9063.8	104	
2	C,V,E	2390.8	92	.001
3	CV,E	736.9	84	.001
4	CV,EV	212.0	72	.001
5	CV,EV,CE	84.8	48	.001

The model excluding a CVE interaction term does not give a good fit to the data. However, we shall see in chapter 4, note 20, that the CVE term is not required once we control for changes in housing tenure over time.
[14] A model containing the terms CV, EV and CE for the five remaining elections alone has a G^2 of 40.8 with 32 degrees of freedom, p‹ .137.
Further log-linear analysis confirms that what can at most be agreed in favour of the class dealignment thesis is that there was a significant difference in relative class voting between 1964 and 1970. A log-linear analysis of the three elections 1964-1966-1970 fitting the model CV,EV,CE produces a G^2 of 36.1 with 16 degrees of freedom, p‹ .003. But there is no evidence of any continuing dealignment after 1970 and, indeed, as the odds ratios in table 3.2 indicate there was some reversal of the 1964-1970 change. The model CV,EV,CE for the five elections between 1970 and 1983 fits the data satisfactorily (G^2 = 35.2 with 32 degrees of freedom, p‹ .320). There is thus no evidence of a long-standing secular trend towards class dealignment. All that has occurred is a change of doubtful meaning between 1964 and 1970.
It is also worth noting that using a very different approach Franklin (1982) identified the period between 1966 and 1970 as the only one in which there was a clear fall in the strength of the class/party alignment.
[15] The change between 1964 and 1983 is equally dramatic if respondents are allocated to the class of the head of household. The figures then become:

TABLE 3.6N Head of Household's Class 1964–1983

	1964	1983
Salariat	19	30
Routine nonmanual	13	15
Petty bourgeoisie	8	9
Foremen and technicians	11	12
Working class	49	34
	100%	100%
N =	1601	3777

For further evidence on the changing occupational structure of Britain see Routh (1980). The reader may have noticed that table 3.2 suggests a decline in the relative size of the class of foremen and technicians between 1979 and 1983. This is almost certainly due to a change in coding procedure in 1983.

[16] The calculation was undertaken as follows. For each party a hypothetical 1983 vote was calculated by multiplying the proportion of each class who reported having voted for each party in 1964 by the 1983 frequencies of those reporting having voted in 1983 in the relevant class. In other words, the 1964 conditional probabilities of voting for a party were weighted by 1983 class frequencies. The 'effect' of the change in the class structure on each party is simply the difference between the hypothetical 1983 vote and the reported vote in the 1964 survey. For an alternative approach to measuring the impact of social change on the parties' electoral fortunes using a much more 'inclusive' approach to class see Kelley et al (1984).

[17] See Steed (1979).

[18] Indeed, if we repeat the calculation for every election since 1964 we find that, with the exception of February 1974, Labour tended to do at least slightly better than would have been expected given the change in the size of the classes. Further, until 1983, their performance in this respect compared with the Conservatives was always better. The fall in the Labour vote in 1983 was thus unique in the extent to which it cannot be accounted for by social change.

[19] The work of Lockwood, Goldthorpe and their colleagues in the 1960s clearly showed the fallacies inherent in the position of writers like Abrams, but the lessons of their work have not been well remembered. See Goldthorpe et al (1968).

[20] Writers such as Hirsch (1977) have suggested that they may actually increase as a result of positional competition, but we would not ourselves go this far. See Ellis and Heath (1983).

[21] On income see Routh (1980), Nicholson (1967); on education see Halsey, Heath and Ridge (1980); on social mobility see Goldthorpe (1980).

[22] There is also a good time-series on self-assigned class. This shows a small decline over the period. In 1964 60 per cent gave themselves either a middle or working-class self-description, compared with 52 per cent in 1983. It is striking how few people gave such a description at either time, but we should note that the interpretation of self-assigned class is not without problems. Respondents are asked "Do you ever think of yourself as belonging to a particular social class?". If yes, "Which class is that?" (Q49a). One trouble with this question is that respondents may not interpret it in quite the same way that the political scientists intend. The manager who says that he is working class may simply be making the point that he works for his living; the manual worker who says he is middle class may simply mean that he has a middle level income. Neither may be expressing the subjective class awareness that the political scientist has in mind.

Chapter 4

Housing

Class remains central to an understanding of contemporary British politics — class differences in interests, values, and support for the political parties continue unabated. The changing shape of the class structure, on the other hand, has serious implications for Labour's electoral future, and to add to Labour's woes there have been further social changes which, it has been argued, work to Labour's long-term disadvantage. Principal among these is the spread of home-ownership.[1]

Ever since academics first began survey research on voting behaviour, council tenants have always proved more likely to support Labour and owner-occupiers to support the Conservative party. Like the class differences, housing differences in voting have been long-standing ones.

For much of the period since 1964 changes in the housing stock were not wholly to Labour's disadvantage. There was a small but gradual increase in the propor-tion of households living in council houses until the end of the 1970s when, at 32 per cent, it was 4 points higher than in 1964. During this period owner-occupation rose even more, from 46 per cent to 55 per cent, but it grew at the expense of private renting rather than of Labour's constituency, the council estate.

With the Conservative victory in 1979, however, the gradual rise in council housing was not only halted but reversed. Helped by the new government's policy of requiring local authorities to sell council houses on favourable terms to existing tenants, the proportion of council tenants fell to 28½ per cent, almost back to the level of 1964. Owner-occupation, meanwhile, continued to grow, indeed at an even faster rate than before 1979, and in 1983 accounted for 60 per cent of house-holds.[2]

Some writers have suggested that these changes undermine Labour's position yet further. Butler and Kavanagh, for example, have argued "Members of the

44

relatively affluent working class who were car-owners, buying their own houses and employed in the private sector, clearly preferred the Conservative party. Home-ownership was particularly significant. MORI found that whereas council house tenants voted 49 per cent Labour to 29 per cent Conservative, the figures were almost exactly reversed among working-class voters owning or buying their homes (26 per cent to 47 per cent). These workers were, according to Ivor Crewe, 'the new working class' and, more significantly, they were the growing part of it" (Butler and Kavanagh 1984: 296-297).

However, we suspect that the political significance of the spread of home ownership has been exaggerated. First, although the *association* between housing and vote is real enough, it is not self-evident that changes in housing lead to changes in vote. The direction of causation may not be what is usually assumed. Second, although the changes in the distribution of housing tenure are also real, once we have taken account of the changing class structure they add little to the story of chapter 3. We agree that, if we take a single snapshot of the electorate, housing tenure does indeed have a strong association with vote, even after controlling for class. But if we take a moving film of the changing electorate, we find that changes in the distribution of housing tell us little that the changes in class structure had not told us already.

Housing and Party

Table 4.1 gives a snapshot of the relation betwen housing and vote in 1983. It shows very clearly the well-established association between the two. Indeed, the importance of housing, according to these data, would seem to be almost greater than that of class. Thus Conservative voting is thirty points higher among owner-occupiers than among council tenants. In contrast table 2.3 showed only a twenty-four point difference between the salariat and the working class.

TABLE 4.1 Housing and Vote

	Conservative	Labour	Alliance	Others	
Owner-occupiers	53	19	27	1	100% (N = 2131)
Private tenants	44	28	23	5	100% (N = 249)
Council tenants	23	55	20	2	100% (N = 797)

Not surprisingly the association between housing and vote persists even when we control for class. We do not disagree with the view of Butler and Kavanagh (and many others) that housing cross-cuts class and that working-class home-owners are more likely to vote Conservative than are working-class council tenants.

Given our stricter definition of class, it is not surprising that our detailed figures in table 4.2 are rather different from the ones quoted by Butler and Kavanagh. But the general story is still the same: housing tenure is strongly associated with vote even after taking account of class membership.[3] The importance (in the statistical not political sense) of housing and class is very similar.[4]

TABLE 4.2 Housing, Class and Vote

	Conservative	Labour	Alliance	Others		
Salariat:						
Owner-occupiers	56	12	31	1	100%	(N = 744)
Private tenants	54	5	34	7	100%	(N = 39)
Council tenants	33	36	28	3	100%	(N = 71)
Intermediate classes:						
Owner-occupiers	59	14	26	1	100%	(N = 844)
Private tenants	54	23	18	5	100%	(N = 112)
Council tenants	25	50	23	2	100%	(N = 252)
Working class:						
Owner-occupiers	39	37	23	1	100%	(N = 463)
Private tenants	28	47	22	3	100%	(N = 83)
Council tenants	20	62	17	1	100%	(N = 441)

Two quite different types of explanation for this relationship between housing tenure and vote can be put forward. One explanation sees housing as an extension of the influence of the workplace. According to this view one's politics are influenced not only by one's own class position but by the class position of those around one. Housing estates are thus assumed to constitute social communities which foster and reinforce class values.[5] Council-house tenants will typically be working-class individuals; by putting them in close proximity to each other the estate fosters networks of friendship and social association which will reinforce the prevailing working-class values of the neighbourhood. Similarly, the private estate will foster the development of a community with middle-class values. We shall look further at this line of argument in chapter 6.[6]

A second line of argument is that an individual's housing tenure will structure his or her individual interests in just the same way that position in the labour market structures class interests.[7] Thus owner-occupiers have made a substantial financial investment in their homes and, historically at least, home ownership has proved to be an important means of accumulating wealth. Home-owners have valuable marketable assets which give them a measure of security and economic advantage. They have an interest in the maintenance of property rights and of a market for housing which preserves the value of those assets. Their interests are thus very like those of the salariat or petty bourgeoisie, and of course in many cases they are the same people.

Council tenants are in a rather different position. They are beneficiaries of collective, nonmarket provision of accommodation. Their houses have no value to them beyond their immediate utility as dwellings. They do not have a marketable asset and thus do not have the same interest in the maintenance of property rights (although to some extent the right to buy one's council house now makes the contrast of interests a less stark one than before).

Tenants who rent their homes from a private landlord rather than a local authority are a category which straddles rather uneasily between the other two. Unlike the council tenants, their housing has been supplied by the market rather than through collective provision but on the other hand, like council tenants, their homes do not represent a financial investment. For some, private renting will be a temporary solution to their housing needs before moving into one of the other two sectors of housing. The group as a whole is likely to be a rather disparate one and the influence, if any, of their current housing situation on political behaviour is unclear.

Housing, then, may be a source of material interests in much the same way that class is, and the character of those interests may be very similar too. Owner-occupiers have advantages in the housing market not unlike those of the salariat in the labour market, and they have a similar interest in protecting their advantages. Council tenants have an interest in collective provision and government intervention in a similar way to the working class. Housing may be an independent source of interests but the structure of the conflict that it generates matches that produced by class.[8]

This argument can in principle be applied to other aspects of individuals' consumption. It can be argued that people who have access to private medicine or private education do not have the same interest in the improvement of the welfare state as do those who have no option but to use the National Health Service and state schools. The same could be said of car-ownership and public transport.[9]

Housing and Values

If this account of housing interests is correct, then we would expect to see the same kinds of differences between council tenants and home-owners in their values as we saw between the classes in chapter 2, and such proves to be the case. Housing has the strongest relationships with precisely the same questions that figured in our class analysis. There are some nuances of emphasis, but the overall picture is the same. The following questions headed the list:[10]

(1) "whether income and wealth should be redistributed towards ordinary working people" (Q34b),

(2) "whether the government should get rid of private education in Britain" (Q35a),

(3) "whether some of the industries that are now nationalised should become private companies" (Q37),

(4) "whether the government should spend more money to create jobs" (Q30d).

(5) "whether the government should do more to help the economy of the area in which you live" (Q40d).

The similarity of this list to the previous one in chapter 2 is almost complete. Three of the four main questions from chapter 2 reappear here — the role of government in creating jobs, the redistribution of income and the public ownership of industry. Only trade union legislation is missing.

Beliefs about the proper scope of government intervention in the economy, then, are the ones that vary most strongly with housing, just as they do with class.

The other topics that we asked about — defence, law and order, freedom of speech, the welfare state and taxation — were less strongly related to either class or housing. Doubtless, if we had asked more specific questions about tax relief on mortgage interest or home improvement grants, we might have found bigger differences. But surprisingly the topic of this kind which was salient in the election and which we did put to our respondents, namely council house sales, showed only a weak association with housing tenure.[11]

TABLE 4.3 Housing and Values

	Percentage opposing redistribution			Percentage favouring privatisation		
	Owner-occupiers	Private tenants	Council tenants	Owner-occupiers	Private tenants	Council tenants
Salariat	52 (868)	50 (50)	26 (85)	53 (840)	43 (44)	48 (75)
Intermediate classes	46 (1008)	39 (143)	15 (333)	54 (916)	42 (118)	31 (272)
Working class	35 (602)	19 (111)	17 (541)	35 (535)	21 (91)	22 (440)

Figures in brackets give cell sizes

More importantly, housing seems to represent an *additional* source of influence on class values. As table 4.3 shows, the association does not disappear when we control for class position. It is not due solely to the overlap between class membership and housing tenure. Within social classes, owner-occupiers are markedly more opposed to government intervention than are council tenants. Conversely, among owner-occupiers, members of the salariat are markedly more opposed to intervention than are members of the working class. Both class and housing tenure appear to foster the same attitudes but to do so independently of the other. They may be two sources of values, but they work in much the same direction.[12]

There is, however, one nuance worth noting. Home-owners are more divided from council tenants in their attitudes to income and wealth redistribution whereas the salariat were more divided from the working class in their attitudes to nationalisation and privatisation. This is hardly surprising. After all, for most owner-occupiers their house is their major capital asset and source of wealth while nationalisation has more to do with the labour market than the housing market. These differences of emphasis are precisely those that we might expect to stem from the material interests that we described above.

However, it is one thing to show an *association* between housing and attitudes towards income redistribution. It is another to demonstrate a *causal* connection. The assumption that the spread of home-ownership has political significance depends on the existence of a causal connection. It has never been properly demonstrated.

In reporting tables 4.1, 4.2 and 4.3 we have been careful always to talk of associations, not influences. Snapshots of the electorate like these tables cannot ever demonstrate causation. It is the political scientist who imputes the causal connection. Now in the case of housing it is quite plausible, and perfectly consistent with the data, to argue that social attitudes influence one's choice of housing rather than the other way round. This will only be true to the extent that there is some choice in the housing market for people of limited financial means. This has not always been the case, and for many people it will not be the case even now. But one of the real consequences of increasing affluence is that more working-class people have the opportunity to purchase their own home. Their values may determine whether they avail themselves of the opportunity or not.

On this account, the increasing availability of mortgages and the right of council tenants to purchase, simply allows people who already favour private property to purchase their own homes. It does not create these values; without such values, people are hardly likely to want to buy in the first place.

We do not suggest that causation is quite such a black and white matter as this. For some people there is no choice anyway. For others the actual purchase of a property may reinforce values that were only tentative to start with. Nor do we suggest that this element of choice is unique to housing. Such an argument would apply even more forcefully to the purchase of private education or private healthcare. It would also apply to some extent to occupational choice, although we suspect that there is now greater choice in the housing market than in the labour market.

There is, however, some evidence which can be brought to bear on this question of causation. In the election survey we asked owner-occupiers whether they had previously rented their current home as a council tenant. 4 per cent of the total sample came into this category. Not all of these people will have bought their council houses since 1979 as some local authorities had been prepared to sell council houses to their tenants before 1979; but most will have done so. Since we also asked people how they voted at the last election, this allows us to test the effect of purchase upon vote.[13]

There are two main findings. First, purchasers of council houses were indeed more likely to have been Conservative voters in 1979 than were council tenants as a whole. The differences are not great, and only just reach statistical significance, but the expected pattern is there.[14] As table 4.4 shows, of current council tenants who had voted in 1979, 23 per cent had voted Conservative and 68 per cent had voted Labour at that election.[15] But of former council tenants who had purchased from the local authority, 40 per cent had voted Conservative and only 52 per cent Labour.[16] This supports (or more strictly fails to refute) the hypothesis that purchasers differed to start with in their political preferences from the majority of tenants.

Second, we find that purchasers were no more likely than other tenants in 1979 to defect to the conservative or to abandon the Labour party. Table 4.4 shows that they did not swing to the Conservatives at all. And while some did abandon the Labour party for the Alliance, so of course did many council tenants. Three-quarters of Labour purchasers continued to vote Labour in 1983—the same proportion as among Labour tenants who did not buy (to be precise, 76 per cent as against 79 per cent). On this evidence, Labour fears (or Conservative hopes) about the electoral consequences of council house sales would appear to be unfounded.[17]

TABLE 4.4 Council House Sales and Vote

		Conservative	Labour	Liberal/ Alliance	Others		
Council tenants who did not buy	Vote in 1979	23	68	6	3	100%	(N = 781)
	Vote in 1983	23	55	20	2	100%	(N = 797)
Council tenants who bought	Vote in 1979	40	52	6	2	100%	(N = 128)
	Vote in 1983	40	40	19	1	100%	(N = 126)

We found precisely the same pattern when we asked people whether they were likely to buy their council houses in future. They were only a tiny proportion of the sample — less than 2 per cent — again suggesting the limited electoral implications of council house sales. And they closely resembled existing purchasers in their politics, 33 per cent voting Conservative in 1983. Housing tenure, at least in the short run, probably reflects rather than causes differences in party preference.

In the long run it might be a different story. Extensive council house sales might weaken the solidarity of erstwhile council estates, particularly if the current generation of purchasers sell to different types of home-owner in future. If the estates change their character as communities, then we could still see long-run consequences stemming from the sales.

Housing and Vote 1964-1983

We have argued, then, that the political implications of the spread of the property-owning democracy may be somewhat reduced, although not perhaps wholly eliminated, if values determine housing choice rather than the other way round. But there are other reasons too for doubting that the spread of owner-occupation presents a major source of political change over and above the change in class structure.

In the first place the spread of home ownership has occurred largely at the expense of private renting rather than of local authority housing. As we saw earlier in this chapter, private tenants constitute a rather disparate group which lies between the owner-occupiers and the council tenants in their values and political preferences. The political significance of the shift from private renting to home-ownership is thus likely to be rather muted.

A second reason for doubting the political significance of the changes in housing over time is that they largely parallel rather than supplement those of the class structure. What has happened is that home ownership has grown as the salariat has grown; council housing has shrunk but so too has the working class.[18] As a result the proportion of home-owners within the salariat increased only slightly between 1964 and 1983, while more importantly the salariat itself almost doubled in size. Similarly, the proportion of council tenants within the working class declined only slightly, but of course the working class itself shrunk by a third.

At first sight the most striking aspect of table 4.5 is the increase in home-ownership from 48 per cent to 66 per cent of the total. The biggest single increase is the ten point jump from 13 per cent to 23 per cent in the proportion of people who are both owner-occupiers and members of the salariat. But the majority of the salariat were already owner-occupiers in 1964, and so the ten point increase tells us little that the expansion of the salariat had not told us already. It is not an additional source of Conservative voting over time.

The next largest increase is the seven point jump in the proportion of people who are both owner-occupiers and members of the intermediate classes. There is only a modest spread of home-ownership *within* the intermediate classes, and consequently only a modest impact on their voting could be expected.

Table 4.5 Class and Housing in 1964 and 1983

1964	Owner-occupiers	Private tenants	Council tenants	All
	(Percentage of the total sample)			
Salariat	13	3	2	18
Intermediate classes	20	7	8	35
Working class	15	12	20	47
All	48	22	30	100
N =	760	346	463	1569

1983	Owner-occupiers	Private tenants	Council tenants	All
	(Percentage of the total sample)			
Salariat	23	1	2	26
Intermediate classes	27	4	9	40
Working class	16	3	15	34
All	66	8	26	100
N =	2489	304	969	3762

In the working class, it is true, there has been a relative growth of home-ownership, but this is more because of the contraction of the working class than because of any absolute increase in the numbers of people who are both working class and home-owners. As table 4.5 shows, as a proportion of the *total* electorate working-class home-owners have grown only from 15 per cent to 16 per cent.

We can make a more precise estimate of the implications of housing change by constructing another simulation on analogous lines to that of chapter 3. We can calculate the 'expected' shares of the vote which would have occurred if party preferences had stayed as they were in 1964 while *both* housing *and* class changed in the way they actually did. On these assumptions we find that the Conservative share of the vote would have increased by 7 per cent to 50 per cent, the Alliance share by 2 per cent to 13 per cent, and the Labour share would have fallen by 8½ per cent to nearly 35 per cent.[19] These figures differ only slightly from those of chapter 3 where our simulation took account only of the changing class structure. There our estimates of change were 5½ per cent for the Conservatives, 1½ per cent for the Alliance and 7 per cent for Labour. The broad outlines of the picture remain the same, although the detail has changed.

We have, then, quite a striking result. Housing seems to be an important factor in explaining how individuals vote in a given election; it looms large in the snapshot. But it has little importance, net of class, in explaining changes over time; in the film it is masked by class. The paradox arises because, in the snapshot, housing cross-cuts class: there are many working-class owner-occupiers (although rather fewer salaried-class council tenants). But in the film their proportions within each class stay roughly constant over time. They do not change much and therefore cannot be a major source of change.[20]

This paradox is not an inevitable one, however. It tells us that housing does not explain Labour's decline or the Alliance rise, once we have taken account of the changing class structure, over the last twenty years. But it does not follow that the role of housing might not become important in future. Thus if the policy of council house sales was pursued even more vigorously, the proportion of the working class who are council tenants might at last fall and bring new problems for Labour. In other words, if the rate of change of housing clearly outstripped the rate of change of class structure, political impact might occur. Conversely, if a future Labour or Alliance government actively pursued a policy of providing council accommodation for the elderly or the single homeless, the impact might work in the other direction. It would do so, of course, only if housing determined values, not the other way round.

Notes

[1] Thus Dunleavy has argued that "It is possible to point to extensive changes in British society which could well have political effects cross-cutting those of occupational class . . . In particular, the changes in consumption patterns in housing and transport, with which we are largely concerned here, raise important questions for political analysis". (Dunleavy, 1979: 410)

[2] These figures are taken from Central Statistical Office (1971, Table 69); Central Statistical Office (1982, Table 3.61) and Central Statistical Office (1985, Table 3.7).

[3] In table 4.2 as in all of the tables in the remainder of this part of the book we have grouped the routine nonmanual class, the petty bourgeoisie and the foremen and technicians together as the 'intermediate classes'. This helps to maintain sample size and reduce the complexity of the tables.

McAllister (1984) shows that the association between housing tenure and voting behaviour is unusually strong in Britain, being much stronger than in either Australia or the United States.

[4] There are several possible measures of relative importance. Perhaps the simplest is to look at the contributions to G^2 in a log-linear analysis. We obtained the following results:

TABLE 4.6N Log-linear Analysis of Housing, Class and Vote in 1983

		G^2	df	$p <$
1	Grand total	3688.7	44	
2	C,T,V	980.8	36	.001
3	CT,V	588.5	28	.001
4	CT,CV	235.6	20	.001
5	CT,TV	217.6	24	.001
6	CT,CV,TV	28.9	16	.024

C represents class (five-fold schema), T represents tenure (three categories) and V represents vote (three categories — Conservative, Labour, Alliance and others).

Comparing models 4 and 5 with 6 we can get an estimate of the unique contributions of TV and NV respectively to G2. On this criterion tenure proves to be slightly more important. Note that a small but significant interaction exists between class, tenure and vote.

Housing and class are of course themselves correlated and it could well be argued that class is causally prior to housing. If that is accepted, it follows that some of the 'effects' of class may be mediated through housing. In other words the effects of housing may not be wholly independent after all and to estimate the 'total effect' of class we would need to include its indirect effect via housing. Of course, different assumptions about causal ordering could also be made, although they would seem less plausible.

[5] See Parkin (1967), Miller (1977, 1978), Garrahan (1977).

[6] We should, however, note here that the association between housing and vote shown in table 4.2 cannot be accounted for by the 'neighbourhood' effect analysed in chapter 5. Even after controlling for the class composition of a neighbourhood, there is still an association between housing and vote.

[7] There is a large and vexed literature on the nature of housing interests. See for example Dunleavy (1979), Rex and Moore (1967), Saunders (1978), Castells (1977), Haddon (1970). We would generally support Saunders' Weberian analysis.

[8] Thus while we agree with Dunleavy (1979) that "consumption patterns . . . in housing . . . raise important questions for political analysis", we disagree that housing has "political effects cross cutting those of occupational class". Housing does not form the basis for a new cleavage in British politics, but rather acts as a separate source for the maintenance of the class cleavage.

[9] See especially Dunleavy (1979).

[10] See chapter 2, note 8, for the list of attitude questions which were analysed.

[11] In the case of council house sales (Q45h) Cramer's V was only .03.

(Notes continue on following page)

[12] This conclusion is more formally confirmed by a canonical correlation analysis between a set of attitudinal variables and a set of structural variables including housing and class. On the first, main variate both home-ownership and membership of the salariat had relatively high coefficients.
The details of the canonical correlation are as follows:

TABLE 4.7 N Canonical Correlations: Structural Variables

	Variate 1	Variate 2	Variate 3
C1	−.48	.12	.15
C2	−.17	.27	.21
C3	−.33	.27	−.24
C4	−.14	.09	−.14
T1	−.44	.38	−.28
T2	−.12	.18	.03
U1	.14	−.61	−.51
E1	−.32	−.57	.60
E2	−.39	−.35	−.25

TABLE 4.8N Canonical Correlations: Attitudinal Variables

	Variate 1	Variate 2	Variate 3
Q23a1	.24	.12	.17
Q23b1	.09	.18	−.14
Q27a	−.17	−.21	.08
Q27b	.02	.03	−.08
Q27c	.09	.11	−.14
Q30b	−.02	−.14	−.04
Q30d	−.14	−.04	−.13
Q34b	−.20	.02	−.38
Q35a	−.12	.19	−.15
Q35b	.05	.07	.10
Q35c	−.02	.11	−.11
Q35d	−.01	−.12	.11
Q35e	−.05	−.04	.04
Q37	−.21	.20	−.01
Q40a	.19	−.34	−.59
Q40b	−.02	.23	.03
Q40c	.06	−.09	.24
Q40d	−.20	−.06	.13
Q42b	−.17	−.20	−.44
Q42c	−.19	−.02	.33
Q42e	−.13	−.16	.34
Q43b	−.21	−.03	.23
Correlation	.53	.34	.21
P<	.001	.001	.001

C1 represents the salariat, C2 routine nonmanual, C3 the petty bourgeoisie, C4 foremen and technicians, T1 owner-occupiers, T2 private tenants, U1 union members, E1 degree holders, E2 other qualified. (Since we are using sets of dummy variables there is no need to enter the final member of each set, eg the working class.) For the attitude questions see the questionnaire, Appendix I.

[13] This analysis is based on respondents' recall of their 1979 vote when interviewed after the 1983 election. Such recall data is known to be prone to systematic error. In particular, respondents have a tendency to make their previous voting behaviour consistent with their current voting behaviour. See especially Himmelweit et al (1978). Panel data are not necessarily, however, superior. Sarlvik and Crewe's (1983) analysis of the representativeness of their October 1974-1979 panel indicates that panel attrition also results in an overestimate of the consistency of voting behaviour (see especially Table A.6). Our analysis is based on the assumption that errors in recall are not distributed differently amongst those who bought their council house and those who did not.

[14] If we combine Liberal with other voters, the difference in their 1979 recalled vote between present council tenants and former tenants who bought their homes from the council is statistically significant. Chi square = 14.6, df = 2, p< .001. However, the design effects for housing are unusually high (see Appendix III) and will serve to reduce the level of significance.

[15] Excludes those too young to vote in 1979, some of whom did report a 1979 vote.

[16] These differences can partly be explained by class differences between purchasers and tenants. Thus people who purchase may do so because their means differ, not just because their values differ.

[17] These results would seem to be at odds with those of Butler and Stokes, whose panel data appeared to show that a change of housing tenure from council to owner-occupation was associated with a change of vote. They do not report the sample numbers on which their conclusion was based, but they would appear to be very small. Only 3 per cent of their panel moved from council to owner-occupied housing which implies just 22 respondents. If the sample numbers were around 22, the conclusions Butler and Stokes draw in the text are worthless. (See Butler and Stokes, 1974: 111-112.)

[18] For a detailed analysis of the Census data on changes in class and tenure between 1961 and 1981 which produces similar results to those in table 4.5 see Hamnett (1984).

[19] In this simulation, as in the rest of the analysis in this chapter, those living in nonprivate households are excluded. We have also collapsed the three intermediate classes into one class.

(Notes continue on following page)

[20] It is also worth noting that, contrary to a number of recent speculations, housing has not become a more important influence on voting at the expense of class over time. We fitted the following log-linear models:

TABLE 4.9N Log-linear Analysis of Housing, Class and Vote 1964–1983

		G^2	df	p <
1	Grand total	6090.8	89	
2	TCE,V	1182.1	58	.001
3	TCE,VE	984.0	56	.001
4	TCE,VE,VC	340.3	48	.001
5	TCE,VE,VC,VT	64.7	44	.023
6	TCE,VE,TCV	30.5	28	.339

C represents class (five-fold schema), T represents tenure (three categories), V represents vote (three categories — Conservative, Labour, Liberal and others), and E represents elections (two categories, 1964 and 1983).

Thus a TVE interaction term is not needed to achieve a satisfactory fit to the data. The null hypothesis that the association between tenure and vote has not changed between the two elections cannot be rejected.

Note also that, in contrast to an analysis of the two elections excluding tenure, a CVE term is not needed either. This adds further fuel to our doubts about the class dealignment thesis. Part of the change in the class-party association that has occurred would appear to be a consequence of the (small) change in the distribution of tenure groups within each class shown in table 4.5.

Chapter 5

Education and Occupation

In addition to the spread of home-ownership, commentators have drawn attention to a number of other social changes which, arguably, may have had consequences for the political parties. These changes are of two broad sorts. On the one hand, it is alleged, there has been the emergence of new divisions of *interest* within the classes, particularly the salariat, while on the other hand some writers have prophesied the spread of alternative *values* which stand outside the conventional left-right dimension of class politics. Both agree that there is a new potential for radical political action among nonmanual workers. Whereas the spread of home ownership was thought to fragment the working class, these new divisions are more often seen to fragment the salariat. If true, they suggest that the future of the Conservative party may not be quite as secure as the changing shape of the class structure and the spread of home ownership might have suggested.

In dealing with the rise of new interests, different commentators have emphasised rather different processes. Some have emphasised the growth of more specialist, technical jobs with their distinctive expertise and 'knowledge base'. These are occupations like computer programmer, systems analyst or research scientist and are sometimes termed the 'new working class'.[1] In the language of organisation theory they are 'staff' rather than 'line' jobs. Their members do not have direct managerial authority and do not therefore have quite the same interests as those of the 'old' middle class. They are more likely to demand the extension of industrial democracy and question the patterns of authority at the workplace.

A second line of argument has focussed on divisions of interest between the public and private sectors of employment.[2] The emphasis here is on the growth of welfare state occupations like teaching, nursing and social work which are funded through taxation. Correspondingly, their members are seen to have a greater interest, like the working class, in government intervention in the economy and government spending on the welfare services.

Both sets of arguments, then, suggest that interests normally associated with the working class may apply to specific sections of salaries workers as well. They retain the conventional 'left-right' view of politics (the view that is also captured by our interventionist-free enterprise continuum) but argue that it does not follow class lines quite so simply as before.

The theories of value change, on the other hand, suggest that there may be a spread of alternative values which have nothing to do with government intervention or free enterprise. Most notably Inglehart has developed a thesis of 'post-materialist' values.[3] He argues that people who have been brought up in an economically secure environment — who have experienced 'formative affluence' with a freedom from want and war — will grow up to place greater emphasis on higher needs such as freedom of speech and a humane society. Conversely those who experienced insecurity in their formative years will come to place more value on materialist needs like a high rate of economic growth, a stable economy, fighting crime and maintaining strong defence forces. The point of the argument is that the affluence of the postwar period will now have produced a generation of 'postmaterialists' with new political potential.

This argument introduces a 'second dimension' into political analysis. It is one that might be thought of as involving social rather than economic radicalism. But while the argument is very different from the interest theory, the two are not wholly unconnected, not least because many of the 'postmaterialist' generation will have found employment in the expanding technical and welfare state occupations of the salariat. To some extent they are dealing with the same people but offering very different explanations of their behaviour and drawing quite different implications about their political potential. Both accounts are also quite similar in looking for realignment rather than dealignment. They suggest that the old class politics will not merely wither away leaving a vacuum but will be replaced either by a new class politics or by a postclass politics.

These theories looked a great deal more plausible in Britain in the early 1970s at a time when class voting appeared to be on the decline and a larger proportion of the salariat seemed to be turning to Labour. But they could in principle apply to the Alliance as much as to Labour. As we suggested in chapter 2, the Alliance probably appeals to a somewhat different section of the salariat from the Conservative party — it may well be the newer, knowledge-based occupations that provide its most promising recruiting ground. Moreover, the Alliance may prove to be a very convenient compromise for members of the salariat. It does not have the commitment to equality and redistribution that would threaten their privileged economic position but it does hold out the prospect of a measure of 'social radicalism' on issues such as the welfare state or industrial democracy.

Indeed, one might go further and ask whether the Social Democratic Party has captured that reformist and meritocratic tradition that used to characterise the right wing of the Labour party. Has there in fact been a realignment within the salaried class not between Conservative and Labour, as was thought in the early 1970s, but between Labour and the Alliance?

Divisions Within the Salariat

Unfortunately, even with a sample of nearly 4000, our numbers are too few to permit useful comparisons of individual occupations. And the constraint of sample size is even more pressing if we wish to extend our analysis backwards to the 1964 study and test for realignment within the salariat. What we have done therefore is to group occupations together to reflect the basic divisions discussed by the commentators. The most practical procedure for analysing the distinction between 'line' and 'staff' occupations is to follow the Office of Population Censuses and Surveys' distinction between 'managers in small establishments' on the one hand and 'ancillary workers' (largely semi-professionals such as teachers, nurses, computer programmers, technicians and the like) on the other.[4] This gives us reasonably large numbers and captures rather well the distinction between old and new occupations in the salariat.

TABLE 5.1 Occupational Divisions Within the Salariat

	Conservative	Labour	Alliance	Others	
Managers in small establishments	68	12	20	1	101% (N = 102)
Ancillary workers	44	19	35	2	100% (N = 302)

Table 5.1 shows clearly enough a difference in the predicted direction in the votes of the two groups.[5] The managers in small establishments are much more 'right-wing', and indeed come very close to the petty bourgeoisie in their voting behaviour. For example 71 per cent of the petty bourgeoisie voted Conservative compared with 68 per cent of the small managers, and the figures for Labour and Alliance voting are almost identical too.

The ancillary workers on the other hand are rather more 'left-wing', lying closer to the routine white-collar workers and the manual foremen in their level of support for the Conservatives. They do however have a markedly higher Alliance vote than any of the five classes described in chapter 2 while their Labour vote is not especially high. It is clear that there is an important division here between these two 'wings' of the salariat and that there may be something of a radical potential among the newer occupations – although whether radical is quite the right term is perhaps questionable. After all, Mrs Thatcher's Conservative party can also claim to be following radical economic policies, and in many respects the Alliance can be said to be following conservative, consensus politics.

This pattern is repeated if we compare public and private sectors within the salariat. Given the concentration of small establishments in the private sector, we are to some extent simply looking at the same people but under a different label. It is not really possible, given our small numbers, to disentangle sectoral from occupational differences. However, it may be worth saying in passing that ancillary workers in the private sector (of whom there were only 64 in our sample)

TABLE 5.2 Sectoral Divisions Within the Salariat

	Conservative	Labour	Alliance	Others	
Private sector	62	9	28	1	100% (N = 441)
Nationalised industries	47	23	30	0	100% (N = 78)
Government sector	46	18	35	2	101% (N = 323)

voted 43 per cent Conservative, 17 per cent Labour and 39 per cent Alliance – almost exactly the same as in the public sector. On this scanty evidence we would give more weight to the occupational account.[6] But on either account, we clearly have two different 'wings' of the salarist with different propensities to favour the Conservatives.

These differences between the two wings of the salariat are reflected in their values, although the pattern does not follow their alleged interests in any simple way. True, the ancillary workers were rather more in favour of industrial democracy and government spending on the National Health Service than were the small managers. For example, 75 per cent of the ancillary workers agreed that the government should "give workers more say in running the places where they work" (Q40b) while only 21 per cent disagreed. But as table 5.3 shows the difference from the managers on this question was only modest. This particular issue hardly constitutes a major new basis of social conflict within the salariat.

TABLE 5.3 Attitudes in the Salariat

	Percentage agreeing with "right-wing" alternative				
	Nationalisation	Defence spending	Income redistribution	Industrial democracy	NHS spending
Managers in small establishments	68	73	59	35	26
Ancillary workers	41	55	40	21	14

There is also an interesting difference in attitudes towards defence spending, but it is on the major class issues of nationalisation and income redistribution that the differences are largest. On both these questions the small managers closely resemble the petty bourgeoisie while the ancillary workers are similar to the routine white-collar workers and the foremen. Indeed this 'new working class' of salaried semi-professionals lies slightly closer, on these two questions, to the 'old working class' of manual workers in industry than it does to the 'old middle class' of the petty bourgeoisie and small managers. Thus on nationalisation there is a 27 point difference between ancillary workers and the small managers but a 17 point difference between the ancillary workers and the working class. On income redistribution the differences are 19 points and 15 points respectively.

We have, then, some sympathy for theories of the 'new working class'. The ancillary workers — the semi-professionals who lack direct managerial authority — do seem to represent a rather different segment of the salariat from the small managers, and do seem to have somewhat greater radical potential. Their radicalism should not be exaggerated however. On the class issues they appear to have rather more in common with the working class than with the managers, but in their voting behaviour they act very differently from the working class. It is the Alliance rather than the Labour party which does well among the ancillary workers, and even so the Conservative party wins more of their votes than does the Alliance. In their voting patterns they look more like a 'new intermediate class' than a 'new working class'.

The distinctiveness of their voting behaviour is not new either. Exactly the same divisions between ancillary workers and small managers were present in the earliest election surveys of 1964 and 1966.[7] In 1964 and 1966 as in 1983, the small managers voted in almost identical fashion to the petty bourgeoisie. And in both years the ancillary workers were less prone to vote Conservative than the small managers but more prone to support the Liberals than were the routine non-manual workers.[8] Relative voting patterns have shown no significant change over the twenty years of the election studies. There has been no realignment within the salariat or between Labour and Alliance. The divisions are long-standing ones.[9]

There is, however, one change worth noting. Ancillary workers have grown in number more rapidly than the managers. In 1964 they constituted roughly a quarter of the salariat. They are now just over a third — hardly dramatic stuff and certainly not enough to account for the rise of the Alliance, but a nudge in their direction all the same.

Postmaterialist Values

While we have some sympathy for the theory of the 'new working class', its quantitative importance would appear on this evidence to be rather exaggerated. We have much less sympathy however with Inglehart's theory, at least with that aspect of it which emphasises formative affluence.

Inglehart's theory is based on the ideas of the psychologist Maslow.[10] Maslow postulates that man has a hierarchy of needs: needs for food and shelter come at the bottom of the hierarchy and tend to receive highest priority until they are satisfied. Once they are satisfied people move on to higher needs culminating in ones such as 'self-actualisation'. Inglehart claims to follow this account and argues that people who experienced 'formative affluence' will grow up to place more emphasis on values such as democracy and freedom of speech.

It is not entirely clear to us that 'self-actualisation' and a belief in freedom of speech have much in common, but our more serious worry concerns the psychologistic assumptions about formative affluence. Just as we are very sceptical about the theories of Abrams and others that affluence would erode class values, so we are sceptical that affluence on its own will create new postmaterialist values. In general we believe that value change requires sociological and political, not economic and psychological, explanations. And there is also, in our view, an important conceptual distinction to be made between needs and values (just as there is between interests and values).

Much of Inglehart's evidence comes from a comparison of generations born and brought up in more and less affluent times. But there is also a more direct test which can be made. While class is not the same as affluence, people's class origins will nonetheless give a fair approximation to the economic circumstances of their upbringing. Accordingly we might expect the 'second generation' members of the salariat to place more emphasis on postmaterialist values than the newcomers from the working class (and indeed from the second-generation members of the working class itself).

Following Inglehart we asked respondents "If you had to choose from among the items on this card, which are the two that seem most desirable to you?
   Maintaining order in the nation,
   giving people more say in important political decisions,
   fighting rising prices,
   protecting freedom of speech." (Q22)
Materialists are defined as those who select 'maintaining order' and 'fighting rising prices'. Postmaterialists are defined as those who select 'giving people more say' and 'protecting freedom of speech'.[11] The majority of people fall in a mixed category, selecting one materialist and one postmaterialist value. And, again as Inglehart found, materialists substantially outnumber postmaterialists.

Contrary to Inglehart's expectations, however, we found that class origins had only the weakest of associations with materialism and postmaterialism. Table 5.4 shows that the differences are in the expected direction, but they are modest in the extreme. Class origins are a far weaker basis of these values than they are, for example, of the more familiar class values.[12] If formative affluence has any part to play in political analysis, it is at best a minor, walk-on part, not one of the starring roles.

TABLE 5.4 Class Origins and Postmaterialism

Class origins	Post-materialist values	Mixed	Materialist values		
Salariat	11	60	29	100%	(N = 609)
Intermediate classes	11	55	34	100%	(N = 1020)
Working class	9	55	36	100%	(N = 1714)

However, while Inglehart's concept of postmaterialism and his major explanatory thrust derive from Maslow's psychology, he also points out that there is a strong correlation between postmaterialism and higher education. This is a much more interesting finding and it does, we believe, provide a serious sociological basis to a 'second dimension'.[13] Interestingly, even the extremely modest association between class origins and postmaterialism disappears once we control for education.

Education and Liberal Values

Education, when it has been considered at all by British political scientists, has usually been thought of as an aspect of class structure rather like housing. Some writers indeed have gone so far as to create composite indices in which education (and housing) are as important as occupation in defining class membership.[14] Such composite indices have a lot in common with the market research classification of social grade, and may have some merit as predictors of life-style. However, they serve to obscure important differences in values and political behaviour.

It is of course true that educational attainment is influenced by one's class origins and affects one's class destination. To that extent class and educational qualifications are intimately connected. However, it is quite misleading to treat education as if it were related to class in the same way that housing is. Although the statistical associations are rather similar, the political significance of education is very different from that of housing. As we saw in chapter 4, ownership tends to promote (or at least to associate with) the same 'free enterprise' values that prevail among the petty bourgeoisie and, to a lesser extent, among the salariat; council housing tends to go with the same interventionist values that prevail among the working class. Housing is not a source of alternative values. But while educational *qualifications* may be a route to advantaged jobs, educational *experience* is also an important source of values which are quite distinct from class values. Higher education does not go with 'free enterprise' values in the way that home ownership does.

The continually changing character of British education makes it rather difficult to achieve a satisfactory classification of educational experience. Because of the raising of the school-leaving age and the spread of comprehensive schools, both years of schooling and type of schooling can mean very different things to different age-groups within our sample. Comparability can most easily be achieved using a measure of qualifications and this is what we have used in table 5.5, although on theoretical grounds we would argue that it is the educational experience as such rather than the acquisition of formal credentials which is likely to shape values.[15] Nevertheless, table 5.5 shows that our measure, although not perfect, differentiates clearly between our respondents. In order not to confuse class differences with educational differences, the table compares educational categories within the salariat.

Table 5.5 reports the questions on which our educational categories differed most strongly, just as table 2.2 reported the questions on which the classes differed most.[16] The two lists, however, are totally different. None of the class questions appears here (and *vice versa*). The top five education questions quite clearly involve a different array of values. They are:

(1) "whether Britain should bring back the death penalty" (Q42c),
(2) "whether [racists] should be allowed to hold public meetings to express their views" (Q23b),

(3) "whether Britain should spend less on defence" (Q27c),
(4) "whether Britain should stay in the Common Market" (Q43b),
(5) "whether people who break the law should be given stiffer sentences"
(Q42e).

TABLE 5.5 Education and Values

	Percentage agreeing with the "liberal" alternative					
Highest qualification	Death penalty	Free speech	Defence spending	Common Market	Stiffer sentences	
Degree	72	84	53	58	30	(N = 145)
'O' level or above	44	67	37	36	14	(N = 598)
Below 'O' level	32	55	24	35	18	(N = 261)

Sample: respondents in the salariat

Whereas formative affluence appears to have little or no association with postmaterialism, the educational differences are every bit as large as the class ones of table 2.2 and a great deal larger than the occupational ones described earlier in this chapter. On this criterion the salariat is far more divided by education than it is by sector or occupation.

The content of this list of 'education values' is very similar to Inglehart's description of postmaterialist values. The one surprising entry on the list is the Common Market (where we have arbitrarily defined the 'liberal ' alternative as remaining in the Common Market without renegotiation). This has often been seen by the left and the Labour party as a class issue; thus the Common Market is sometimes portrayed as an institution that develops greater markets for capitalist multi-national companies. As such it would seem to rest uneasily alongside support for free speech and doubts about defence spending. Presumably, however, our graduate respondents inclined to a rather different view; we interpret their responses as indicative more of a support for international political institutions than for multinational companies.

Descriptively, then, our education values come very close to Inglehart's. We agree with him that we have here a major attitudinal dimension which cross-cuts class and provides a potential basis for political divisions within the salariat. But our interpretation of the results is that they have little to do with psychology or 'formative affluence' and more to do with the distinctive cultural values associated with the 'liberal arts' tradition of our universities and grammar schools (a tradition now being recreated in sixth form colleges and many comprehensives). As Musgrove has suggested, it has been one of the gross over-simplifications of sociology to suppose that grammar schools have simply been the purveyors of 'bourgeois' values. We would agree with Musgrove that schools, and even more so universities with their long-standing traditions of academic freedom and the pursuit of knowledge for its own sake, provide a home for nonmaterialistic values.

Writing about his time as a teacher at Mansfield's Queen Elizabeth's Grammar School for boys he said:

> "Middle-class parents, whatever their wealth, family, or Masonic connexions, knew that educational credentials mattered . . . They wanted their sons crammed . . . [but] probably the deepest, most genuinely shared and abiding value that we held as a staff was that 'spoonfeeding' was bad for the intellect and worse for the soul. And more generally 'getting on' was really rather a discreditable preoccupation. The Senior Science Master was thought also to be the Careers Master, but undue concern about jobs was rather immoral. This was not, in fact, a middle-class culture; it was a gentry culture" (1979: 10-11).

Since we are unconvinced by Maslow's hierarchy of needs and by Inglehart's notion of formative affluence, we shall not use the expression postmaterialist values. The layman's use of 'liberal' (with a small l) suits our purposes quite well, particularly given its association with the notion of 'liberal arts' in our educational system.

Whichever term is used, we should also recognise that we are dealing, as with class values, with a rather loose collection of values. The questions on free speech, the death penalty, and sentencing can be thought of as a single continuum analogous to the class continuum of nationalisation, private education, income redistribution and job creation. Attitudes to defence spending and the Common Market cross-cut it to some extent, just as attitudes towards trade union legislation cross-cut the government intervention-free enterprise continuum![7]

Nevertheless, loose though they may be, these liberal values do provide the basis of a second axis which divides the salariat (and to a lesser extent the other classes) and provides an alternative basis to political alignment to that provided by the class values.

To some extent, therefore, we do accept Inglehart's hypothesis that values, rather than class interests, may be a source of alternative political divisions. We would not, however, want to exaggerate the contrast between values and interests or between education and occupation. While we see experience of sixth-form and higher education as the social source of these liberal values, it is also a route of advancement into the salariat, particularly into the professional and semi-professional jobs of the salariat. 37 per cent of the small managers for example had low, or lacked any, qualifications compared with only 15 per cent of the ancillary workers. The educational division thus overlaps the occupational one.

True, it may be that people choose their jobs in the light of their values. Graduates in particular may have a measure of choice in the kinds of jobs they do. But we would also suggest that different occupations may provide more (or less) favourable environments for the maintenance of these values. Values may influence job choice, but the job chosen may also reinforce, or fail to reinforce, those values.[18] In other words, there may be a congruence between the two, just as there is a congruence for example between self-employment and free enterprise values.

Education and Vote

As might be expected, higher education is not only associated with liberal values but also with a vote for the Liberal (or Social Democratic) party. Indeed, the tiny group of graduates in our sample show the highest level of Alliance voting of any social group that we have considered, although even here they are not actually in the lead. As social bases go, higher education looks to be a rather insecure one.

TABLE 5.6 Class, Education and Vote

	Conservative	Labour	Alliance	Others	
Salariat					
degree	42	16	41	1	100% (N = 131)
'O' level or above	54	12	33	1	100% (N = 501)
below 'O' level	60	17	22	2	101% (N = 231)
Intermediate classes					
degree	—	—	—	—	— (N = 21)
'O' level or above	57	17	25	1	100% (N = 441)
below 'O' level	49	25	24	2	100% (N = 748)
Working class					
degree	—	—	—	—	— (N = 4)
'O' level or above	40	36	22	2	100% (N = 169)
below 'O' level	28	52	20	1	101% (N = 815)

In some ways, the more striking feature of table 5.6 is the weakness of the relation between education and voting. Whereas education is as strongly associated with liberal values as class is with free enterprise values, its association with vote is much weaker than that of class. For example, within the salariat, there is a 19 point 'education difference' in Alliance voting. But, among the unqualified, there is a 32 point 'class difference' in Conservative voting. While society is as much divided on the liberal values as it is on the class values, these divisions are not equally translated into political action.

One might suggest that there is a potential here for political action that is not fulfilled in the way that the class potential is. Of course, this is partly because some of the 'moral' issues like abortion, divorce and the death penalty are the subjects of 'free votes' in the House of Commons rather than matters of party whips (as they are in some other countries where religion is a major basis of political representation). Britain has partly defined 'paarty politics' as being more about the class issues than the moral ones.

Still, although education is in general rather weakly associated with vote, table 5.6 shows that it is a stronger basis of the Alliance vote than is class. For example, among those with no or low qualifications there is virtually no class difference at all in the Alliance vote: 22 per cent of such people in the salariat voted for the Alliance compared with 20 per cent in the working class. The class differences are somewhat greater among those with intermediate level qualifications. But these class differences in Alliance voting are still smaller than those within the salariat;

41 per cent of the graduates here supported the Alliance compared with 22 per cent of the unqualified. If class is the basis of the Conservative and Labour parties, education is the basis (albeit a weaker one) of the Alliance.

Whether this educational basis of the Liberal vote is a new one is doubtful. Unfortunately the number of graduates in the earlier surveys is far too small to permit useful analysis (to be precise there were only 9 such respondents in 1964). Moreover the earlier surveys did not ask about qualifications such as 'A' and 'O' level, although they did ask about the type of school attended. Since we are interested in educational experience this will suffice as a measure.

First it is clear that the educational basis of liberal values is longstanding. If we equate a selective education in 1964 with 'O' level qualifications and above in 1983, we find almost exactly the same relation between education and attitudes to the death penalty in the two years. In 1964 27 per cent of those who attended selective schools (largely grammar and private schools) favoured abolition compared with 14 per cent of those who had attended elementary and secondary modern schools. In 1983 the proportions opposed to the death penalty had increased but the gap had remained the same: 39 per cent of those with qualifications such as 'O' level opposed its restoration compared with 26 per cent of those with lower (or no) qualifications.[19]

There is nothing new therefore about the 'second dimension' and its relation to education. We are also doubtful whether its relation to Liberal voting is new, although the small number of Liberal voters in the 1964 and 1966 surveys makes this rather harder to detect.[20]

Notes

[1] This is the term used by Serge Mallet (1963). We should distinguish these theories from those of Braverman (1974) and others who deal with the 'proletarianisation' of routine nonmanual work. For a useful collection dealing with both sorts of theory see Hyman and Price (1983).

[2] See Dunleavy (1980). Dunleavy's sectoral argument suggests that these divisions should cross-cut the intermediate and working classes as well as the salariat.

[3] See Inglehart (1971, 1977, 1981). The character of Inglehart's theory seems to have been changing slowly over the years. He now places his main emphasis on two key hypotheses:

> "1 A Scarcity Hypothesis. An individual's priorities reflect the socioeconomic environment: one places the greatest subjective value on those things that are in relatively short supply.
>
> 2 A Socialisation Hypothesis. The relationship between socioeconomic environment and value priorities is not one of immediate adjustment: a substantial time lag is involved, for, to a large extent, one's basic values reflect the conditions that prevailed during one's preadult years" (1981: 881).

[4] 'Managers in small establishments' are those in socio-economic group 2.2; 'ancillary workers' are those in socio-economic group 5.1. For further details see Office of Populations Censuses and Surveys (1970). These two groups together are only a subset of the whole salariat. We have chosen managers in small rather

than large establishments because they are more distinctively Conservative in their voting. It is thus the most favourable test for the theories of the new working class.
[5] Throughout this chapter we have used respondents' own occupation, sector and education and have not attempted to construct measures, analogous to those of class, where respondents are allocated to their spouse's occupations, if they are not themselves economically active or retired.
[6] It is perhaps worth noting that the sectoral divisions do not cross-cut class in quite the way predicted by the theory.

TABLE 5.7N Class, Sector and Vote

	Conservative	Labour	Alliance	Others	
Salariat					
private sector	62	9	28	1	100% (N = 441)
nationalised industries	47	23	30	0	100% (N = 78)
government sector	46	18	35	2	101% (N = 323)
Intermediate classes					
private sector	55	21	23	1	100% (N = 836)
nationalised industries	40	29	27	4	100% (N = 99)
government sector	43	27	28	2	100% (N = 247)
Working class					
private sector	34	47	19	1	101% (N = 650)
nationalised industries	17	62	18	3	100% (N = 147)
government sector	29	46	24	2	101% (N = 167)

Table 5.7N shows that, in the working class, it is only the nationalised industry sector that is distinctively more prone to vote Labour. The government sector is almost indistinguishable from the private sector.
[7] To be fair we should point out that Mallet's book on the new working class was published in 1963 before either of these elections. However, our main point is that these are not new developments which could explain a realignment in the 1970s after the alleged class dealignment.
[8] The numbers involved in both years are small, so we should be cautious in our interpretations. We should also note that in the 1964 and 1966 surveys the ancillary workers were combined with nonmanual foremen, who tend to be a rather more Conservative group. The differences between the two wings of the salariat were rather larger in 1966 than in 1964. In 1966 they were as follows:

TABLE 5.8N Divisions Within the Salariat in 1966

	Conservative	Labour	Liberal	Others	
Managers in small establishments	66	21	13	0	100% (N = 51)
Ancillary workers and nonmanual foremen	48	29	21	1	99% (N = 78)

[9] Absence of realignment is shown by the fact that the Labour/Alliance odds ratio in 1966 was 1.2 and in 1983 was 1.1. It is of course true that Labour did better than the Liberals in the salariat as a whole in 1966, whereas the positions were reversed in 1983, but this can be accounted for largely by the overall changes in their respective fortunes.

[10] See Maslow (1954).

[11] This is the procedure followed by Inglehart in the first of his papers (1971). In his major study (1977) he uses a more elaborate 12-item measure, but we did not have room in our questionnaire for this (particularly in view of the marginality of Inglehart's interests to our own).

[12] Table 5.9N shows the relation between class origins and current attitudes to nationalisation. It confirms our claim that class origins have a stronger association with class values than with postmaterialist values. These data suggest social mobility may have an important effect on politics. We shall examine this in a subsequent paper.

TABLE 5.9N Class Origins and Attitudes to Nationalisation

	Percentage favouring		
	Nationalisation	No change	Privatisation	
Class origins				
salariat	11	35	54	100% (N = 576)
intermediate classes	15	36	49	100% (N = 959)
working class	22	42	36	100% (N = 1548)

[13] Inglehart actually takes education to be a measure of formative affluence. He writes:

"Throughout the United States and Western Europe those with higher incomes, more education, and better jobs are two or three times as likely to have Post-materialist values as those who are less fortunate. Of the three socio-economic status variables, education is the strongest predictor of values, because it (far more than one's present income) reflects the relative prosperity of the family during one's youth and childhood – the period of life we hypothesised, when one's values are most malleable. Education is also an indicator of exposure to specific forms of indoctrination which may also help shape one's values, just as Flanagan claims. But to attempt to separate these influences by controlling away all the variance linked with education is to perform surgery with a meat ax . . ." (1982: 471-472).

The difficulty with this line of reasoning is that, once we control for education, the association between class origins and postmaterialism wholly disappears. Our own views are much closer to those of Flanagan (1982), who writes:

"We would also expect education to be independently associated with changes in value preferences, since education implies a process of enlightenment whereby traditional folkways are gradually replaced by the more modern and current concepts of society. Thus even within the same age cohorts, we would expect those with less education to cling to the more traditional societal value preferences. As previously noted, however, we would not expect individual affluence to be related to this kind of value change, because the environmental changes that prompt the authoritarian-libertarian reorientation are not limited to one economic stratum" (Flanagan 1982: 418).[14] See, for example, Rose (1980).

[15] Our three educational categories are defined according to the highest qualification a respondent claimed to have in response to Q62 of the questionnaire.

'degree' contains only those who claimed to hold a degree.

'O' level and above' includes those who claimed to hold at least one of the following, but did not claim to hold a degree: CSE Grade 1, GCE 'O' level, Scottish (SCE) lower, School Certificate, GCE 'A' level, Scottish (SCE) higher, City and Guilds craft/ordinary level, City and Guilds advanced/final level, City and Guilds full technological, ONC, OND, BEC or TEC ordinary/general, HNC, HND, BEC or TEC higher level, teachers training qualification, nursing qualification, other professional qualification, other diploma/certificate.

'below 'O' level' includes all remaining respondents including those who claimed to have CSE Grades 2-5, RSA or similar clerical or commercial qualification or a full apprenticeship qualification.

Because of our lack of knowledge about the content of the educational experience involved, overseas qualifications were ignored in allocating respondents to these categories. This affected only a small number of respondents.

[16] The 'liberal' alternatives are taken to be disagreement with the reintroduction of the death penalty, agreement that racists should be allowed to hold public meetings, that Britain should spend less on defence, and that "Britain should stay in the Common Market anyway", and disagreement with stiffer sentences.

[17] The three questions Q23b, Q42c and Q42e form a reasonable Guttman scale, coefficient of reproducibility 0.90 and coefficient of scalability 0.65. In the general factor analysis of all attitude questions, these three items had high loadings on the second main factor (the first factor being interpreted as a left-right dimension akin to our interventionist-free enterprise continuum). The questions

(Notes continue on following page)

on defence and the Common Market had relatively higher loadings on the first factor, probably because they are more 'politicised' and are more strongly associated with party allegiance. The results of the factor analysis are as follows:

TABLE 5.10N Factor Analysis of Attitude Questions

	Factor pattern after oblique rotation	
	Factor 1	Factor 2
Q23a1	.00	−.26
Q23b1	−.07	−.16
Q27a	.29	.28
Q27b	.17	−.17
Q27c	.45	−.20
Q30b	−.09	.20
Q30d	.38	.01
Q34b	.52	.01
Q35a	.54	−.04
Q35b	.20	−.04
Q35c	.16	.03
Q35d	−.44	.22
Q35e	.26	.00
Q37	.58	−.06
Q40a	−.50	.33
Q40b	.22	−.06
Q40c	−.41	.23
Q40d	.25	.20
Q42b	−.13	.52
Q42c	−.09	.55
Q42e	−.14	.46
Q43b	.42	.22
Eigenvalue	3.03	1.70
Percentage of variance explained	48%	27%

[18] One of the factors that may be involved in such a process is the degree of unionisation of an occupation. Members of the salariat working in the government sector, such as people in welfare state occupations like teaching and social work, are much more likely to be members of a trade union than those in the private sector. Their trade unions might help to promote or maintain their radical attitudes. Certainly there is evidence that trade unionists in the salariat are rather more radical than nonunionists with respect to both class and liberal values. However, this finding is not repeated in the working class. We incline to the view that, in the salariat, where union membership is more voluntary, values determine union membership (rather than the other way round). In the working class

union membership 'goes with the job' and is not therefore determined by values (nor promotes them) (see Daniel and Millward 1983).

[19] These figures are slightly different from those of table 5.5 because we have not controlled for class here as we did in table 5.5.

[20] Certainly there is no substantial evidence that the association between education and Alliance voting is a distinctive contribution made to the Alliance by supporters of the new Social Democratic Party. Although those who reported an attachment to the Social Democratic Party were slightly more likely to be better educated the difference was not statistically significant. Indeed, there appears to have been no statistically significant difference in the social base of Liberal and Social Democratic attachment. Slight tendencies for Social Democratic supporters to be more likely to own their own homes, to be employed in a nationalised industry and to be a member of a trade union were all insignificant. So far as its social base is concerned, we are therefore able to analyse the Alliance as a single entity.

But while we have identified a social base to Alliance support, it does not necessarily follow that we can now also account for a significant part of the increase in support for the Liberal and the Alliance since 1964. Although it is likely that the association between education and support for the Liberal party predates the formation of the Alliance and that, therefore, the expansion of university education since 1964 has helped to expand the size of the Alliance's strongest constituency, the size of the expansion is small relative to the increase in the Alliance vote. The proportion of school leavers going on to degree courses increased from 6.7 per cent between 1966/7 to 7.6 per cent in 1979/80 (Social Trends 1982 edition). But even after allowing for the lack of Liberal candidates in half of the constituencies in 1964, the increase in Alliance support is 9½ points.

Chapter 6

Neighbourhood, Region and Vote

Since the 1955 general election there has been an important change in the regional distribution of Conservative and Labour strength.[1] The Conservative party's vote has become more concentrated in the South of England and in rural constituencies while Labour support has become more distinctively a feature of constituencies in the North of England and Scotland and in urban areas. Between 1955 and 1983 there was an overall swing to Labour of 6½ per cent in Scotland; in the North of England there was little change in the two parties' relative strength; but in the South and in the Midlands there was an average swing of 13 per cent to the Conservatives. Similarly in the most urban seats there has been a swing to Labour of 1½ per cent while within the most rural ones the Conservatives have benefitted from a 19 per cent swing.[2] Labour's decline, therefore, has not been a national one but concentrated in certain parts of the country. And while the Conservative share of the vote was much the same in 1964 and 1983, this hides marked changes of support in different types of constituency.

Table 6.1 shows the regional distribution of the vote in 1983 (as reported by the respondents in our survey.)[3] In Scotland there was a huge Labour lead and in the South an even bigger Conservative one with Labour trailing in third place. Wales, the North and the Midlands lie in between politically as well as geographically. To talk of 'two political nations' is therefore something of an oversimplification, but it captures the spirit of a major geographical dimension to the vote.

This division of Britain into two political nations has also had important consequences for the operation of the electoral system. In particular it means that Labour's loss of votes has not been reflected in the number of seats that it holds in the House of Commons. The number of seats won by the Conservatives in 1983 was considerably smaller, and the number won by the Labour party considerably greater, than would have happened if the 1983 shares of the vote had occurred in the 1950s or earlier.[4] For example, in 1931 Labour gained 31 per cent of the vote but won only 52 seats. In 1983 it gained 209 seats from 28 per cent of the vote. The increasing geographical concentration of Labour strength saved the Labour party from parliamentary rout.

TABLE 6.1 Region and Vote

	Conservative	Labour	Alliance	Others		
Scotland	22	45	23	10	100%	(N = 280)
Wales	34	40	23	3	100%	(N = 167)
North	39	37	24	0	100%	(N = 812)
Midlands	52	27	22	0	101%	(N = 573)
South	53	19	28	0	100%	(N = 1217)

Regional Differences in 1983

The most natural explanation of geographical differences in a party's support is the geographical distribution of those social groups which are most inclined to support it. In our survey, 41 per cent of the respondents in Scotland were working class compared with 24 per cent in the South. Similarly, 54 per cent of our Scottish respondents were council tenants, but only 20 per cent of those in the South. These differences alone would produce quite large regional differences in vote.

We can easily calculate the hypothetical differences in vote that would be expected to follow from these regional differences in class and housing. This is done in table 6.2.

TABLE 6.2 Hypothetical Regional Differences

	Conservative	Labour	Alliance	Others	
Scotland	36	39	23	2	100%
Wales	48	26	26	1	101%
North	44	31	24	1	100%
Midlands	46	29	25	1	101%
South	47	25	26	2	100%

Table 6.2 shows that class and housing differences are only part of the story. They generate some regional variations in vote, with Scotland proving particularly distinctive, but these hypothetical differences are nothing like as large as the actual ones. For example, in our survey, there was an *actual* 31 point difference in Conservative voting between Scotland and the South, but the *hypothetical*

gap is only 11 points. In other words class and housing explain about a third of the political difference between the two regions. They do even worse in explaining the low level of Conservative voting in Wales and the North.[5]

The calculations of table 6.2 assume that the way an individual votes depends solely on his or her own social characteristics. However, political scientists have suggested that the social environment too may be important. It has been argued that in a predominantly working-class area, both working-class and middle-class voters are more likely to vote Labour than in a socially mixed area, while in a predominantly middle-class area, voters of both classes will be more likely to vote Conservative. In other words, voting may be 'contagious'. How you vote may depend on how the people round you vote. This kind of environmental influence would tend to accentuate the prevailing patterns of political support. It would tend to make Scotland even more Labour-orientated, and the South even more Conservative-orientated, than would otherwise be expected.[6]

Analysis of 'neighbourhood effects' has, however, been dogged by one important difficulty — the lack of appropriate data. In order to demonstrate a neighbourhood effect two kinds of data are required. First, we need data on the social background and electoral behaviour of the individual. These are produced by a social survey such as ours. Secondly, data are needed on the social character of the neighbourhood in which each individual interviewed in the survey lives. Only the census of population, normally conducted every ten years, is able to provide this information for each and every neighbourhood in Britain. Linking these two sources of information is a difficult task. Each respondent has to be allocated to an appropriately sized Census district. The identification of the correct area is usually a complex and tedious task and researchers in the past have either contented themselves with using information on a respondent's constituency, a much larger area than can reasonably be called a neighbourhood[7] or, more commonly, they have employed advanced statistical methods designed to bypass the need for linking individual with Census data.[8] However, we have been able to derive information from the 1981 Census on the social composition of the local government ward in which each of our respondents lived.[9] Wards are a considerable improvement on parliamentary constituencies, and we would thus claim to have a reasonably accurate and appropriate measure of the social character of the immediate area in which our respondents lived.

Neighbourhood, Region and Vote

In table 6.3 we use our linked data to test the relation between social milieu and vote. We have divided local government wards into three types — those which contained relatively many members of the salariat, those which contained relatively many members of the working class, and a residual category of more mixed neighbourhoods.[10]

Table 6.3 gives persuasive evidence that social milieu as well as individual class position is associated with the way one votes. Social milieu seems to be most important for working-class individuals. The minority of working-class people who live in 'salaried' neighbourhoods are much more like salaried than working-class individuals in their voting behaviour. 49 per cent voted Conservative and 28

TABLE 6.3 Class, Neighbourhood and Vote

	Conservative	Labour	Alliance	Others		
Salaried individuals						
in salaried wards	55	10	34	1	100%	(N = 419)
in mixed wards	60	16	24	0	100%	(N = 233)
in working-class wards	48	22	30	0	100%	(N = 156)
Intermediate-class individuals						
in salaried wards	60	15	25	0	100%	(N = 413)
in mixed wards	57	19	23	1	100%	(N = 407)
in working-class wards	41	33	26	1	101%	(N = 290)
Working-class individuals						
in salaried wards	49	23	28	0	100%	(N = 177)
in mixed wards	37	40	24	0	101%	(N = 264)
in working-class wards	22	61	17	1	101%	(N = 435)

per cent for the Alliance, proportions that come very close to those for the salariat in general (given in table 2.3). Conversely working-class individuals in working-class neighbourhoods are much more strongly Labour-voting. The 61 per cent of these people voting Labour approaches the figure that Labour obtained twenty years ago in the working class as a whole (given in table 3.2). Among the salariat, however, the neighbourhood 'effect' is very much weaker. Labour's vote is only 12 per cent higher among those members of the salariat living in working-class wards than among those living in salaried wards.

Of course, we cannot be sure that the 'neighbourhood differences' shown in table 6.3 are actually 'neighbourhood effects'. They might simply be the consequences of individual characteristics which we have omitted to measure. As we saw in chapter 4, the working class is divided by housing whereas the salariat is not. Clearly we need to check that the 'neighbourhood differences' are not just the familiar housing differences masquerading under another name.

This can easily be checked. We find that the 'neighbourhood difference' persists even when we control for the individuals' housing. Indeed they are not even much reduced in scale. For example, in the case of working-class owner-occupiers, 52 per cent in working-class wards voted Labour but only 18 per cent in salaried wards. By controlling for housing we have reduced the neighbourhood difference from 39 points to 34 points. It remains a substantial difference, and we feel it is unlikely that other individual characteristics will be any more successful in reducing it.

We also find that it adds little to our analysis of neighbourhoods if we take account of their housing mix as well as their class composition. The finding is analogous to the discovery in chapter 4 that the spread of housing over time added little once we had taken account of changing class structure. And it occurs for much the same reason. Predominantly working-class neighbourhoods, for example, are also likely to be ones with a larger proportion of council tenants. By adding housing mix to our analysis we merely pick out the same neighbourhoods as before but give them a different label.

The class composition of a neighbourhood is thus strongly associated with support for the Conservative and Labour parties (although not for the Alliance) and it is this which largely accounts for the regional variation in support for those parties.[11] As might be expected there are more predominantly working-class neighbourhoods in the North of England and Scotland than in the Midlands and the South, while the opposite is true of salaried neighbourhoods. Similarly, working-class neighbourhoods are more likely to be found in urban constituencies and predominantly salaried-class ones in rural constituencies.

Neighbourhood and Values

It is not perhaps surprising that the character of one's neighbourhood should affect one's political attitudes and behaviour. Consider, for example, the position of self-employed shopkeepers living and working in an economically depressed inner-city area. Their individual economic position would incline them towards a 'free enterprise' political ideology and the Conservative party. But they may also perceive that business success depends upon that of the local economy as a whole and, consequently, might favour government intervention to promote the economy of their area. Indeed, they might go even further and favour at least some collective political action designed to advance the interests of the working class, since an increase in local wages will generate more money to spend in that neighbourhood.

The social and economic character of a neighbourhood might then be expected to influence individuals' attitudes towards the role of government activity in the economy. It might be expected to have most influence on attitudes towards regional policy but it may also influence more general attitudes towards broad class issues.

In order to test this hypothesis we examined the relationship between the class composition of a neighbourhood and the class values described in chapter 2. We also looked at answers to the question "Should the government do more to help the economy of the area in which you live?" (Q40d). As we had anticipated it was replies towards this question which were the most strongly associated with the class composition of a neighbourhood. Within each class, people living in a predominantly working-class neighbourhood were much more likely to favour government help for their local economy than those living in a predominantly salaried one.[12]

On the general class values, however, there was a somewhat different pattern. Here the association was confined to the intermediate and working classes. As table 6.4 shows, intermediate and working-class people living in salaried neighbourhoods were more likely to adopt a 'right-wing' position on issues such as income and wealth redistribution and nationalisation. For example, among members of the working class living in salaried neighbourhoods 38 per cent were opposed to the redistribution of income and wealth while in working-class neighbourhoods this fell to 20 per cent. Among the salariat, however, neighbourhood seemed to make little or no difference.

TABLE 6.4 Neighbourhood and Class Values

	Percentage opposing redistribution			Percentage favouring privatisation		
	Salaried wards	Mixed wards	Working-class wards	Salaried wards	Mixed wards	Working-class wards
Salariat	53 (489)	46 (268)	47 (190)	53 (469)	56 (260)	48 (181)
Intermediate classes	48 (487)	43 (490)	32 (379)	55 (466)	52 (435)	40 (321)
Working class	38 (222)	30 (341)	20 (559)	40 (193)	33 (288)	24 (484)

Figures in brackets give cell sizes

The fact that the class composition of the neighbourhood has had little effect upon the values and behaviour of the salariat is probably because their 'life chances' are less affected by the character of their locality. Compared with the working class, members of the salariat (teachers and civil servants for example) are more likely to have their work governed by national arrangements, while their chances of finding promotion and advancement are less likely to be confined to their immediate area. Indeed, geographical mobility may be an essential ingredient of their career advancement.[13]

Change Over Time

While the character of the neighbourhood may explain regional differences in voting behaviour in 1983, we need more evidence before we can account for the changes over time. As we suggested earlier, the division into two political nations has become steadily more important over the last thirty years but neighbourhood differences have surely always been a feature of British society. How might we account for the change?

We can posit three possible sources of change.[14] First, economic growth (and decline) and the associated processes of migration and social mobility may have altered the class composition of the regions themselves. We need to ask whether the expansion of the salariat has proceeded faster in the South and the Midlands than in the North and Scotland.

Second, the mix of neighbourhoods in each region may have changed, particularly with the building of new private estates. The South may now have fewer homogeneous working-class neighbourhoods while in the North the mix may be much as it was before. Third, the neighbourhood effect itself may have become stronger over time. Most obviously economic inequalities between neighbourhoods may have been accentuated as unemployment has grown more rapidly in some areas than others.

These three possibilities are by no means mutually exclusive. Indeed it is quite likely that if the first were true and the class composition of the regions had changed, then the mix of neighbourhoods would have changed too.

Unfortunately, it has not proved possible to link respondents to Census information on their localities for earlier election surveys. We cannot therefore assess the relative importance over time of the three explanations in any categorical way. However, there is sufficient evidence available for us to make some progress, particularly on the first possible explanation.

The hypothesis that there have been regional differences in the rate at which the class structure has changed receives only modest support. Table 6.5 shows the differences in the extent to which the working class has contracted. For example, in 1964 54 per cent of the Scottish respondents in the sample were working class. By 1983 this had fallen to 41 per cent, giving the change of 13 points shown in the table. This contraction was of very similar magnitude to the ones found in the other regions. The differences are clearly insufficient to account for the major political change that has occurred.

Changes in housing, also shown in table 6.5, are rather more distinct, with an increase in the proportion of council tenants in the North and Scotland but clear declines in the South and Midlands.[15] Taken together, these two sources of change go a little way towards explaining the development of 'two nations'. We can simulate the effects of these changes in class and housing on vote just as we did in chapters 3 and 4. The result of this exercise suggests that in Scotland social change was worth a swing to the Conservatives between 1964 and 1983 of 1½ per cent while in the South and the Midlands the Conservative gain was between 5 per cent and 8 per cent.[16]

TABLE 6.5 Regional Changes 1964–1983

	Change in percentage working class	Change in percentage council tenants
Scotland	−13	+6
Wales	−14	−12
North	−10	+2
Midlands	−14	−7
South	−15	−6

While these figures indicate that the social structure has moved in the Conservatives' favour to a greater extent in the South than in the North and Scotland, it is also clear that this social change alone cannot account for the whole of the political change. The actual difference in the swing between Scotland and the Midlands and the South between 1964 and 1983 was 20 per cent; our hypothetical difference is no more than 6½ per cent. [17]

This still leaves us needing either our second or third explanations to account fully for the widening of the regional gap. As we have already mentioned the changing shape of the regional class structures is also likely to change the mix of neighbourhood in each region. However, despite the plausibility of this argument we are not in a position to test it ourselves and, as far as we are aware, no-one else has yet worked on it.[18] Our results suggest that such an analysis should be placed on the agenda for future research.

So far we have concentrated on the possibility that the change in the geographical distribution of support for the Conservative and Labour parties can be accounted for by social changes. But as with the Alliance rise or Labour's decline in Britain as a whole, there is no reason in principle why social change should be the whole explanation. More political factors could be at work too.

That the two social factors considered so far are not the whole explanation is suggested by the result of the October 1974 general election. That election occurred only eight months after its predecessor and on the same electoral register. The swing between the October and the February 1974 elections could not therefore have been much influenced by change in the class composition or homogeneity of constituencies. But there was still a difference in the swing between urban and rural areas. City constituencies swung by an average of 3.6 per cent to Labour while rural seats swung by only 2.2 per cent.[19]

It is possible therefore that the association between neighbourhood and vote may have strengthened. Certainly, the economic condition of Britain over the last 25 years has encouraged such a change. The period has seen both a stagnant national economy while (with the exception of the development of the oil industry in Scotland) the more depressed parts of the country in the 1950s have remained relatively depressed in the 1970s and 1980s. In such circumstances, those living in less affluent neighbourhoods might increasingly despair of the ability of the free market to provide economic advancement and be persuaded of the value of government intervention.

Notes

[1] The swing between 1955 and 1959 marks the beginning of the change. At each election from 1959 onwards there has either been an urban/rural and/or North/South pattern to the swing between Conservative and Labour. The swing at the 1951 and 1955 elections, in contrast, was uniform across the country. See Curtice and Steed (1982: 256). The pattern of swing in Wales has not fitted into either the pattern typical of Northern Britain or that of Southern Britain. Until 1970 Labour performed better than the national average but since then the principality has swung towards the Conservatives. Because of this, and because of the smallness of the size of our sample in Wales, most of the analysis in this chapter excludes consideration of the Welsh case. For an analysis of voting in Wales see Balsom et al (1983).

[2] Curtice and Steed (1982); Curtice and Steed (1984a); Curtice and Steed (1984b). Two-party swing is defined as the change in the Conservative share of the combined Conservative and Labour vote in a constituency. It thus measures changes in relative strength.

[3] Regions are based on the standard regions as defined by the Registrar General on the basis of the pre-1974 local government boundaries. South includes the South East and South West standard regions; Midlands includes East Anglia, East Midlands and West Midlands; and the North includes Yorkshire and Humberside, North West and the Northern regions. The regional pattern of the actual vote is similar to that in table 6.1. See Butler and Kavanagh (1984: 301).

[4] For further details see Curtice and Steed (1982); Curtice and Steed (1984a).

[5] The Scottish and Welsh vote does, of course, have an added distinctiveness in the incidence of support for nationalist parties.

[6] The most popular explanation for a neighbourhood effect has been provided by Butler and Stokes who suggest that the social psychology of a neighbourhood is important. They suggest that electors can be divided into two groups. The members of the first group derive their political information primarily from national sources such as the mass media; the others derive their information primarily from local sources, particularly from conversations with friends and neighbours. It is this latter group whose behaviour will be influenced by their immediate social milieux. In a working-class area their political sources of information will be predominantly Labour voters, and conversations will consequently tend to be imbued with a predominantly pro-Labour bias. The voter's political view will be influenced accordingly. See Butler and Stokes (1974: 130-137 and 140-151). See also Parkin (1967) for a more structural explanation. For a review of the literature on the neighbourhood effect see Taylor and Johnston (1979, chapter 5). For a reanalysis of Butler and Stokes' data see Bodman (1983).

[7] See, for example, Butler and Stokes (1974). Clearly it is quite possible, for example, for an individual in a predominantly working-class constituency to live in a predominantly middle-class local neighbourhood. If inter-personal influence

is the mechanism behind the neighbourhood effect it is difficult to believe that the social character of the neighbourhood beyond an individual's immediate neighbourhood is of any importance. Where linkage has been achieved at a lower level this has been achieved with a local rather than a national survey. See Bealey et al (1965: 179-186).

[8] See, for example, Miller (1977, 1978), Johnston (1983a, 1983b), Crewe and Payne (1976).

[9] It was not, however, possible at the time of writing easily to assemble the necessary data for Scotland. These respondents are therefore excluded from this analysis. We are grateful to the Economic and Social Research Council Data Archive for supplying the Census data and to the Office of Population Censuses and Surveys and the many electoral registration officers we contacted for their assistance in identifying the 1981 ward of our respondents.

[10] Salaried wards were defined as those where the percentage of economically active and retired persons in socio-economic groups 1,2,3,4 and 5 was 28 per cent or more. Working-class wards were defined as those where the percentage of economically active and retired persons in socio-economic groups 9, 10, 11 and 15 was 42½ per cent or more. (These two definitions proved to be mutually exclusive and give the best possible approximation to our definition of the salariat and the working class available from Census data.) Mixed wards constitute all other wards.

TABLE 6.6N Class, Neighbourhood, Region and Vote

	Percentage voting Conservative	
	North	South
Salaried individuals		
in salaried wards	54 (78)	54 (269)
in mixed wards	51 (40)	60 (140)
in working-class wards	40 (81)	— (14)
All salaried individuals	48 (199)	57 (423)
Intermediate-class individuals		
in salaried wards	56 (87)	63 (251)
in mixed wards	60 (79)	53 (236)
in working-class wards	39 (142)	40 (28)
All intermediate-class individuals	49 (308)	57 (515)
Working-class individuals		
in salaried wards	46 (22)	49 (106)
in mixed wards	31 (57)	40 (145)
in working-class wards	20 (235)	19 (40)
All working class individuals	24 (314)	40 (291)

Figures in brackets give cell sizes

[11] To test whether this is the case so far as the North/South variation is concerned we have to compare voting patterns controlling simultaneously for individual class membership, ward composition and region. As a result the numbers in some

cells of the required table become almost vanishingly small. What we have done therefore is to restrict ourselves to our two largest (numerically) regions, namely the North and the South. Table 6.6N shows the percentages voting Conservative.

It is apparent that the neighbourhood differences very largely account for the regional ones. This is most strikingly the case for working-class individuals, 24 per cent of whom voted Conservative in the North but 40 per cent in the South. This 16 point difference wholly disappears when we compare working-class individuals in working-class neighbourhoods. If we undertake the same kind of analysis for urban and rural constituencies we acquire similar results; once one takes into account the class composition of a neighbourhood those living in urban and rural areas in the same class generally differ only a little in the way in which they distribute their support between Conservative and Labour. Among members of the working class living in mixed or working-class neighbourhoods, however, there is a marked preference for Labour rather than the Conservatives in urban areas as compared to rural ones. [12] The details are as follows:

TABLE 6.7N Class, Neighbourhood and Attitudes to Regional Aid

	Percentage agreeing the government should do more to help the economy of the area in which they live		
	Salaried wards	Mixed wards	Working-class wards
Salariat	58 (472)	71 (256)	84 (185)
Intermediate classes	71 (440)	75 (452)	88 (362)
Working class	82 (210)	85 (317)	94 (543)
Figures in brackets give cell sizes			

[13] This feature of upward social mobility was identified by Watson who coined the term 'spiralists' for those whose upward social mobility was associated with residential mobility. See Watson (1964).

[14] The same arguments may also be applied, *mutatis mutandis*, to the increased urban/rural differences as well as to the regional ones.

[15] These figures are based on the 1964 and 1983 election surveys and are thus subject to sampling error. This is particularly true of Wales where the number of respondents in both surveys is smallest. But their broad message is confirmed by official statistics. Between 1966 and 1981 the percentage of economically active and retired persons in socio-economic groups 9, 10, 11, 15 and 16 fell by 7.9 per cent in the North and in Scotland, 9.0 per cent in the Midlands and 8.1 per cent in the South. (Calculated from the 1966 and 1981 Censuses. See Table 30, General Registrar Office London and Edinburgh (1969); Table 46, Office of Population Censuses and Surveys/Registrar General Scotland (1983)). In the same period the proportion of council tenants increased by 6 per cent in Scotland, by 5 per cent in the North-west and by 4 per cent in Yorkshire and Humberside and the Northern

Region. Elsewhere the increase was no more than 2 per cent. (Sources: Table 6.2, Central Statistical Office (1976); Table 3.3, Central Statistical Office (1983).

[16] The hypothetical falls in the Labour vote within each region produced by this exercise (between 1½ per cent and 6½ per cent) are less than the overall fall for Labour calculated in chapter 4 because the South has also been growing in population relative to the North.

[17] Further evidence that social change alone cannot account for the emergence of the two nations is also shown in table 6.8N. This shows the association between class and Labour vote separately for each region in 1964 and 1983. The behaviour of the intermediate classes differed little from one region to another in 1964 while in 1983, there was a 23 per cent difference in the level of support for Labour between Scotland and the South. Meanwhile, amongst the working class the difference in support for Labour between Scotland and the South increased from 21 per cent to 30 per cent. Quite clearly, then, those in the same class position were more likely to vote differently from one part of the country to another in 1983 than in 1964.

[18] We are very grateful to Chris Hamnett of the Open University and Barry Morgan of King's College, London for their help on this point. The truth of the hypothesis could be examined by comparing the spatial distribution of the classes at ward (or a similar) level as measured by the 1961, 1971 and 1981 Censuses, but no nationwide study of this sort has been conducted. See, however, Hamnett's (1976) study of the change in the social structure of Inner London between 1961 and 1971 which showed little increase in the spatial segregation of those in professional and managerial occupations from those in other socio-economic groups. It is doubtful, however, whether the findings can be generalised to other cities; the process of 'gentrification' which helped to counteract any tendency towards increased segregation is unusually important in London.

[19] Curtice and Steed (1982: 263).

(Table 6.8N appears on following page)

TABLE 6.8N Class, Region and Vote 1964–1983

Percentage voting Labour

	1964				1983			
	Scotland	North	Midlands	South	Scotland	North	Midlands	South
Salariat	10 (23)	24 (62)	19 (42)	20 (133)	15 (60)	17 (199)	18 (140)	11 (424)
Intermediate classes	30 (46)	29 (143)	38 (93)	28 (192)	40 (103)	27 (308)	20 (229)	17 (514)
Working class	83 (77)	72 (209)	70 (152)	62 (204)	64 (117)	60 (313)	39 (206)	34 (291)

Figures in brackets give cell sizes

PART 2

POLITICAL CHANGE

Chapter 7

Policies

In part 1 we have seen that class remains a major basis of political conflict. The *absolute* level of class voting has declined as Labour has become less successful, but the *relative* level of class voting shows few signs of secular decline. Class has by no means withered away.

Nevertheless the class structure has changed in several respects. The working class has contracted, reducing Labour's electoral base. The salariat has expanded, in particular its liberal wing of educated, public sector professionals who are out of tune both with the free enterprise ideology of the entrepreneur and with the interventionist ideology of the working class. This group provides fertile soil for the Alliance, although as yet the Alliance crop of voters remains a rather sparse and poorly nourished one.

These structural changes provide part, but only part, of the explanation for the long-run changes in British politics. Our various simulations suggest that they could account for half of Labour's decline between 1964 and 1983, but only a small part of the Alliance rise; and they also suggested that it was not just the Labour party that has lost its potential voters; the Conservative party should have benefitted from the changes, but its vote has instead stayed remarkably constant.

We must, therefore, look beyond these structural changes if we are to account both for the long-run political changes and for the immediate results of the 1983 election. We need an account of *political* change to supplement our account of social change.

Accounts of political change usually concentrate on the ways in which the political parties themselves change or behave. How people vote will depend in part on the relation between their interests and the appeals which the parties make to them. To continue the agricultural analogy, social structure provides the soil, the political parties constitute the climate. How well a particular crop grows will depend not only on the soil conditions but also on the climate.

We can think of the parties' performance in office, their image and their styles of leadership as analogous to the climate. The Labour and Conservative parties may have done worse than expected because they have not put forward the right policies to capture the enthusiasm of their potential voters, or because they have failed to implement those policies in office, or because the electorate doubts their ability to implement their policies in future. Our objective in Part 2 is to explore these factors.

Party policy, particularly Labour party policy, has been singled out by many commentators as an explanation of political success or failure. It has been argued that Labour had unpopular policies in 1979, failed to learn the lessons of defeat, and so went down to even worse defeat in 1983.[1] Similarly, whereas the Conservatives may have had unpopular policies on unemployment, they more than made up for this by their popularity on other important issues of the day. As one commentator put it immediately after the election:[2]

"Unemployment damaged the Conservative vote without repairing Labour's; at best it prevented Labour's disaster turning into catastrophe. Other issues, ranked lower in importance, actually made a bigger impact, compensating the Conservatives for what they lost on jobs. Defence is the prime example . . . There was, in fact, only one issue apart from unemployment on which Labour was preferred to the Conservatives — the Health Service — but this was something that consciously affected only one voter in ten. On the remaining issues asked about — prosperity, peace, the EEC, crime, strikes, taxation — the Conservatives were the public's first choice, usually by a wide margin" (Crewe, 1983a).

This line of argument has been suggested as an explanation not only for the Labour defeat in 1983 but also for the long-run decline of Labour and the rise of the Liberals and the Alliance. Thus in the 1950s it was widely held that the policies of the Labour and Conservative parties had begun to converge around the centre. This was the era of Butskellism, a term coined by The Economist to describe the centrist economic policies of the Conservative Chancellor R A Butler and the Labour leader Hugh Gaitskell. Butler and Gaitskell appeared to agree broadly on many major issues; they shared a belief in government intervention in the economy to maintain growth and full employment but they also shared a suspicion of too much intervention, such as nationalisation.[3] Although the 1950s are now believed to have witnessed a high level of class voting, it was paradoxically seen by commentators at the time as the era of consensus politics when the parties agreed on fundamental objectives and the major question was which party provided the better management team.[4]

In many respects, Harold Wilson's governments in the 1960s and the Conservative opposition confirmed the Butskellite tradition. It was not until after the 1966 election that the two major parties began once more to diverge. In particular Edward Heath began a Conservative move away from government intervention and in favour of the free play of market forces. His experiments were shortlived; a sharp increase in unemployment in 1972 led to his famous U-turn back to government controls and interventionism. But Labour too swung away from the centre in 1974 with more extensive promises of nationalisation than had been seen in Labour manifestos for a long time.

As the two major parties moved apart, so the centrist voter, it was held, turned to the Liberals giving them in the February 1974 election their finest haul of votes for forty-five years. As Ivor Crewe and his colleagues put it: "the electorate was well aware of the return to the politics of class conflict and did not like it".[5] According to this account, the 1979 and 1983 elections then marked two more steps along this unpopular route. As Conservative and Labour moved further apart, so there was more room in the centre for Alliance voters. Moreover since the Labour party had moved further to the left than the Conservatives had moved to the right, it was the Labour party that lost more votes.[6]

In principle this is not an implausible account. It is clear that both Conservative and Labour manifestos were a great deal more radical in 1983 than they had been in the 1950s and 1960s, but we doubt whether this is the whole story, or even much of the story.[7] Indeed, the evidence we present here suggests that, had people voted according to the detailed stances of each party on the most important issues of the day, Labour would not in fact have gone down to defeat at all. Its policies on the important issues were not nearly so unpopular as commentators have imagined. As we shall show in this chapter, if voters had decided between the parties according to their policy preferences, there would actually have been a dead heat between Conservative and Labour.

The Consumer Theory of Voting

The view that election results are determined by the detailed stands which the competing parties take on the issues of the day has become the vogue in recent years. This vogue has been largely a result of the failure of the previous orthodoxy (the 'expressive' theory of voting) to account for the electoral changes of the 1970s. The old orthodoxy had emphasised the importance of childhood socialisation in the development of political allegiance. Long term political change occurred as one political generation was replaced by another — as older voters died, young voters with different identities and allegiances entered the electorate. In an elegant piece of analysis Ivor Crewe and his colleagues showed that this theory failed to account for the results of the 1970 and 1974 elections.[8] The consumer theory of voting then filled the resulting vacuum.[9]

The consumer theory is one of the family of instrumental theories described in chapter 1. Whereas the expressive theory held that people vote according to group loyalty, the instrumental theory holds that people vote as rational individuals who want to maximise their self-interest. Two distinct versions of the instrumental theory, the consumer theory and the investment theory coexist.[10] They differ according to their treatment of self-interest. The investment theory assumes that the voter invests in the party that is likely to bring him or her the greatest stream of benefits in the future; self-interest is thus defined as future well-being, and is usually given a highly materialistic slant. It is not perhaps too much of a parody to say that the investment theory assumes that voters will vote for the party which they judge most likely to raise their own standard of living. We shall provide some evidence on this theory in chapter 11. As we shall see, there is something, but not a great deal, to be said in its favour.

The consumer theory is not quite so materialistic. In essence it is based on the axiom that individuals vote for the party they prefer; no limit is set in principle on the range of party characteristics that may be taken into account. As Himmelweit, a major proponent of the consumer theory puts it:[11]

"In a 'consumer' model of parties, a choice has to be made on the basis of the relative preferences a voter has for each party . . . restricting the evaluation to changes in personal welfare is too limited. For some voters, the prestige of the country or the need to safeguard fundamental values concerning toler-ance and justice might well be important in their evaluation of the policies, irrespective of whether this would bring about changes in the voters' personal welfare" (Himmelweit et al 1981: 116-117).

On this account, the act of voting is analogous to the purchase of a consumer good. Parties are treated as competing products; voters are assumed to be dis-criminating consumers who weigh up their likes and dislikes about the alternative parties and choose accordingly. Emotional ties such as party identification or class loyalty do not come into it.

On the face of it, the consumer model does provide a good 'explanation' of how people vote. The preferences which people report for the parties' policies do correspond very closely with the way they vote. However, there is a serious problem with this kind of evidence. The questions place more emphasis on the parties than on the policies. They cannot be used to show that evaluations of policy determine vote since the policies themselves are not actually specified in the questions. For example, the Gallup poll questions which Crewe used as the basis for the Guardian article quoted at the beginning of this chapter asked re-spondents "Would you say which party you think would be best at reducing unemployment?". A respondent could, of course, answer this question without knowing anything about any of the parties' policies on unemployment. Answers to this kind of question do in fact associate highly with how one votes, but how are we to interpret this association? Exponents of the expressive theory would argue that people who identify with a particular party would loyally express support for its policies and that the causal link runs from party allegiance to policy prefer-ences rather than the other way round.[12]

There is a great deal of evidence in support of this expressive interpretation. In particular, questions which ask respondents to rate a party's policy, or its handling of an issue, obtain much higher associations with vote than do questions which ask respondents to rate the policy itself. Thus the question "Should the government spend more money to create jobs?" has a much weaker association with vote than the question "Which party's views on unemployment would you say came closest to your own views?".[13] The more a question is loaded with partisan cues like the expression 'best party' the more it is likely to be tapping *generalised* support for the party rather than *specific* support for the policy in question. When Crewe found that on a large range of issues the Conservatives were the public's first choice by a wide margin it is possible that he has done no more than confirm that the public gave, by a wide margin, more support to the Conservatives than to the other parties. He has restated the election result, not explained it.

Were Conservative Policies Really Preferred?

To determine whether it was party policy that determined the election outcome, we must rely on less loaded questions than those which ask about 'the best party' on each issue. To be fair we should point out that in the 1974 and 1979 election studies Crewe and his colleagues pioneered more neutral questions. They placed before respondents a series of detailed policy statements, for example:

"The best way to tackle unemployment is to allow private companies to keep more of their profits to create more jobs";

"it doesn't matter much either way";

"it is mainly up to the government to tackle unemployment by using tax money to create jobs" (Q25a, 1979 British Election Study).

They then asked respondents first to say how strongly they themselves agreed or disagreed with the statements and second how strongly the parties agreed with the statements. This approach facilitates rather more independent measures of the respondent's own position and of his or her perception of the parties' positions on the issues in question. While it does not eliminate the problem of causal direction, it does produce less loaded descriptions of the electorate's attitudes towards the issues.

In the 1983 study we followed the same general principles as those pioneered by Crewe and his colleagues, but for technical reasons changed the format of the questions somewhat.[14] (Since the context of the issues had in several cases changed quite dramatically, the question wording necessarily had to be changed. This is one of the problems of looking at issues; they are rarely precisely comparable over time.) We used a set of scales to measure the respondents' own views and their perceptions of the parties' positions on each of the major issues of the election. For example, in the case of unemployment and inflation we gave respondents a 21-point scale (running from -10 on the left through zero to +10 on the right) and introduced the question by saying that "people who are convinced that *getting people back to work should be the government's top priority* will put a tick in the last box on the left [the -10 box] and those who are convinced that *keeping prices down should be the government's top priority* will put a tick in the last box on the right [the +10 box]". People who held intermediate positions were asked to tick a box somewhere in between.

We then asked respondents where they would place themselves and where they would place the Conservative party, the Labour party and the Alliance respectively. The distribution of responses for the three party groupings is shown in diagram 7.1.

As can be seen from diagram 7.1, there was broad consensus among our respondents that the Labour position lay on the extreme left of the scale. In that respect the perceived thrust of Labour's policies apparently got across to the electorate rather better than did that of Conservative or Alliance policies on which there was apparently considerable ambiguity. A rather higher proportion (15 per cent in the case of the Alliance compared with 4 per cent in the case of the Conservatives) said that they did not know at all where to place the Alliance on the issues of unemployment and inflation. But among those who did claim to know where the parties were there was actually more disagreement about the Conservative position. The median respondent placed it about halfway between the centre and the extreme right, but there was a substantial minority who placed it well over to the left.

DIAGRAM 7.1 Where the Parties were Believed to Stand

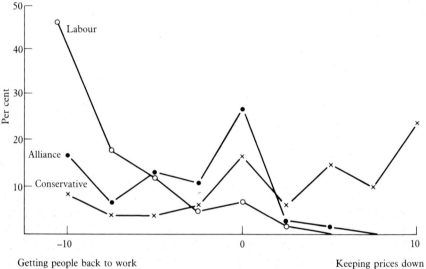

Getting people back to work
should be top priority

Keeping prices down
should be top priority

In itself this is an important result. It shows that perceptions of party positions are themselves variable. Party policy is not an objective phenomenon universally recognised by the electorate. It cannot therefore be 'the' cause of election results, as implied by the consumer theory, for there must be further causes of the variation in perception. In the language of statistics, perceptions of party policy are as much a dependent as an independent variable.

One of the major correlates, and a possible cause, of variations in perception is where the voter places him or herself on the scale. The distribution of our respondents on unemployment and inflation is shown in diagram 7.2 together with the parties' positions (as seen by the median respondent).

On all the issues that we covered in the scales, there were peaks in support at the centre and at the two poles, but on the unemployment-inflation scale there was a particularly pronounced peak on the left, close to the perceived Labour position, with only a very minor peak on the right. At first sight, therefore, diagram 7.2 suggests that the Labour party was, by a wide margin, the electorate's first choice on unemployment and inflation, the two issues which our respondents claimed were the most important to them in deciding their vote. Indeed 49 per cent of the sample placed themselves closer to the median Labour position than to either of the other two parties; next came the Alliance — 32 per cent placed themselves closest to the median Alliance position; and the Conservatives trailed in third with only 16 per cent.[15]

DIAGRAM 7.2 Where the Electorate Stood on
Unemployment and Inflation

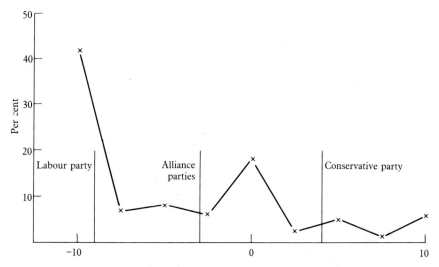

Getting people back to work
should be top priority

Keeping prices down
should be top priority

However, these calculations ignore the fact that where one places oneself and
where one places the parties are not independent phenomena. In particular,
Conservative voters who placed themselves on the left of the scale were quite
likely to place the Conservative party there as well. This is the explanation for the
Conservative peak on the left in diagram 7.1. In contrast, Labour voters who
placed themselves on the left were quite likely to place the Conservative party well
over to the right. Party preference seems to influence how party policy is perceived.[16]

We cannot, therefore, conclude that Labour's policy on unemployment was so
overwhelmingly preferred by the electorate as our initial calculation implied. As
we have shown, some of the people who placed themselves on the left thought that
they were expressing agreement with Conservative policy. They may well have
agreed with Mrs Thatcher's dictum that 'there is no alternative' — that her
policies of controlling the 'evil' of inflation were the only sound basis for
managing the economy and controlling unemployment in the long-run. If this
was their rationale it would clearly be wrong to include them as supporters of
Labour policy.

A second set of calculations is therefore required, based on where the *individual* respondent rather than the *median* respondent placed each party. These
calculations reduce the Labour party's lead on unemployment and inflation, but
still leave it well ahead. 40 per cent now placed themselves closest to Labour,
compared with 32 per cent to the Alliance, while the Conservatives were still in
third place with 28 per cent.[17] Whatever the causal processes that lay behind these
perceptions and evaluations, there has remained a clear preference for Labour

policy on the two (apparently) most important issues of the 1983 election. If people had voted on the basis of these two issues alone, there would have been a Labour landslide.

After unemployment and inflation, the next most important issue in the election was judged by our respondents to be government spending on health and social services.[18] We pitted this against its natural opponent — tax cuts — to create another set of scales (Q31). We realised, of course, that health spending and tax cuts were not necessarily logical opposites; health and social services comprise only a proportion of total government spending, being dwarfed, for instance, by government expenditure on unemployment benefit and social security;[19] in principle, a redistribution of government expenditure is all that is needed to increase spending on health and social services. Nonetheless, we needed to confront our respondents with a pair of alternatives in order to discriminate usefully between them. Everybody is in favour of spending more on the National Health Service, other things being equal, and everybody is in favour of tax cuts, other things being equal. But other things rarely are equal and political choices have to be made. So our question attempted to capture the spirit of these choices, as commonly posited, and as they were frequently posited in the election campaign itself. Our respondents seemed to accept the scale on these terms.[20]

DIAGRAM 7.3 Where the Electorate Stood on Government Spending and Tax Cuts

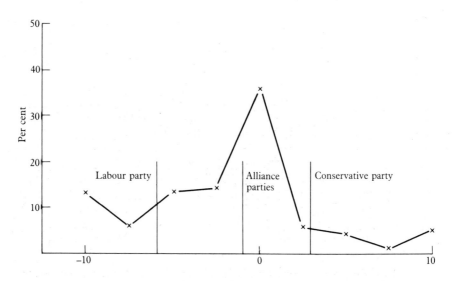

Putting up taxes and spending more on health and social services should be top priority

Cutting taxes and spending less on health and social services should be top priority

Diagram 7.3 shows the distribution of the sample on this tax and social services scale and indicates where the median respondent placed each of the main party groupings. As with unemployment and inflation we have three peaks, at the centre and at the two poles. And as before the electorate tends towards the left rather than the right of the scale, although the peak at the centre is now much the largest. Superficially, this suggests that the Alliance position was the most popular, but again many people (19 per cent) did not know where to place the Alliance, while many supporters of the other two parties also placed them at the centre.

Once again, then, we must compare the individual respondent's position with where he or she placed the parties. On these calculations the Alliance position is still preferred by 38 per cent with Labour and the Conservatives sharing second place on 31 per cent.[21] We have yet to find a Conservative victory on an issue, leave alone a wide margin of victory.

The Conservatives did, however, fare rather better on the next most important issue, defence. As diagram 7.4 shows, unilateral nuclear disarmament did not prove to be a popular policy. Labour's views were generally perceived to be perilously close to the extreme of the scale while the electorate found the centre to be a much more attractive resting point.

DIAGRAM 7.4 Where the Electorate stood on Nuclear Weapons

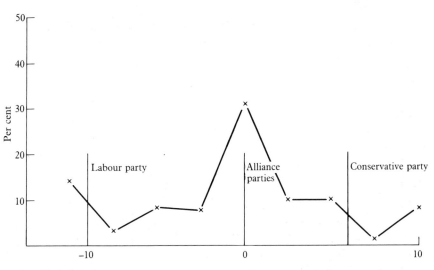

Get rid of all nuclear weapons in Britain without delay

Increase nuclear weapons in Britain without delay

As with the first two scales, the respondents on average placed Labour nearer to the extreme left than they did the Conservatives to the extreme right.[22] But while on the first two scales a position near the extreme left did not seem to be a particular electoral handicap, in the case of of nuclear disarmament it did seem to be one. Only 26 per cent placed themselves closest to the Labour position on disarmament whereas 37 per cent preferred the Conservative position and a further 37 per cent preferred the Alliance position.[23] All the same, this could hardly have been the grave electoral handicap that commentators at the time supposed. Even on Labour's apparent Achilles heel, the Conservatives had still failed to win an outright victory. Since they tie with the Alliance on nuclear defence, even this issue can hardly explain the margin of their electoral success. We have reached the fourth most important election issue, according to our respondents, before the Conservatives even so much as share the lead.

These results seem to challenge the consumer theory's contention that the policies of the parties on the important issues of the day determine election results. True, on the other scales we included, a nationalisation-privatisation scale, and a law and order scale, the Conservative party did well. But these were comparatively minor issues in relation to the other four. It was not only our respondents but political commentators during the election campaign and the political parties themselves who seemed to agree that the issues of unemployment, inflation, taxation, government spending and defence were indeed the dominant ones in the 1983 election and the ones around which the election seemed to turn. But on none of them was the Conservative party clearly in the lead.

What the Result Might Have Been

It is interesting to speculate what the result of the election might have been if the consumer theory had been literally correct. Let us suppose that people vote solely on the basis of their preferences for party policies. Let us assume too that the six issues covered by our scales had been the only ones that really mattered. The latter is by no means a fanciful assumption; after all, these six issues included the ones on which the parties had concentrated heavily during the campaign and around which the election was widely thought to have turned. If a set of issues which includes unemployment, inflation, health and social services (and taxation), defence, law and order, and nationalisation (and privatisation) does not contain the issues that mattered in the 1983 election it would be surprising indeed.

In table 7.5 we show the calculations necessary to pursue this hypothetical question. Since they involve rather heroic simplifying assumptions, we ought to make them explicit in advance. First, and most heroically, we have assumed that people vote for the party that comes closest to their own position on the issue they regard as most important. Thus in accordance with the spirit of consumer theory we asked our respondents "Which one of the six issues on the card would you say was most important to you in deciding about voting?" (Q20b). For each issue we have included in our analysis only those people who regarded it as most important.

Next, we have calculated the distances (assuming an equal interval scale) between people's own position and the position that they themselves assigned to each party. The closest party is then taken to be the party of their choice. If two or more parties were equidistant from their position, the calculations split the vote equally between the equidistant parties. Finally, if people were unable to nominate a most important issue, we have simply excluded them from the table. This applied to fewer than 5 per cent of the respondents.

The top part of the table shows the numbers of people who came closest to each party on the issue they regarded as most important. The bottom part translates

TABLE 7.5 Closest Party on the Most Important Issues

Closest party		Unemployment/ inflation	Defence	Taxes/ Social Services	Law and Order	Nationalisation/ privatisation	Total	%
Conservative	N =	368	333	69	183	67		
Alliance	N =	346	182	105	51	18		
Labour	N =	638	71	147	30	7		
Conservative and Alliance	N =	67	64	15	40	4		
Conservative and Labour	N =	54	15	12	11	1		
Alliance and Labour	N =	320	21	63	26	1		
Conservative, Labour and Alliance	N =	187	4	59	51	2		
N =		1980	690	470	392	100		

EXPECTED VOTE

		Unemployment/ inflation	Defence	Taxes/ Social Services	Law and Order	Nationalisation/ privatisation	Total	%
Conservative	N =	490	373	102	226	71	1262	35
Alliance	N =	602	226	164	101	21	1114	31
Labour	N =	887	91	204	65	8	1255	35
N =							3631	101

these figures into an 'expected vote'. The result, as can be seen, is more or less a dead heat between the Conservative and Labour parties with the Alliance only barely behind. Even with the vagaries of the British electoral system, the result could hardly have been other than a hung parliament.

We accept, of course, that these sorts of hypothetical calculations are a *reductio ad absurdum*. But they are useful as an analytical tool with which to assess the claims of competing theories. We also accept that different assumptions would lead to somewhat different conclusions, although we doubt if alternative ones could lead to radically different conclusions unless they did violence to respondents' own reports of their preferences and priorities.

We did, moreover, explore the effects of changing the most heroic of our assumptions. We realise that it is a gross over-simplification to pretend, as we did, that people vote on the basis of their one most important issue. Many people might indeed have regarded unemployment as the single most important issue and (agreed with the Labour position on that issue) while preferring the Conservative position on, say, health and defence. That being so, it might have been rational for them to vote Conservative even though they judged these two issues to be of lower importance. Two or three 'quite important' issues might outweigh one 'extremely important' issue.

The consumer theory allows that people do make this kind of rational calculus of competing policies. But how are we to ascertain what trade-offs people make? The consumer theory is not very helpful on this.[24] The usual method in studying how people choose real consumer goods is to observe a series of actual choices under different conditions and infer their trade-offs. But in the analysis of an election we have only one choice to study — the vote itself. It would be unjustified to tinker with hypothetical trade-offs until we were able to make them generate the 'right' election result. This would render the analysis circular as we would have to assume the truth of the theory in order to test it! What we need is *independent* evidence about trade-offs in order to test the consumer theory.

We do in fact have some independent evidence ourselves since we asked our respondents not only which issue was most important to them when deciding about voting but also which came next. If we give equal weight to the two issues judged most important by the respondents, we are probably erring on the side of generosity. In so doing we allow trade-offs a good opportunity to display themselves.

The main consequence of such calculations is to pull the Alliance up at Labour's expense. The expected outcome now becomes 35 per cent of the vote for the Conservatives, 32 per cent for the Alliance and 33 per cent for Labour.[25] This is still a long way from the actual election result.

One could go on tinkering with the assumptions *ad infinitum* in order to get a closer approximation to the actual result, but, as it turns out, the most effective way of getting the 'right' answer is to ignore respondents' own judgements of importance altogether. As we shall show in the next chapter, issues like nationalisation, which respondents almost universally described as unimportant in deciding their vote, actually prove to be the best predictors of voting behaviour.[26]

It seems to us that this is bad news indeed for the consumer theory of voting. The theory surely cannot rely on respondents' reports of their policy preferences but then reject their reports of their relative importance. Why should one set of reports be so unduly privileged?

In our view, the consumer theory is based on the misconception that voting is based on a discrete, deliberate decision. The fact that people will answer a survey question that asks them what was 'the most important issue in deciding about voting' does not means that they actually reach their decision in that way. It is well known that respondents have an infuriating (and gratifying) habit of answering questions that have little or no relevance to their behaviour simply in order to be cooperative.

Our data suggest to us that voting choices are not made on the basis of a conscious weighing in the balance of alternative policies (although respondents will quite happily evaluate alternatives if one asks them to). As we shall try to show in the following chapters, electoral choice is based on a much broader, more 'synoptic' evaluation of parties than the consumer theory allows for. We accept the conclusions of the 'expressive' theory that these electoral choices and evaluations will in many cases be long-standing ones, perhaps even inherited from childhood socialisation. But they are not solely inherited. We do not want to replace a one-sided instrumental theory with a return to a one-sided expressive theory. Events and personalities may also shape perceptions: there is a 'political construction of reality' as well as a 'social construction of reality'.

But these constructions are not detailed appraisals of party manifestos and policies. Rather they are more global or 'synoptic' perceptions of the overall character of a party. Factors such as policies, record in office, putative ability to implement a programme, leadership, unity of purpose may all come into it, but none is paramount. Thus a new leadership with the same avowed policies might well convey a different impression of party character, as might the same leadership in new political circumstances. It is the fit between the general character of the party and the voter's own general ideology which, we believe, best accounts for electoral choice. But we do not believe that there is any one simple causal process that underlies this fit. The expressive theory held that parties shape electors' values; the instrumental theory held that electors' attitudes determine party choices. Both are right but both are too simple.

Notes

[1] For this kind of explanation of the 1979 result see Crewe (1982a).

[2] To be fair we should point out that Crewe modified his position somewhat in his later writings on the 1983 election (Crewe, forthcoming).

[3] Our souce for this is Butler and Stokes (1974: 196).

[4] This was primarily an American account of 'the end of ideology' (see Bell, 1960; Lipset, 1960) but British commentators tended to follow this lead. For an analysis of British party manifestos which supports the claim that the Conservative and Labour parties moved closer together in the 1950s and early 1960s see Charlot (1975).

[5] Crewe, Sarlvik and Alt (1977: 172).

[6] This kind of account fits naturally into the classic instrumental theory of voting advanced by Downs (1957). It does however leave unanswered the question why the parties themselves should behave so irrationally. In the Downsian model both electors and parties are assumed to be rational, instrumental actors. Robertson

(1976) attempts to give a more sophisticated account of party motivation within the overall Downsian framework.

[7] This view is confirmed by the content analysis of party manifestos undertaken by Laver (1984).

[8] We take Butler and Stokes (1974) to represent the old orthodoxy. The main critique of the account of generational replacement is Crewe, Sarlvik and Alt (1977). See also Crewe (1974) for another critique of Butler and Stokes.

[9] Not only has the consumer theory become more popular among academics. but it has also been claimed that, as class solidarity declined, the electorate is now more likely to behave in accordance with its postulates. See, for example, Franklin (1983).

[10] This distinction comes from Ferejohn and Fiorina (1974). Downs' original formulation of the economic theory of democracy represents an investment theory; in it electors accept the cost of voting if it is outweighed by the expected utility of future benefits. Riker and Ordeshook's (1968) reformulation represents a consumption theory; voting itself is assumed to yield 'psychic pleasure'.

[11] Himmelweit might not accept the simple outline of the consumer model which we offer in the text. She herself says her theory is a model "not of voting but of parties: voting for a party 'purchases' the party" (1981: 116) We find the distinction opaque. Confusingly, Himmelweit's consumer model of voting is not the same as the consumer approach to politics described in chapter 2 and attributed to Abrams et al (1960). Abrams' view has more in common with the investment theory, since it suggests that people will vote for the party that makes them better off.

For a critique of Himmelweit's work see Dunleavy (1982), and for a general critique of rational choice theories see Heath (1976).

[12] This is one of the oldest claims in political science literature, and exponents of instrumental theories usually accept it too. See for example Sarlvik and Crewe (1983). As Sarlvik elegantly puts it "it is as though individuals were looking at the issues and the parties' policies through tinted spectacles with the effect of making the party one sympathises with look a bit better and the opposite party a bit worse" (1983: 220). However, he then ignores the implications of this for an instrumental theory of voting.

[13] Cramer's V for the association between vote and Q30d (". . . the government should spend more money to create jobs") is .25 and for the association with Q20d2 ("Which party's views on unemployment would you say come closest to your own views?") is .56.

[14] In particular we wanted to get a better approximation to Downs' notion of ideological distance. The questions developed by Crewe et al run the risk of confusing the salience of an issue to the respondent with his or her position on the issue. We would however accept that the two are not unrelated. Respondents who feel strongly about an issue often adopt a more extreme position on the issue. It is perhaps worth noting that Sarlvik and Crewe also interpret their measures as ones of distance.

[15] In making these calculations we have had to assume an equal interval scale, but it is doubtful if alternative assumptions would radically modify our interpretation.

[16] The relation between vote, own position and perceived party positions is shown in the following table. For ease of presentation we have collapsed the scales to five categories only. The table covers Conservative position on the unemployment/inflation scale.

TABLE 7.6N Own Position and Perceived Party Positions

	Perceived Conservative position						
	−10	−9 to −1	0	1 to 9	10		
Conservative voters' own position							
−10	36	17	21	10	15	99%	(N = 374)
−9 to −1	1	44	11	39	5	100%	(N = 292)
0	2	7	38	40	13	100%	(N = 343)
1 to 9	0	6	10	69	16	101%	(N = 251)
10	7	2	11	12	68	100%	(N = 142)

	Perceived Conservative position						
	−10	−9 to −1	0	1 to 9	10		
Labour voters' own position							
−10	13	10	18	18	40	99%	(N = 559)
−9 to −1	1	22	7	55	15	100%	(N = 158)
0	2	7	27	29	35	100%	(N = 85)
9 to 1	0	20	8	68	8	104%	(N = 25)
10	22	11	22	19	30	104%	(N = 27)

It can be seen that the further 'left' a Conservative respondent places himself or herself on the scale the greater the likelihood that the respondent regards the Conservative party as being on the left.

See also Alt et al (1976) in which it was demonstrated that party identification was as important an influence upon which party a voter regarded as the best on an issue as which party he placed closest to himself on an issue scale.

[17] These calculations again assume an equal interval scale. Respondents who placed themselves equidistant between two or more parties are divided equally between the relevant parties. Respondents who did not know where to place a particular party (usually the Alliance) are retained in the analysis but cannot of course be closest to the missing party. The basis of our calculations is as follows:

TABLE 7.7N Closest Party on Unemployment and Inflation

Closest single party on the unemployment-inflation scale	Conservative	21.5
	Alliance	19.1
	Labour	27.8
Equidistant between	Conservative and Alliance	4.7
	Conservative and Labour	2.6
	Labour and Alliance	14.4
	Conservative, Labour and Alliance	10.0
		100.1%
N =		3808

We then calculate that the Conservative party wins 21.5% + 2.35% + 1.3% + 3.33% of the voters, ie 28%. Similar calculations yield the figures of 32% for the Alliance and 40% for Labour.

A simpler set of assumptions yields not dissimilar results. Thus 36 per cent placed themselves in exactly the same position as Labour, 32 per cent in the same position as the Alliance and 21 per cent in the same position as the Conservative party.

[18] This judgement depends on which criterion of importance one takes. Thus 62 per cent of respondents said that health and social services were extremely important compared with 40 per cent for defence. But 17 per cent said that defence was the single most important issue compared with only 13 per cent for health and social services (which had more second choices).

[19] In 1982/3 defence spending amounted to 13 per cent of public expenditure, education to 12 per cent, health and personal social services to 12 per cent but social security to 29 per cent (Imber and Todd, 1983, table 3).

[20] We subjected a number of interviews to interaction coding analysis and this did not reveal any particular problems with this scale. See Morton-Williams (1977).

[21] The assumptions are the same as before. The figures on which they are based are given in Table 7.8N.

[22] However, we should note that when respondents were asked "On the whole, would you describe the Conservative party as extreme or moderate?" "And the Labour party nowadays, is it extreme or moderate?" identical proportions of our respondents described the two parties as extreme, 49 per cent in the case of the Conservative party and also 49 per cent in the case of the Labour party (Q18a). We believe that this supports our distinction between the perception of policies and the perceptions of parties as institutions.

[23] The assumptions are the same as before and the calculations are based on the figures in Table 7.9N

[24] Himmelweit, for example, assumes that voters take into account as many as 21 issues in reaching an overall preference for a party. She appears to assume that they all have equal weight (1981: 118). The choice of 21 issues appears to be based on the fact that improved predictions of aggregate voting are achieved when all 21 are included, but of course this does not prove that any one individual takes into account all 21 issues. Indeed each voter could in theory take account of only one issue; provided different voters took account of different single issues, a large number of issues in total would still be needed to predict aggregate voting.

[25] The calculations for the 'next most important' issue are given below in table 7.10N. We have then averaged the 'expected outcomes' of Tables 7.5 and 7.10N to obtain the figures quoted in the text.

[26] This is not a new finding. Sarlvik found that the same held true in the 1979 election (Sarlvik and Crewe, 1983: 224). He attempts to rescue the consumer theory by making a distinction between salience and decisiveness. An issue like nationalisation may thus have been decisive to voters but not salient. This is almost certainly true, but it renders the theory circular. Sarlvik is no longer predicting votes from people's views but inferring their views from their votes.

TABLE 7.8N Closest Party on Taxation and Social Services

Closest single party on the tax and social services scale	Conservative	24.1
	Alliance	26.7
	Labour	21.2
Equidistant between	Conservative and Alliance	6.5
	Conservative and Labour	2.5
	Labour and Alliance	11.0
	Conservative, Labour and Alliance	8.0
		100.0%
N =		3703

TABLE 7.9N Closest Party on Nuclear Defence

Closest single party on the nuclear weapons scale	Conservative	32.0
	Alliance	29.8
	Labour	20.4
Equidistant between	Conservative and Alliance	6.2
	Conservative and Labour	2.4
	Labour and Alliance	6.1
	Conservative, Labour and Alliance	3.1
		100.0%
N =		3750

TABLE 7.10N Closest Party on the 'Next Most Important Issue'

Closest party		Unemployment/inflation	Defence	Taxes/Social Services	Law and Order	Nationalisation/privatisation
Conservative	N =	296	224	149	225	82
Alliance	N =	279	166	257	82	18
Labour	N =	379	77	241	57	10
Conservative and Alliance	N =	70	36	36	51	5
Conservative and Labour	N =	36	9	32	27	1
Alliance and Labour	N =	184	23	122	39	4
Conservative, Labour and Alliance	N =	127	17	75	98	2
N =		1371	552	912	579	122

EXPECTED VOTE

		Unemployment/inflation	Defence	Taxes/Social Services	Law and Order	Nationalisation/privatisation	Total	%
Conservative	N =	391	252	208	297	86	1234	35
Alliance	N =	448	202	361	160	24	1195	34
Labour	N =	532	99	343	122	12	1108	31
N =							3537	100

Chapter 8

Ideology

We have suggested that it is unsound to view the voter as a consumer in the marketplace, choosing between parties on the basis of their detailed policy proposals. The notion that the elector makes up his or her mind in the course of the election campaign on the basis of the important issues of the day simply will not do.

But we do not want to revert to the old orthodoxy of voting theory. People do not, and probably never have, voted simply out of loyalty to a party. Our theory, which we shall try to document in this chapter, is that it is also the 'fit' between the voters' general values and their overall perceptions of what the parties stand for — their general ideologies rather than their specific policies — which affects how they vote and how strongly they are attached to a party. It is not the small print of the manifesto but the overall perception of the party's character that counts. If that character is seen to change, perhaps when a new team of leaders takes over, then support for the party will change too.[1]

In general, we believe the character of the parties to be rather stable. Benney, for example, writing in the 1950s, saw the Labour party as standing for public ownership of the means of production and for the development of the National Health Service, while the Conservative party stood for tax cuts and privatisation. Thus he and his colleagues wrote:

"There is no doubt that the Conservatives' stand on nationalisation and their strong feelings about it were well known. That the Conservative Party was similarly identified by public opinion with the cause of reducing taxation is highly probable. Apart from the parties' past records, the Conservatives had made the reduction of taxation one of their election battle cries, while Labour had seldom mentioned the subject. We have positive evidence that the Labour Party was credited with the greatest concern for the problem of unemployment, not only by its supporters, but also by many Conservative voters. Promises to maintain and improve the Health Service were freely given by both parties during the election campaign, but it seems unlikely that those of the Conservatives could shake the faith of Labour voters that their own party was the more seriously concerned about what was one of the principal achievements of the Labour Government" (Benney et al 1956: 198). A very similar account would be given today, some thirty years on.

The emphases which the two parties place on these different aspects of their underlying ideologies may change from time to time. Harold Wilson for example played down public ownership (after steel renationalisation); his administrations concentrated more on social services (with the Seebohm report), comprehensive schooling and other social reforms. Even so, in the public mind the parties remained differentiated throughout the 1960s on these major criteria of public ownership, the welfare state, and taxation.

These general philosophies are both enduring and fundamental aspects of the Labour and Conservative parties' characters. With the Labour party they are of course enshrined in the party's constitution.[2] They constitute the major basis of each party's character and therefore of its appeal to different groups in the population. The electors' attitudes towards these political philosophies provide a key to their voting behaviour not only in 1983 but also in all the earlier general elections on which we have the relevant data. They are of course attitudes and appeals which derive to a large extent from the class basis both of the electorate and of the two major parties. We must however emphasise that the relationship is a two-way one: the parties' appeals may help to shape class values too.[3]

Conservative and Labour Voters

Let us begin by comparing the attitudes of Conservative and Labour voters towards these general features of party philosophy and ideology. As we described in Part 1, in the course of the 1983 election study we asked our respondents not only about the campaign issues but also about a range of less prominent policies on which the parties take fundamentally different stands. These included the class issues such as private education, trade union legislation and income redistribution which we described in chapter 2, and also nonclass issues like civil liberties, free speech and the death penalty, described in chapter 5. The questions on which Conservative and Labour voters expressed the most divergent attitudes are shown in table 8.1.

In table 8.1 we report the percentage of Labour and Conservative voters who expressed agreement with the 'right-wing' alternative on each question.[4] In the third column of table 8.1 we give the index of dissimilarity.[5] This is an overall measure of the difference between Conservative and Labour voters on each question. The index takes into account the proportions who were 'not sure', or who could not choose between the options given, in addition to those who gave 'left-wing' responses. This is important in the answers to the job creation question and in this case the index gives a better guide to the difference of opinion than the first two columns in table 8.1 provide on their own.

TABLE 8.1 The Attitudes of Conservative and Labour Voters

| | Percentage agreeing with "right-wing" alternative | | |
	Conservative voters	Labour voters	Index of dissimilarity
Nationalisation	66	12	54
Trade union legislation	84	29	55
Income redistribution	59	12	49
Defence spending	82	37	45
Private education	87	43	44
Job creation	35	2	42
N (minimum)	1383	837	

As we can see, the two sets of voters differ most in their attitudes towards nationalisation and trade union legislation, followed by income redistribution, defence and private education. The major issue of the campaign — unemployment — comes relatively low in the list. Few respondents described nationalisation as an important issue in the election, and hardly any had said that trade union legislation was important (although it figured quite prominently in the Conservative manifesto).[6] But the close relation between the unions and the Labour party is not only part and parcel of its constitution, it is also widely recognised as part of its character. Indeed, over one half of Labour's current Members of Parliament are officially sponsored by trade unions.[7] Labour's relationship with the unions (even when it is strained) is an integral part of the party's character. People's perceptions of the party reflect this (just as they reflect each party's general stance on public ownership) almost regardless of manifesto commitments.

Income redistribution and the abolition of private education were also largely absent from the explicit campaign debate.[8] But again these issues sharply divide Conservative from Labour voters, more so indeed than does job creation, which was a campaign issue. Both are also long-standing concerns for the two parties. Almost every Labour election manifesto in the postwar period has had some reference to them. The search for a more equal society is a central article of Labour faith; "Socialism is about equality" was a standard dictum of the left-wing intelligentsia in the 1950s. And the role of private schools in maintaining social divisions has always been anathema to the Labour faithful, although they have not always been entirely clear what should be done about them.

These themes of public ownership and free enterprise, the reform of trade unions and private schools, social equality and individual incentives have been persistent sources of disagreement between the parties since the Labour party's formation. Along with defence they are also the themes on which their supporters diverge most strongly. They constitute the main ideological divisions between the parties. They should be distinguished from issues such as full employment or the

National Health Service where the parties agree on the overall goals but disagree on the means.[9] True, the means that people choose to achieve these agreed goals also reflect their values. Decisions about means are rarely pure, technical decisions. The distinction is one of degree rather than kind.

The ideological content of different policies varies, therefore. And it is those where ideology is most visible that differentiate most strongly between the rival sets of voters. This was true not only in 1983 but also in 1979.[10] (We also suspect that if we could take the analyses further back they would tell us the same story.) Trade union reform, nationalisation and income redistribution headed the list in both years. Their importance (as predictors of vote) does not seem to vary according to their prominence in the electoral campaigns: despite the fact that the 1979 election occurred immediately after the 'winter of discontent', attitudes towards the unions were no more important than they were in 1983. The main change that has taken place is that the two sets of voters are now somewhat more polarised than they were before, although this may simply be an artefact of the growth in the number of centre party supporters.[11]

More interestingly, we find that these ideological themes are also the ones that best predict how the floating voter will cast his or her vote. Their importance is not confined to the party loyalists, or to those who are more ideologically committed. Tables 8.2 and 8.3 compare the two types of voter, floating voters being defined as those who reportedly made up their minds "during the election campaign" itself, party loyalists as those who had made up their minds which way to vote "a long time ago" (Q8a).[12]

TABLE 8.2 The Attitudes of Party Loyalists

	Percentage agreeing with "right-wing" alternative		
	Conservative voters	Labour voters	Index of dissimilarity
Nationalisation	70	11	59
Trade union legislation	87	26	61
Income redistribution	65	12	57
Defence spending	86	36	50
Private education	91	41	50
Job creation	39	2	47
N (minimum)	901	584	

TABLE 8.3 The Attitudes of Floating Voters

	Percentage agreeing with "right-wing" alternative		
	Conservative voters	Labour voters	Index of dissimilarity
Nationalisation	59	13	46
Trade union legislation	71	40	31
Income redistribution	47	15	31
Defence spending	69	41	28
Private education	78	50	28
Job creation	22	5	26
N (minimum)	202	125	

We can see that the two sets of loyalists are a long way apart from each other on these issues: the lowest index of dissimilarity is 47 points in their case. The two sets of floating voters are rather closer to each other, and their greatest dissimilarity is only 46 points. But the *relative* importance of the different issues is much the same for both loyalists and floating voters. It is not true that floating voters make up their minds on the basis of the campaign issues while loyalists vote out of habit or commitment. That would have been a rather neat solution. We could then have postulated that the instrumental theory worked for floating voters and the expressive theory for committed voters. But it was not to be.

Instead we suggest that in both cases people's underlying social and political values affect how they evaluate the parties and their proposals. People's responses to questions about nationalisation, income equality and so on are simply tapping these general values. For the floating voters there is a less close 'fit' between their own values and their perceptions of where the parties stand. The 'floating' Conservatives were more likely to report that they lay to the left of their party while 'floating' Labour voters tended to lie to the right of the Labour position.[13] They were therefore not so completely in tune with the parties' ideologies as the loyalists; hence their relative indecisiveness. But it is still their general values which best explain their eventual vote.

We do not however interpret any of these findings as evidence that people consciously weighed up nationalisation or trade union reform instead of (or as well as) the campaign issues they claimed were on their minds. Instead, as we said in chapter 2, we interpret these questions as tapping people's underlying values, values which they most often take for granted but which nonetheless shape their perceptions and evaluations of specific events, personalities and policies. As we argued earlier, our questions on nationalisation, income redistribution and private education are not so much tapping discrete issues as a general ideological dimension the respective poles of which are support for government intervention on the one hand and free enterprise on the other.

Positions along this ideological dimension are probably quite stable, but by no means immutable.[14] They derive from, among other things, people's class positions. The list of questions in table 8.1 that differentiates Conservative from Labour voters has a striking resemblance to the list in table 2.2 which differentiates members of the five classes. This is not perhaps surprising, given the substantial overlap between class and vote. However, we should note that defence did not appear as one of our top class issues. Instead, it figured as one of the 'liberal' issues in chapter 6. Even with the Labour and Conservative parties, then, we should not make the simple equation that 'class equals party'.

The comparison between tables 2.2 and 8.1 shows also that the political parties are more polarised than the classes. Thus on the nationalisation question the index of dissimilarity between Conservative and Labour voters is 54 points; but the index between members of the petty bourgeoisie and the working class is only 36 points. Thus, it is not the parties which are pale reflections of the classes, but the other way round. This lends weight to our view that the parties help to shape class values. In representing different classes, the parties may well help to define what counts as class interests and class politics.

The presence of these 'taken-for-granted' class values in the background of voters' thinking helps to explain (although only in part) why Labour has done so badly of late, despite the electorate's favourable attitude towards its stand on unemployment and the welfare state. We do not mean by this that the electorate rejected Labour (either consciously or unconsciously) because it did not like the party's specific nationalisation proposals. And we certainly do not take the view that all would be well for Labour if it simply abandoned its generally unpopular stand on this issue. After all, attitudes towards nationalisation have always been a good predictor of Labour voting, even for instance in 1966 when there was little difference between the parties on this particular issue. We doubt if Labour would fare better if it merely dropped nationalisation from the manifesto but retained its left-wing character overall. Our interpretation, rather, is that in 1983 there were relatively few people towards the left-wing end of the interventionist-free enterprise continuum. Changing the details of policy would not have affected matters greatly.

Nor do we wish to imply that changing Labour's left-wing character is the only remedy available for the party. The consumer theory of political choice may treat attitudes as 'independent' variables which 'determine' voting behaviour; its proponents conclude from this that the Labour party must change its policies if it is to regain office. But our conception of political choice treats values as 'dependent' variables which can be shaped, both by political and by social processes. We give some evidence for this in chapter 9. For the moment we must emphasise that we are simply describing the level of support for left-wing or interventionist principles that happened to exist in 1983. This cannot, without further assumptions, yield prescriptions for what the parties ought or ought not do to increase their appeals in future.

Alliance Voters

Liberal voters have been regarded in the past as a rather amorphous group without a distinctive attitudinal profile or ideology. The most that could be said for them, earlier research suggested, was that they lay approximately in the middle of the road, occupying the ideological space between the Labour right and the Conservative left. A rather more radical view was that Liberal voters were essentially protest voters reacting against specific policies or failures of their 'natural' parties rather than positively attracted by the Liberal party itself. The party's centrist political character was thus to some extent immaterial, since its supporters were not positively attracted to the centre as such. They simply found themselves there by virtue of transient disagreements with particular aspects of Labour or Conservative policy.[15] Himmelweit and her colleagues have argued this point most cogently:

"The Liberal voters in one election are rarely the same people in another. Each election produces a new crop of Liberals thrown up by the vagaries of the two main parties. This makes the paradigm, appropriate for discussing the changing fortunes of the Conservative and Labour party, inappropriate when discussing changes in the fortunes of the Liberal party. A more appropriate paradigm is one which looks, not so much at what attracts the voter to the Liberal party, but rather at what draws the voter away from the party for which he or she had previously voted. *The Liberal vote is a vote of disaffection; it represents movement away from a party rather than movement to the party; it is a vote signifying departure rather than arrival.*" (Himmelweit et al, 1981: 159. Italics in original)

Himmelweit's account in many ways fits the facts of Liberal voting quite well. The Liberal vote has been notoriously 'soft' in the past. Relatively few Liberal voters were loyal to the party between one election and the next. Compared with the Conservative and Labour parties it had many more temporary adherents. Whereas the 25 per cent drop in the Labour vote between 1979 and 1983 was greeted with some surprise the similar drop in the Liberal vote between 1974 and 1979 was rather taken for granted. It was assumed to be in the nature of the Liberal vote that it could collapse as quickly as it rose. And even when the aggregate Liberal vote stayed relatively constant, as in October 1974, it was still marked by high 'turnover' of individual voters.[16]

It is also true that the identification of Liberal voters with their party has been on average much lower than that of Conservative and Labour voters. And this remains true of the Alliance voter in 1983. Whereas 35 per cent of Labour voters and 24 per cent of Conservative voters reported very strong identification with their parties, the equivalent figure in the case of Alliance voters was only 10 per cent. Party identification has in the past been a good predictor of voting stability.[17] It appears that the Alliance vote is still relatively vulnerable.

It is not however self-evident that this 'softness' means that the Liberal vote requires a different kind of explanation from that of the Labour or Conservative vote, as Himmelweit would have us believe. It could equally be argued that a centrist vote is, by its nature, subject to double jeopardy. It is vulnerable to assault on both flanks, from left and right, while a right-wing or left-wing party is

seriously vulnerable on only one of its flanks. Moreover, the notion that the
Liberal vote signifies departure rather than arrival is a rather curious one. If
people wish to express disaffection there are many other equally or even more
potent ways in which to do it — staying at home on polling day, for example, or
voting for an extremist party like the National Front or for one of the many fringe
candidates who appear, particularly at by-elections.[18] The fact that voters chose
the Liberal party as the vehicle for their protest suggests an element of attraction
as well as disaffection.[19]

In any event, whatever may have been true in the past, we shall show that the
Alliance vote in 1983 was not an amorphous one without any distinctive character. The Alliance vote can be explained in much the same way as that of the
Conservative or Labour parties — it depends on the 'fit' between the ideological
position of the voter and that of the Alliance parties.

Table 8.4 takes the questions which most differentiated Labour and Conservative voters and plots the Alliance responses. The two sets of indices of dissimilarity then show by how much these Alliance responses diverged from the Labour
and Conservative ones that we reported in table 8.1.

On the two class values which head the list — nationalisation and trade union
legislation — the Alliance voters lie almost plumb in the centre, halfway between
the Conservative and Labour voters. This finding is more or less repeated for two
of the other class values on the list — private education and income redistribution. Only in the case of unemployment do Alliance voters come closer to
Labour. With this one exception, it seems fair to regard the Alliance voter as lying
at the centre of the main ideological continuum that differentiates both the classes
and the Conservative and Labour parties. So on these class values, the conventional view that the Alliance is a centrist formation is broadly correct.

But this does not appear to be the whole story. Table 8.4 also shows that
Alliance voters are much closer to Labour than to the Conservatives on defence,
and as we saw in chapter 6 defence has a somewhat different character to the class
issues. The story is thus more complicated than a simple narrative of the middle
ground. We therefore explored the attitudinal questions in our data set in greater
depth to see what other issues differentiated Alliance voters from Labour and the
Conservatives.

First, comparing Alliance voters with Labour voters we found them to be far
apart on the Common Market. Alliance voters were strongly in favour of remaining in the EEC, and in this respect they were only little different from Conservatives. It would be quite wrong to think of them as occupying the centre ground on
this issue. On the index of dissimilarity they were 23 points from Labour but only
7 from the Conservatives.

Again it is striking that the Common Market turned out to be one of the best
predictors of whether someone would vote Labour or Alliance, despite the fact
that it was hardly a dominant issue in the election campaign.[20] But support for the
Common Market has always been an important article of faith inside the Liberal
party.[21] It was also a key source of division in the pre-1981 Labour party and the
Limehouse declaration which announced the formation of the Social Democratic
Party included a strong and manifest endorsement of EEC membership.[22] We
would argue that here is a fundamental difference of principle between the parties
which provides an enduring basis of division.

TABLE 8.4 The Attitudes of Alliance Voters

	Percentage agreeing with "right-wing" alternative	Dissimilarity from Labour	Dissimilarity from Conservative
Nationalisation	36	29	30
Trade union legislation	56	26	28
Income redistribution	32	22	27
Defence spending	48	11	34
Private education	66	23	21
Job creation	11	12	30
N (minimum)	743		

Apart from the Common Market, the questions that divide Labour from the Alliance are the ones on the class issues. But the questions that divide Alliance voters from Conservative voters are more akin to those on the liberal issues described in chapter 5. In addition to defence and unemployment, Alliance voters were relatively further away from the Conservatives and relatively closer to Labour on health and education spending, on the death penalty and police power, and on the Falklands. The differences between the parties on these questions are shown in table 8.5.

In table 8.5 we show the percentages agreeing with the more 'liberal' alternative on each of these questions.[23] On all of them the Alliance voters are much closer to Labour than to Conservative voters, and on the two at the top of the list they are actually slightly more 'liberal' than Labour voters. These are the questions which, as we saw in chapter 6, tended to divide the salariat and to follow educational rather than class lines.

There is, moreover, a correspondence between this group of issues and the general stance of the two Alliance parties. Analysis of Liberal manifestos in the postwar period suggests that the party has consistently taken more liberal stands on these non-class issues just as it has taken a more pro-EEC attitude than even the Conservatives.[24] However we doubt whether these precise stances have been apparent to the electorate *en masse*. As we reported earlier, many voters seemed to be unaware of the Alliance policies on such issues as defence and health. And diagrams 7.3 and 7.4 show that our respondents placed the Alliance at the centre (and closer to the Conservatives than Labour) on the nuclear disarmament and government spending scales. The Alliance does not seem to have got its message across on these issues.

It is also true that the differences between Alliance, Labour and Conservative voters on these 'liberal' issues are smaller than those between the educational categories described in chapter 6. On the death penalty, for example, the index of dissimilarity between graduates and the unqualified was 39 points; but between the Alliance and Conservatives it is only 13 points.

The reason for this discrepancy may well be that, apart from defence, these issues have not been 'politicised' to anything like the same extent as the class issues have. So although the Alliance, both in its policies and in its support, does stand for a set of 'liberal' views, it has not captured the issue of the welfare state or civil liberties in the way that the Conservatives have captured free enterprise or Labour has captured public ownership. There is as a result a much looser fit between 'liberal' values and Alliance support. The class dimension is still the primary one around which British politics is organised, although a one-dimensional map of British politics is too simple.

A Two-dimensional View of the Electorate

In table 8.6 we have drawn a two-dimensional map of the British electorate.[25] We have used the nationalisation scale as the basis of the main east-west axis representing class values and we have used the nuclear disarmament scale as the basis of the north-south axis representing liberal values. To simplify the presentation we have reduced the scales to three points to represent 'left', 'centre' and 'right'-wing

TABLE 8.5 The 'Liberal' Questions

	Percentage agreeing with the "liberal" alternative			Alliance dissimilarity from Labour	Alliance dissimilarity from Conservative
	Conservative	Labour	Alliance		
Police power	40	49	53	5	13
Death penalty	27	40	40	1	13
Education spending	54	79	77	2	23
Falklands negotiations	52	70	69	1	17
Private medicine	33	72	61	11	30
National Health Service spending	77	98	92	6	15

positions.[26] We should emphasise that this choice of scale to represent the two axes is illustrative only. We have chosen these two largely because they are the most 'politicised' of the class and liberal issues respectively, but other questions would have done almost equally well. Attitudes to income redistribution would be a good measure of the east-west axis, and attitudes to health and social services would do quite well for the north-south axis.[27]

TABLE 8.6 A Map of Ideological Position

Percentage of all respondents (N = 3636)

11	11	12	reduce nuclear weapons
3	12	18	no change
5	6	23	increase nuclear weapons
nationalise private companies	no change	sell off nationalised industries	

Table 8.6 shows the distribution of our respondents over the different areas of the map.[28] For example, the figure of 11 per cent in the north-west corner of the map indicates that 11 per cent of our sample favoured *both* further nationalisation and nuclear disarmament. This area of the map can therefore be thought of as representing a Labour heartland whose inhabitants are more or less in sympathy with these two elements of Labour philosophy, and in practice they are likely to agree with most of the others as well.

Conversely, the figure of 23 per cent in the south-east corner of the map indicates that 23 per cent of the sample tended to favour *both* stronger nuclear defence *and* further privatisation. We can think of this area as the Conservative heartland whose inhabitants are in sympathy with the principles of free enterprise and strong national defence. Too much should not be made of the fact that the Conservative heartland is so much larger than the Labour one; to some extent this is an artifact of the particular measures which we have employed to represent the two axes. If we had used income redistribution to represent the east-west axis, the western area of the map would have been more thickly populated. If we had used government spending to represent the north-south axis the northern area would have been more thickly populated.

On the usual one-dimensional view of politics voters would be expected to cluster along the main diagonal running from the Labour heartland in the north-west down to the Conservative heartland in the south-east. And indeed the two parties like to present their programmes as internally coherent but mutually exclusive packages. Nonetheless, large proportions of the electorate lie off-centre. Not surprisingly, the south-west area of the map is sparsely populated; few people favour a programme of increased public ownership combined with an increased nuclear arsenal (although the policies of the Soviet Union might suggest that there is nothing intrinsically implausible about such a programme). In contrast, the north-east corner is more thickly populated; a large proportion of the electorate favours the historically unusual package of free enterprise combined with nuclear disarmament.

It is no real surprise then that in this area of the map support for Conservative and Labour is weakest and for the Alliance relatively strong. Table 8.7 shows the pattern of voting in the different areas of the map.[29]

TABLE 8.7 Ideological Position and Vote

Percentages

Labour	78	47	21	
Alliance	12	41	37	reduce
Conservative	9	11	41	nuclear weapons
N	(315)	(326)	(345)	
Labour	53	36	8	
Alliance	29	33	20	
Conservative	16	30	72	no change
N	(109)	(338)	(547)	
Labour	50	20	5	
Alliance	17	26	17	increase
Conservative	32	52	77	nuclear weapons
N	(129)	(177)	(695)	
	nationalise private companies	no change	sell off nationalised industries	

Figures in brackets give cell sizes
Percentages do not always sum to 100 because of the presence of a few voters for 'other' parties.

The Labour party is clearly at its strongest in the north-west area of the map where it secured 78 per cent of the voters. For respondents here, we would argue, there is a close fit between their own ideology and the stance of their party. Similarly, the Conservative party is at its strongest in the south-east area of the map. An equally high proportion — 77 per cent — of respondents here voted Conservative. There is again a good 'fit' between the party and its supporters.

Elsewhere in the map there is a less good fit. Both Labour and Conservative votes fall off as we move away from their respective heartlands. While the fall-off is more dramatic along the east-west axis, it is quite clearly there on the north-south axis too. For example, the Labour vote falls off from 78 per cent to 21 per cent as we move along the northern edge of the map, but it also falls off from 78 per cent to 50 per cent as we move down the western edge. The 'two-dimensional' view of politics, therefore, helps our understanding of the Labour and Conservative vote as well as that of the Alliance. The Conservative and Labour parties cannot rely on the votes of people who share their ideological position on the class issues; disagreement on the liberal questions can lose them votes.

The Alliance vote is never as high in any area of the map as are the Conservative and Labour votes in their respective heartlands. But neither is the Alliance vote randomly distributed across the map. As Table 8.7 shows, it has a distinctive contour extending from the centre towards the north and north-east. Though relatively strong in the middle ground, it is not purely a party of the centre. Nor is it equally strong among all 'off-centre' voters. It is almost at its weakest in the 'off-centre' south-west corner among the few voters who adopt a left-wing position on nationalisation but a right-wing position on defence.[30] That being so, it is very implausible that the Alliance vote is simply one of disaffection. Its voters tend to lie, just as the voters of the other parties do, in the area of the map where the Alliance itself happens to lie — in the centre on nationalisation and the other class issues but tending to the north of our map on defence and the liberal issues.

This comes out even more clearly if we look at the level of constancy in each area of the map — respondents who voted for the same party both in 1979 and 1983. This is shown in table 8.8. (Percentages have not been calculated where the cell sizes are below 25).

TABLE 8.8 Constant Voters

Percentage voting the same way in 1979 and 1983

Labour	91	67	64	reduce
Alliance	64	96	90	nuclear weapons
Conservative	62	43	74	
Labour	—	65	42	
Alliance	—	82	79	no change
Conservative	—	78	91	
Labour	—	55	30	increase
Alliance	—	74	69	nuclear weapons
Conservative	—	84	92	

nationalise	sell off
private no change	nationalised
companies	industries

Here we see that the parties could be most certain of retaining the votes of the members of their respective heartlands. Defections from each party increase as one moves across the map to areas which are out of line with its ideology. For example, of people who voted Labour in 1979, 91 per cent remained loyal in the Labour heartland of the north-west corner, but in the north-east a third defected. Loyalty to the Conservatives was highest in their heartland too. But Alliance constancy (or more accurately Liberal constancy since there was no Alliance in 1979) was almost as localised. 96 per cent of people who voted Liberal in 1979 and who placed themselves in the north of the map turned out for one of the Alliance parties again in 1983, and Alliance defections increase just as markedly as do those of the other parties when one moves away from the heartland. On this criterion the Alliance heartland is every bit as distinctive as those of the other two parties.

A Protest Vote?

Whatever may have been true in previous elections, in 1983 there appears to have been some coherence to the Alliance vote. The conclusion that the old Liberal vote was based on protest, on 'departure rather than arrival', was based partly on the amorphous character of Liberal voters. There were, it was said, no distinctive values or principles which united its voters. Liberals seemed to have a variety of characteristics with little in common other than their dislike of the other parties. Thus, one commentator argued, the Liberal vote included defectors from the Labour party because they did not like its anti-Market policy and defectors from the Conservative party because they did not like its pro-Market stand.[31] Even such a basic and longstanding element of Liberal policy — its Europeanism — apparently failed to unite its supporters.

It is still true that there is no single principle which both unites Alliance voters and distinguishes them from Conservative and Labour supporters. For Conservative and Labour parties such issues can be found. Thus 84 per cent of Conservatives believed in stricter trade union legislation while both Alliance and Labour supporters were more divided on the issue. Labour voters, on the other hand, were united in their belief in government spending to create jobs (85 per cent) while the proposition found a more mixed response from the supporters of the other two parties.

This absence of a distinctive and overriding Liberal or Social Democratic principle may be part of the explanation for the paucity of strongly committed supporters of the Alliance. It may be hard for people to feel a passionate belief in moderation. Although there are individual principles upon which Alliance voters agree, for example full employment or increased spending on education, neither of these is a uniquely Alliance cause. Labour voters are even more strongly united on these issues and one might believe that the Labour party would be a more vigorous champion of full employment and a more vigorous opponent of spending cuts. Someone who feels passionately about either of these might well more appropriately vote Labour. Until the Alliance can find one or more distinctively and 'passionately' Alliance principles, it is unlikely that it will rival the other parties in its number of committed supporters.

However, although the Labour and Conservative parties may each have clearer unifying principles than the Alliance has, they also contain deep divisions among their voters in relation to other elements of their programmes. Table 8.9 shows the levels of agreement on different aspects of party policy.[32]

TABLE 8.9 Party Agreement

| | Percentage broadly agreeing with own party's position | | |
	Conservative	Labour	Alliance
Nuclear weapons	62	62	63
Unemployment/inflation	56	84	69
Taxation/social services	48	72	65
Nationalisation	82	53	60
Law and order	69	63	62

On the Labour side disagreement is greatest on nationalisation. Labour's supporters are far from united on what is after all a key aspect of Labour philosophy. On the Conservative side disagreement (at much the same level) is greatest on taxation and social services. Many Conservative supporters are at odds with what they perceive to be their leadership's position on this issue.

At first sight it is surprising that it is government spending on social services rather than unemployment on which Conservative voters are most at odds with their party. Perhaps they were more persuaded by Mrs Thatcher's assertion that 'there is no alternative' to her economic policies than by her claim during the election campaign that 'the National Health Service is safe with us'. It is arguably easier for Conservative supporters to accept a long-term strategy for the return of full-employment as they are rather less likely to have to bear the immediate burdens of such a strategy. Members of the salariat, however, obtain disproportionate benefits from the welfare state. There is now a great deal of evidence that some of the welfare state services are not particularly redistributive. The salariat consult their doctors and dentists more, and their offspring make much greater use of free university education.[33] Cuts in education and health spending hurt Conservative supporters at least as much as they hurt Labour supporters.

Be that as it may, it is clear from table 8.9 that there are themes on which Conservative and Labour voters are deeply at odds with party policy, and these areas of disagreement are by no means ones that are marginal to party philosophies. On the multi-dimensional view of politics, therefore, it appears that all three party groupings are disunited. If we describe the Alliance as an amorphous group of individuals, so too should we describe Labour and Conservative voters.

This can be seen by referring back to the two-dimensional analysis of table 8.7. Labour is relatively strong in its heartland of the north-west corner of the map, but this area contains fewer than one third of all Labour voters — a relatively low proportion, it may be thought, to accept two fundamental elements of Labour policy. If we adopt a more generous definition and include the three adjacent cells immediately to the south and east, the proportion rises to 70 per cent.

The Alliance fares little worse than this; true, only a fifth of its voters lie in the north-east corner but the proportion rises to 65 per cent if we include the three adjacent cells. Agreement between the Conservative voters and their party was rather higher on these two issues of nationalisation and defence. 81 per cent lay in the heartland of the south-west corner or the three cells adjacent to it. But if we add the more controversial items such as unemployment or government spending, Conservative unity falls close to the level of the other parties'.[34]

Voting Histories

While we believe that these two-dimensional analyses help us to make sense of the Alliance vote, we must not make exaggerated claims for the map. Just as the consumer theory failed to predict the election result, greatly underestimating the Conservative total, so our ideological theory is not sufficient on its own, this time greatly overestimating the Alliance vote. As a number of writers have pointed out, the Alliance fails to harvest its full crop of potential voters. Whereas Conservative and Labour secure upwards of three-quarters of the vote in their respective heartlands, the Alliance never does better than two-fifths. Even people who, according to their answers on our scale questions, were in precise agreement with the Alliance position as they saw it, failed in large numbers to cast their votes for an Alliance party.

The most natural explanation for this is that people remain attached to their previous parties even when they have moved out of line with them on major political principles. Thus the centre and north-east areas of the map contain many potential Alliance voters (as judged by ideological position), but as table 8.8 shows both the Labour and the Conservative parties were quite successful in retaining the votes of people in these areas. Even after we have taken account of where people stand on the major principles, how they voted before (and even how their parents voted before them) is still a good predictor of how they will vote in the future.

To this extent we support the expressive theory rather than the instrumental theory of voting. Loyalty to one's party is not a vacuous concept. However, theorists of the 'expressive' school of thought have tended to exaggerate the importance of childhood and early adulthood socialisation into a 'party identity' and have been wrong to look to the replacement of one generation by another as the major source of electoral change. In that respect we agree with the critics of the expressive theory. We found little consistent evidence that older voters, who are likely to have longer histories of voting for a particular party, were less likely to defect to the Alliance than were younger voters.[35] Party loyalty may act as a brake on electoral change, but it slows it down rather than stopping it altogether. Loyalty is unlikely to be wholly unconditional and none of the parties should count on the loyalty of those who lie far away from its heartland.

Notes

[1] In some respects our view is similar to that of Butler and Stokes (1974: 338) who write:

". . . the behaviour of the electorate [is] shaped by generalised attitudes and beliefs about the parties far more than by any specific policy issues. People respond to the parties to a large extent in terms of images they form from the characteristics and style of the leaders and from the party's association, intended or not, with the things government may achieve."

But in contrast to Butler and Stokes we believe that the generalised perceptions that the electorate have of the parties do have an important ideological component. They are not simply based on general qualities such as perceptions of a party's 'strength', 'modernity' or 'dullness'.

[2] Clause IV of the Labour party constitution declares that party objects are

"1 To organise and maintain in parliament and in the country a political labour party.

2 To cooperate with the General Council of the Trades Union Congress, or other kindred organisation, in joint political or other action in harmony with the party constitution and standing orders.

3 To give effect as far as may be practicable to the principles from time to time approved by the party conference.

4 To secure for the workers by hand or by brain the full fruits of their industry and the most equitable distribution thereof that may be possible upon the basis of the common ownership of the means of production, distribution and exchange, and the best obtainable system of popular administration and control of each industry or service.

5 Generally to promote the political, social and economic emancipation of the people, and more particularly of those who depend directly upon their own exertions by hand or brain for the means of life" (Report of the Annual Conference of the Labour Party 1983: 291).

[3] It is worth remembering that public ownership was adopted by the Labour party in 1918 to appeal specifically to potential supporters in the professions and to soften Labour's image as a sectional party. (See McKibbin 1974: 91-106.) The support for nationalisation that does now exist amongst working-class Labour supporters has probably arisen because it was a part of Labour party philosophy rather than the other way around. We are grateful to Hugh Berrington for bringing this point to our attention.

[4] In the case of nationalisation we report the percentages agreeing that "Some industries that are now nationalised should become private companies" (Q37); in the case of trade unions they are the percentages agreeing that "The government should introduce stricter laws to regulate the activities of trade unions" (Q40a); in the case of income redistribution it is the percentages disagreeing that "Income and wealth should be redistributed towards ordinary working people" (Q34b); in the case of private education they are the percentages disagreeing that "The government should get rid of private education in Britain" (Q35a); in the case of defence they are the percentages disagreeing that "The government should spend less on defence" (Q27c); and in the case of unemployment they are the percentages disagreeing that" The government should spend more money to create jobs" (Q30d).

An alternative comparison of like with like is to compare the scales. These, whether in absolute or relative form, confirm the robustness of our findings described in table 8.1. Thus the correlations between the respondents' positions on the scales and Conservative vote are:

Q24a nuclear weapons .45
Q28a unemployment-inflation .39
Q31a taxes and social services .33
Q36a nationalisation .57
Q41a law and order .15

(These correlations are based on five-point collapse of the scales and cover Conservative and Labour voters only.)

If we 'relativise' the scales (ie calculate respondents' positions relative to where they themselves placed the parties), the correlations all increase but remain in almost the same rank order:

Relative position on nuclear weapons .55
Relative position on unemployment-inflation .46
Relative position of taxes-social services .48
Relative position on nationalisation .59
Relative position on law and order .32

We also considered the questions (Q45a to Q45l) which asked whether various changes had 'gone too far'. The ones which discriminated best between Conservative and Labour voters were Q45a (welfare benefits — dissimilarity 38 points), Q45i (comprehensive schooling — dissimilarity 31 points) and Q45e (nuclear power — dissimilarity 37 points).
[5] To compute the index of dissimilarity we sum the differences (of the same sign) between the percentages of Conservative and Labour voters in each category. Thus in the case of job creation the percentages are:

TABLE 8.10N Attitudes to Job Creation

	Agree that government should create jobs	Not sure	Disagree that government should create jobs	
	Percentages			
Conservative	53	12	35	100% (N = 1443)
Labour	95	3	2	100% (N = 915)

Thus the index is the sum of (35-2) and (12-3), ie 42. (This is of course the same as 95-53.) It can thus be seen that we need to take account of the proportions in the 'not sure' category as well as in the 'right-wing' category to get an index of the *overall* difference between Conservative and Labour voters. Simply comparing the difference giving the 'right-wing' response understates the overall dissimilarity.

[6] We did not ask people directly about the importance of trade union legislation, but as a supplementary question we asked "Besides the six issues on the card, are there any other things that were at least as important as these were to you in deciding about voting?" (Q20e). This way of asking will have discouraged answers in comparison with the six issues on the card, so direct comparisons should not be drawn. More appropriately we should note that of the total of 859 people who mentioned one or more 'other things' only 36 mentioned unions or strikes.

[8] 168 respondents mentioned education as important, but by no means all these references were to private education.

[9] As in chapter 2 we are here following Butler and Stokes' distinction between position issues and valence issues. See Butler and Stokes (1974: 292).

[10] For the 1979 and 1983 Election Studies we regressed vote on the following list of attitude questions (restricting the analysis to Conservative and Labour voters only). The standardised regression coefficients are given in table 8.11N.

TABLE 8.11N Multiple Regression of Conservative Vote on Attitudes

	Standardised regression coefficients	
	1979	1983
Nationalisation	.24	.19
Trade unions	−.28	−.28
Redistribution	.19	.18
Government services	.15	.06
Unemployment	.07	.13
Defence	.06	.17
Common Market	.03	.14
Death penalty	−.01	−.02
R^2	.45	.56

[11] This is shown both by the fact that R^2 was higher in the 1983 regression (.56) than in 1979 (.45). The index of dissimilarity for nationalisation also increased from 47 in 1979 to 54 in 1983. Of course these statistical changes cannot tell us which is cause and which is effect.

[12] This distinction excludes respondents in two intermediate categories who reported making up their mind "sometime this year", or "sometime last year".

[13] 65 per cent of Labour loyalists placed themselves to the right of their party on the nationalisation scale compared with 75 per cent of Labour floaters. Similarly, 35 per cent of Conservative loyalists placed themselves to the left of their party on nationalisation but 47 per cent of Conservative floaters did.

[14] Panel studies have shown that answers to the *individual* questions, for example on nationalisation, are unstable over time, but this may be due to the measurement error that is bound to exist. If a *battery* of questions is used to measure ideological position we would expect to find more stability as the errors in individual questions may cancel out. We plan to investigate this further in future research. For further discussions of these points compare Butler and Stokes 1974, chapter 13 and Inglehart 1977, chapter 4.

[15] For a review of the previous literature on the character of Liberal support see Curtice (1983).

[16] Thus only 48 per cent of Liberal voters in February 1974 voted Liberal again in October 1974, compared with 72 per cent of Labour supporters. (Sarlvik and Crewe, 1983: 46-47). See also Butler and Stokes (1969: chapter 14), and Alt et al (1977).
According to our respondents' recall of their 1979 vote, the picture was unchanged in 1983. While amongst those who voted in 1983 the percentage of 1979 Liberals who voted Alliance in 1983 was, at 82 per cent, higher than the proportion of 1979 Labour voters who voted Labour again (67 per cent), it was still lower than the equivalent figure for the Conservative party (85 per cent). This is despite the fact that overall Conservative support fell between 1979 and 1983 while the Alliance vote was a considerable improvement on the 1979 Liberal vote.

[17] Thus of voters with very strong party identities, 97 per cent of 1979 Conservatives voted Conservative again in 1983, 92 per cent of 1979 Labour voters again voted Labour in 1983 and 91 per cent of 1979 Liberals voted for the Alliance in 1983. The comparable figures for those with 'not very strong' party identities were 73 per cent, 43 per cent and 71 per cent respectively. We have measured party identity in the same way as previous election studies using question 13.

[18] Analysis of aggregate election results suggests that in the absence of a Liberal candidate, some people who might have voted do abstain or vote for an extremist party. See, for example, Steed (1974: 334 and 336), Steed (1978). However, even in this situation, the number of voters using this alternative form of protest is small.

[19] See also Curtice (1983: 107).

(Notes continue on following page)

[20] When we used multiple regression to discriminate between Alliance and Labour voters, attitudes towards the Common Market came lower in importance only than nationalisation and trade unions. The results were as follows:

TABLE 8.12N Multiple Regression of Alliance Vote on Attitudes

	Standardised regression coefficients	
	Alliance vs Conservative (1)	Alliance vs Labour (2)
Nationalisation	−.09	.24
Trade unions	.18	−.19
Redistribution	−.13	.13
Government services	−.09	.01
Unemployment	−.15	.09
Defence	−.22	.04
Common Market	−.05	.18
Death penalty	.09	.03
R^2	.27	.26

The coefficients in column 1 are those obtained when the sample is restricted to Alliance and Conservative voters; the coefficients in column 2 are those obtained when the sample is restricted to Alliance and Labour voters.

[21] On the Liberal party's attitude towards the Common Market see Butt Phillip (1983).
[22] The Limehouse declaration, signed by Williams, Jenkins, Rodgers and Owen, states

"Britain needs to recover its self-confidence and be outward looking, rather than isolationist, xenophobic or neutralist. We want Britain to play a full and constructive role within the framework of the European Community, NATO, the United Nations and the Commonwealth. It is only within such a multilateral framework that we can hope to negotiate international agreements covering arms control and disarmament and to grapple effectively with the poverty of the Third World".

(For the full text of the Limehouse declaration see Stephenson 1982: 185-186.)
[23] In the case of the police the percentages given are those disagreeing that "the police should be given more power" (Q42b); in the case of the death penalty the percentages are those disagreeing that "Britain should bring back the death penalty" (Q42c); in the case of the Falklands it is those agreeing that "The government should negotiate with Argentina over the future of the Falklands" (Q27b); in the case of private medicine it is those disagreeing that "The government should encourage the growth of private medicine" (Q35d); in the case of the National Health Service it is those agreeing that "The government should put more money into the National Health Service" (Q35e); in the case of education spending it is those agreeing that government spending on education has "Not gone far enough" (Q45d).

[24] See Laver (1984).

[25] A rather similar two-dimensional view of politics has been used extensively by Robertson (1984), Rokeach (1973).

[26] Points -10 to -1 on each scale have been combined to give the 'left' position; 0 remains as the centre position and +1 to +10 have been combined to give the 'right' position.

[27] Using different questions to tap the dimensions will change the distribution of respondents somewhat but has little impact on our assessment of the areas of relative voting strength for each party.

[28] We should note that there is some tendency for attitudes on the two axes to be associated. If they were statistically independent we would expect to find only 7 per cent in the north-west corner and 18 per cent in the north-east corner. The axes are not therefore strictly orthogonal.

[29] Nonvoters, refusals, etc, have been excluded. The percentages thus tell us what proportion of voters in each area of the map voted Labour, Alliance or Conservative. The percentage voting for other parties can be obtained by subtracting the three-party total from 100.

[30] The small numbers mean that the difference is not significant in this south-west corner. However, the concentration of Alliance voters in the centre, north and north-west is significant. This can be seen most easily from the pattern of residuals from the model which assumes vote is independent of position. Thus fitting the log-linear model NT,V (where N represents respondent's position on the nationalisation scale, T that on the taxation scale and V represents vote) we obtain the following residuals. (A residual of 2 can be regarded as significant.)

TABLE 8.13N Ideological Position and Relative Support for the Alliance

Alliance residuals

−4.6	5.9	4.8	reduce nuclear weapons
1.0	3.0	−2.4	no change
−1.7	0.2	−4.1	increase nuclear weapons
nationalise private companies	no change	sell off nationalised industries	

[31] See Lemieux (1977).

[32] To calculate broad agreement we collapsed the scales into three categories representing left (-10 to -1), centre (0) and right (1 to 10). Broad agreement is then defined as any case where the respondent placed both himself and the party he voted for in the same category.

[33] See Reid 1981, chapter 4.

[34] Less difference in party unity appears if we use respondents' position on the scales relative to their party's. Thus 19 per cent of Conservatives were in exact agreement with their party on both the nationalisation and nuclear disarmament scales; 19 per cent of Labour voters were also in precise agreement with their party's position and 18 per cent of Alliance voters.

[35] Among those who said they voted Labour in 1979 and who reported having voted in 1983, there was no association between age and switching to the Alliance (see table 8.14N).

TABLE 8.14N Age and Switching to the Alliance

Vote in 1979	Percentage switching to the Alliance			
	Under 29	30–44	45–59	60 and over
Conservative	17 (144)	15 (382)	11 (358)	7 (384)
Labour	26 (143)	26 (336)	22 (290)	24 (313)

Figures in brackets give cell sizes

There was an association among former Conservative voters, though this in part reflected a greater propensity among those in the two middle age groups to switch to Labour rather than stay with the Conservatives. Only amongst the oldest age group was loyalty to the Conservatives noticeably higher.

Chapter 9

Ideological Change in the Electorate

Although our two-dimensional map of the electorate is still too simplified, it offers some understanding of the ideological sources of support for the Alliance.[1] It also perhaps offers some clues to the decline in commitment to the Labour and Conservative parties, and the growth of support for the Alliance, over the last twenty years.

As we saw in chapter 3, the class structure has been changing shape over the last twenty years with a contracting working class and an expanding salariat. We might therefore expect a shift of the electorate along the east-west axis of the map. Fewer people than before might now favour government intervention in the economy. Chapter 5 also suggested that the expansion of higher education might lead to a shift along the north-south axis. More people than before might now adopt liberal attitudes. The net result of these two movements would be a shift in the contours of our map as more electors come to be found in the northern and eastern areas of the map. On this account, there are gains and losses for both the Labour and Conservative parties; Labour benefits from the northward drift of the electorate but loses from the eastward drift while the Conservative party makes the opposite gains and losses. The major net beneficiary of these movements is of course the Alliance with an expanded north-eastern area of the map in which to search for voters.

The shift to the right or east on the class axis has been well documented and has been seen as a major source of Labour's decline.[2] The shift to the north on the liberal axis is both more controversial and more problematic. Many commentators have taken a one-dimensional view of ideology and believe that the shift to the right has been general. Even writers like Inglehart who take a two-dimensional view do not expect postmaterialist values to spread under conditions of economic recession. However, we see no reason in principle why change on the second axis should parallel that on the first. If we are correct, orthodox forecasts of the parties' prospects may be in need of substantial revision: the position of the Conservative party may be less secure than is currently assumed while that of Labour may not be quite so dismal.

The Class Values

A standard question has been asked in all but one of the election studies about one of the key class values, namely nationalisation. [3] Respondents were asked whether "A lot more industries should be nationalised", "only a few more industries should be nationalised", "no more industries should be nationalised, but industries that are now nationalised should stay nationalised", or "some of the industries that are now nationalised should become private companies" (Q37). We have combined the first two categories, the distinction between them being more interesting in 1964 than it is now. Table 9.1 shows the changing distribution of responses over time. [4]

TABLE 9.1 Attitudes to Nationalisation 1964–1983

	Percentage favouring				
	Nationalisation	No change	Privatisation		
1964	28	51	21	100%	(N = 1604)
1966	29	49	22	100%	(N = 1631)
Feb 1974	28	47	25	100%	(N = 2103)
Oct 1974	32	46	22	100%	(N = 2109)
1979	17	43	40	100%	(N = 1751)
1983	18	40	42	100%	(N = 3486)

The major feature of table 9.1 is the rather sudden change between October 1974 and May 1979. In 1979 for the first time more people favoured privatisation than further nationalisation, although the *status quo* was still (although only just) the most popular option. The balance tipped the other way in 1983, when privatisation took over as the most popular option.

However, even though the same question wording was used in all the election studies, the interpretation of the answers is not wholly straightforward. The questions may have stayed the same, but the context — in particular the extent of public ownership — has not. Some companies have been nationalised, others privatised. The electorate may not have changed its mind at all about the preferred extent of public ownership; it may simply be reacting in a perfectly consistent way to the institutional changes. In other words, the changed responses to the nationalisation question between 1974 and 1979 could be interpreted as a condemnation of the extension of the public ownership that had taken place under the 1974 Labour government, not as a true 'shift to the right'. It is not the public's liking for nationalisation which changed, it could be argued, but the amount of nationalisation itself.

It is not possible to check this interpretation in any definitive way, but a look at the recent history of nationalisation is nonetheless illuminating. The major landmarks were as follows. In 1967 the Iron and Steel Act renationalised the industry, which had been first nationalised in 1949 by Labour and then denationalised by the Conservatives in 1953. This was the only major piece of nationalisation carried out by the Wilson governments, which otherwise left things much as they were. As table 9.1 shows, public opinion also remained much as it was throughout the Wilson years.

The Heath government was also fairly modest in its accomplishments. The lame duck of Rolls Royce was taken into public onwership in 1971 following its bankruptcy but some modest privatisation took place too. In 1971-2 some of BOAC's routes were allotted to British Caledonian, and in 1973 Thomas Cook's travel agency and the Carlisle state breweries were sold to the private sector. Overall, there was little change and public opinion too remained much as it was.

The Labour government which followed was much more active, (as indeed its manifesto promised). Another lame duck — British Leyland — was rescued and the majority of its shares acquired by the government in 1975. The National Enterprise Board was also established in that year with the objective of playing an active, interventionist role in the economy. In 1977 the British National Oil Corporation was established and large sections of the aerospace and shipbuilding industries were taken into public ownership with the formation of British Aerospace and British Shipbuilders.

Although the 1974 Labour government has not normally enjoyed the reputation of being a radical, socialist administration, this was by far the most extensive programme of nationalisation since the 1945 government. Public opinion however 'responded' (although we should not assume that it was a simple matter of cause and effect) with a substantial swing in favour of privatisation. It would not be implausible to infer that many people simply preferred the earlier *status quo* of the 1966 Wilson administration.

However, it is doubtful if the changes in attitude towards nationalisation were caused purely by the institutional changes. Mrs Thatcher's administration in 1979 restored the *status quo*, but public opinion did not move back in step with the institutional changes. British Aerospace, Britoil, the National Freight Corporation, Amersham International, Cable and Wireless, and the British Transport Docks Board were all privatised (although British Airways, British Telecom and British Shipbuilders were left for the 1983 Parliament). But public opinion remained in favour of privatisation. As table 9.1 shows, the electorate did not revert to its earlier preferences. If Mrs Thatcher completes her programme, she will have pushed back the frontiers of public ownership behind their 1964 boundaries. It is quite possible that public opinion will swing back again, but at the time of writing we are forced to agree that there has been a net shift to the right on nationalisation.

It is in theory possible that this net shift to the right is due simply to the changing shape of the class structure; a smaller working class means that there are fewer potential supporters of public ownership. However, as table 9.2 shows, the shift between 1964 and 1983 is far greater than can be explained by the changes in the class structure alone. In all classes alike there have been shifts in favour of privatisation. Mrs Thatcher, it would seem, has made converts to the free enterprise philosophy.

TABLE 9.2 Class and Nationalisation 1964–1983

| | Percentage respondents favouring privatisation | | Index of dissimilarity |
	1964	1983	
Salariat	21 (278)	52 (973)	31
Routine nonmanual	25 (276)	43 (785)	18
Petty bourgeoisie	35 (112)	66 (270)	32
Foremen and technicians	24 (146)	44 (254)	19
Working class	15 (666)	29 (1073)	14

Figures in brackets give cell sizes

If this analysis is correct, we must not treat ideological change purely as a consequence of social change. We must avoid a naive 'sociological determinism'. Public attitudes can be shaped by political leadership as well as by social change. The political parties can perhaps help to define what counts as class ideology. Parties are not the prisoners of social change and social structure; they are probably one of the major agencies which help to shape subjective awareness of class interests and to translate these into class values. We would, for example, expect class values to take a rather different form in a country such as the USA where the two major parties have less conflicting class ideologies.

But while political parties may help to shape class values, they cannot shape them just as they please. A privatisation programme of the kind espoused by Mrs Thatcher's Conservatives will fall on readier ears among the petty bourgeoisie or the salariat than in the working class. This can be seen from table 9.2. Thus, although all classes have moved to the right since 1964 on nationalisation, the movement is far from even. The working class has been relatively immune to the blandishments of free enterprise with an increase of only 14 points in favour. The petty bourgeoisie and the salariat have responded more enthusiastically with increases of 32 and 31 points. The shift to the right could perhaps be described as a successful attempt by the Conservatives to articulate the latent interests of their natural supporters.

However, we must not place too much weight on a single question if we wish to measure ideological change. On some of the other questions which make up the class axis there was much less net movement.[5] We do not have comparable data over time on attitudes towards job creation, but since 75 per cent of our respondents in 1983 favoured government intervention to create jobs, it is rather more likely that there has been a move to the left than to the right — again perhaps in response to the actual rise in unemployment.

There is rather firmer evidence on income redistribution. Similar questions were asked on this in 1974, 1979 and 1983. In 1974 56 per cent favoured redistribution, and this fell, but only modestly, to 55 per cent in 1979 and 47 per cent in 1983. The net change of 9 points is more in keeping with the small change in the shape of the class structure over the ten years in question (although it cannot wholly be explained by structural change).

These results suggest that while nationalisation may have become increasingly unpopular to many voters, support for other elements of working-class ideology is both higher and more stable. By focussing on nationalisation, we highlight the movements at the extremes of the ideological continuum. But we should not forget that this affects only a minority of people. Even in the case of nationalisation the overall dissimilarity of 21 points between the 1964 and 1983 distributions is quite small. It is a lot smaller for example than the dissimilarity between working-class and petty bourgeois respondents in 1983. It means that there must be a great deal of overlap between the two distributions. The extent of ideological change must not be exaggerated therefore. If we take into account the other class values (particularly income redistribution and job creation), our estimate of ideological change will be further reduced.

Our interpretation therefore is that the minority on the far left of the ideological continuum has declined somewhat in size while that on the far right has grown proportionately. But the bulk of the electorate remains in the centre, favouring some measure of job creation and income redistribution but with ambivalent views towards both nationalisation and privatisation.

Such an interpretation has rather less momentous implications for the political parties than one which concentrates purely on nationalisation. Attitudes to the latter may show the most dramatic change, and it is true that (in a cross-sectional analysis) they are the best predictors of vote, but the other class values are not wholly unimportant and they appear to have been more stable.[6] Moreover, even in 1983 more people shared Labour's views on income redistribution than shared the Conservatives', just as there were still more people in the working class in 1983 than in the salariat. A *shift* to the right is not the same as a *majority* on the right.

The Liberal Values

The best time-series available on the liberal values consists of respondents' changing attitudes towards the death penalty. Questions about this were asked in four of the election studies, although the wording necessarily changed after 1969 when the death penalty was finally removed from the statute book.[7] The time trends are shown in table 9.3.

TABLE 9.3 Attitudes to the Death Penalty 1966–1983

	Percentage favouring			
	Abolition	Retention/ restoration		
1966	18	82	100%	(N = 1783)
1970	19	81	100%	(N = 1094)
1979	25	75	100%	(N = 1713)
1983	37	63	100%	(N = 3515)

The picture is quite different from that of table 9.1 on nationalisation. There is a slight drift from 1966 to 1979 in favour of abolition followed by a more marked shift, in the same direction, in the course of the last Parliament.[8] Despite Mrs Thatcher's views in favour of the restoration of the 'ultimate deterrent', the electorate showed no sign of following her on this as they did on privatisation. Instead, as we would expect from the growth of sixth-form and higher education, the balance of movement has been away from the authoritarian end of the continuum and towards the liberal one.[9]

The rather abrupt change between 1979 and 1983, it must be admitted, is greater than can be explained in educational terms alone, although the overall change from 1966 is more in line with educational expansion. We have no specific explanation for the abrupt change, but it is quite plausible that values will in general change abruptly rather than smoothly. Values must be thought of as *social* phenomena rather than *individual* ones. There needs to be some social process in order to crystallise a change. The rhetoric of a political party may perform this function, but other processes could do the same job. For example, values may also be shaped by the development of new social networks, as with the university expansion of the 1960s and the spread of more 'permissive' values at that time.

As with the class values, however, we should not rely on a single question to measure change. This is particularly important as the death penalty is one of the least 'politicised' of issues. We need some confirming evidence to be sure of movement along the north-south axis of our map.[10] We repeated a number of questions that had been asked in the 1979 Election Survey about issues that might be regarded as liberal ones. These confirm the picture given by the death penalty question of a clear shift in a liberal direction. As in 1979 we asked our respondents whether a number of social changes had gone too far. We asked, *inter alia*, about "attempts to give equal opportunities to women in Britain" (Q45b), "attempts to give equal opportunities to black people and Asians in Britain" (Q45g) and "the availability of abortion on the National Health Service" (Q45e). The results for 1979 and 1983 are given in table 9.4.

TABLE 9.4 Changes in Social Attitudes 1979–1983

	Percentage agreeing that changes had gone too far		
	Equal opportunities for women	Equal opportunities for blacks and Asians	Abortion on the National Health Service
1979 (minimum N = 1714)	23	30	44
1983 (minimum N = 3287)	9	20	32

In all three cases the movements are of very similar magnitude to those with the death penalty question and are in the same direction. Interestingly, there was little movement (again in all three cases) in the percentages who thought that the changes had *not* gone far enough. Rather, the increase was in the proportion who felt that the changes were about right. It is the *status quo*, not radical change, that has become more popular.

A longer, although technically less satisfactory, time series can be constructed on attitudes to tax cuts and spending on social services. Government spending on the welfare state may seem an unlikely candidate for measuring liberal values as, at first sight, it would seem to have more in common with the interventionist-free enterprise values. However there is an important distinction which must be made between the universal benefits, such as health, education and pensions which are available to everybody at some stage of their lives and the selective ones, such as supplementary benefit, which go only to those with specific needs. The universal benefits tend to be much more popular than the selective ones.[11] For example, 64 per cent of our sample in 1983 thought that government spending on education had not gone far enough, while only 28 per cent thought that welfare benefits had not gone far enough.

It is not difficult to explain the difference in popularity. The universal benefits appeal to everyone's self-interest; and they go to the salariat as much as, if not more than, to the working class. The selective benefits on the other hand go only to a minority, mainly the working class, and appeal to the altruism rather than the self-interest of the bulk of the electorate. In line with this, we find that attitudes towards the selective benefits are quite closely related to class position, whereas those towards the universal benefits are not. For example, in response to our question on welfare benefits there was quite a marked difference between the classes; 40 per cent of the working class thought that "welfare benefits . . . have not gone far enough" (Q45a) whereas only 22 per cent of the salariat gave the same answer. But on education spending the differences were almost non-existent, 69 per cent of the working class and 66 per cent of the salariat agreeing that it had not gone far enough, while on pensions and the Health Service there were modest class differences.

It is a mistake therefore to treat the welfare state as a single entity or to regard it as a straightforward class issue. As we saw in chapter 8, spending on health and education were two of the questions on which Alliance voters were closer to Labour than to the Conservatives, and we are inclined to see these particular aspects of the welfare state as ones which to some extent cross-cut class interests.[12]

Unfortunately, because of wording differences, we cannot directly compare the welfare state question in the 1966 survey, which asked about spending on "social services" with the 1979 question on "government spending" or the 1983 question on "health and social services" (Q31a). The questions suggest a modest increase in support for spending — from 40 per cent in favour in 1966 to 45 per cent in 1983 — but we cannot read too much into this.

Fortunately, there is some more direct evidence. The proportion of the electorate saying that the government spends too little on the health service increased from 30 per cent in 1960 to 66 per cent in 1979 and to 85 per cent in 1983.[13] And the proportion agreeing that "government services such as health, education and welfare should be extended, even if it means some increase in taxes" increased from 39 per cent in 1978 to 50 per cent in 1983.[14]

As with nationalisation, these changes could reflect changes in government expenditure rather than real changes in people's values. There were much publicised expenditure cuts under both the 1974 Labour government and the 1979 Conservative government, so again people may be expressing their opposition to these changes rather than altering their own values. But while this may be part of the story, particularly of the last few years, it is unlikely to be the whole of it. Over our period as a whole, from 1964 to 1983, government spending has increased from 36 per cent of Gross Domestic Product to 47 per cent, and within the total the proportion given to education and health has stayed fairly constant.[15] Our interpretation is that this increase in spending has met with general approval and that attempts to reverse it are disliked.[16]

We suspect, then, that very different processes have been at work with nationalisation and government spending. In the case of nationalisation, there has been increased support for cutting back on public ownership; in the case of welfare-state spending there has been increased opposition to cut-backs. There is, we believe, nothing inherently inconsistent in these divergent trends. In principle there is no reason why trends on the first question should run parallel with those on the second.

Changing Contours of the Map

Our assumptions, therefore, that there have been net movements of the electorate to the east (or right) on the class axis of our ideological map and to the north on the liberal axis appear to be sound. They have almost certainly been helped by the changing class structure and the expansion of higher education, but equally certainly they have not been purely passive consequences of social change. Government action and political conversion have played a part too.

It is difficult to make any accurate estimate of the actual amount, rather than the direction, of change. If we take the two questions on which we have the best time-series, namely nationalisation and the death penalty, we obtain the following picture of change:

TABLE 9.5 The Changing Map 1966–1983

	nationalise private companies	no change	sell off nationalised industries	
oppose death penalty	−1	+6	+10	
no change	0	+1	+4	
favour death penalty	−11	−17	+7	

Table 9.5 shows the change in the proportions of the total samples who favoured each possible combination. Thus in 1966 20 per cent of the total sample were in favour *both* of further nationalisation *and* of the retention of the death

penalty. By 1983 this had fallen to 9 per cent of the total sample, giving us our figure of -11 in the south-west corner of the map.

Too much weight should not be placed on individual figures, but the relative decline of population in the south-west and the growth in the north-east is clear enough. Table 9.5 also makes clear that the changes have not been entirely to Labour's disadvantage. While Labour's heartland has contracted (although only slightly) and the Conservatives' has expanded, the areas immediately adjacent to the heartlands show a different pattern: potential Conservative recruits in the south have dwindled in number while potential Labour recruits in the north have grown.

We should not exaggerate the impact of these changes, since attitudes towards the death penalty are very weakly related to voting behaviour. Even if we use the alternative, more politicised criterion of defence for measuring the second axis (as in chapter 8), it still proves to be only of secondary importance. In other words the increased numbers of people who share their attitudes on the class values have been a more valuable asset to the Conservative party than the increased numbers of like-minded people on the nonclass issues have been to Labour. Labour have not gained as much on the roundabouts as they lost on the swings.

But the main beneficiary of the ideological shift towards the north-east of our map is likely to be the Alliance. As we showed in chapter 8 this area of the map seems to be the Alliance heartland. We can attempt to estimate the size of the Alliance gain by assuming that the preferences of the inhabitants of each area of our ideological map had remained constant but that the numbers in each area changed in the way they actually did. Our best estimate is that the Alliance vote has been increased by between a minimum of 1 point and a maximum of 5 points by this drift to the north-east.[17] Such Alliance gains would have been drawn more from Labour than from the Conservative party, but only just. If the Alliance had gained the full five points, we estimate that three would have come at Labour's expense and two at the Conservatives' expense.

Notes

[1] A three-dimensional view might be preferred. Compare the results of the canonical correlations in chapter 4, note 12 and of the factor analysis in chapter 5, note 16.

[2] See the discussions in Sarlvik and Crewe (1983), Crewe (1982a).

[3] The same question was also asked of panel members in the remaining election study (1970). However, the small numbers involved and the problem of selective attrition in panel studies means that less weight can be attached to the results. For further details of the panels see Appendix II.

[4] There is also some interesting material on attitudes to nationalisation in 1949 quoted in Abrams et al (1960: table 20). This showed 27 per cent of the electorate in favour of further nationalisation, a very similar percentage to the 1964 one.

[5] We must emphasise that we we are here dealing only with net movements. Panel studies have shown that aggregate movement is a great deal higher, but that the large number of individual movements tend to cancel out.

[6] As we saw in chapter 8, note 10, nationalisation and trade union legislation are the two best individual predictors of Conservative or Labour voting, but the questions on income redistribution and job creation make further quite substantial increments to variance explained.

[7] The death penalty was abolished temporarily in 1965. After a review period it was permanently abolished in 1969. In the 1966 and 1970 studies the wording was "Did you want to see the death penalty kept or abolished?" (1966, Q27; 1970, Q29). In 1979 it was "I am going to read out a list of things that some people believe a government should do. For each one you can say whether you feel it is: very important that it should be done, fairly important that it should be done, it doesn't matter either way, fairly important that it should not be done, very important that it should not be done. . . . What is your view about bringing back the death penalty?" (1979, Q38f), and in 1983 "Please say whether you agree or disagree with each of these statements, or say if you are not sure either way: . . . Britain should bring back the death penalty" (Q42c).

[8] We should note however that in the pre-election study of 1963 a question on the death penalty was asked and showed a rather lower percentage (78 per cent) in favour of retention. This casts doubt on whether there actually was a slight drift to a more liberal position between the early 1960s and 1979.

[9] The 1983 Social Attitudes survey, a national probability sample carried out shortly before the election survey, tends to confirm the level of support for the death penalty given in table 9.3. Thus, 70 per cent of the Social Attitudes respondents favoured the death penalty for terrorist murders, 66 per cent for murder of a policeman and 59 per cent for other murderers (Jowell and Airey 1984). It is thus unlikely that our result is due to a quirk of our sample or our question.

[10] A rather shorter time series can be constructed using Inglehart's measures of 'postmaterialist' values. He has obtained estimates of the number of postmaterialists in Britain in 1970, 1973 and 1976, and as described in chapter 5 we repeated his measures in 1983. The changes over time parallel those shown in table 9.3 on the death penalty. In the 1970s the distribution of materialists and postmaterialists was rather stable with around 36 per cent of the former and 8 per cent of the latter (Inglehart, 1977: table 4.1). But the 1983 results show a small movement in the direction of postmaterialism. Our survey yielded 10 per cent postmaterialists and 35 per cent materialists, a minor change to be sure but modest confirmation of our story.

[11] For further discussion and evidence on this point see Taylor-Gooby (1983, 1984).

[12] It is quite possible that there has been a trend against welfare benefits (as with the other class issues) but in favour of health and education. This would help to reconcile our findings with those of Sarlvik and Crewe (1983), although our data actually suggest increased support for welfare benefits between 1979 and 1983.

[13] Again we must be cautious in interpreting this trend since it comes from different sources. The 1960 and 1979 figures are from Gallup (quoted in Crewe (1982a)). The 1983 figure comes from our election survey (Q35e).

[14] These are the most reliable indicators of change since they come from standard Gallup polls with identical question wording. They are quoted in Butler and Kavanagh (1984) and in Taylor-Gooby (1984). There is further evidence in Rose (forthcoming) pointing in the same direction.

[15] For details see Imber and Todd (1983).

[16] This trend in favour of welfare state spending would seem to be in direct contradiction to the findings of Harris and Seldon (1979) who suggest that there has been a steady decline in support for the welfare state. However, we should note that Harris and Seldon's evidence for their claim was that an increased proportion of their samples favoured the statement "The state should continue the present service but allow people to contract out, pay less contributions and so on and use the money to pay for their own services" Harris and Seldon (1979: 45).

[17] Unfortunately, the results of this exercise are not very robust. Estimates of the likely benefits to the Alliance are rather sensitive to the assumptions we make about preferences, and in the case of the Alliance we are dependent on rather small sample sizes. One problem is that in 1966 the probability of voting Liberal was very weakly related to position on the ideological map (as we shall see in chapter 10). If we use the 1966 conditional probabilities, therefore, the changing cell frequencies make virtually no difference to the expected Liberal vote. An alternative is to work backwards from 1983, assuming that the 1983 conditional probabilities had occurred in 1966 as well, and this is the strategy we have followed.

A second problem is that even in 1983 attitudes to the death penalty are more weakly related to vote than, say, attitudes to government spending. We get larger estimates of the Alliance gain if we use the latter as the source for the conditional probabilities. If we had data on attitudes to defence over time, the imputed Alliance gains might turn out to be even larger.

The estimate of the 1 point Alliance gain is based on 1983 probabilities of Alliance voting conditional on attitudes to the death penalty (and to nationalisation). The estimate of the 5 point Alliance gain is based on 1983 probabilities of Alliance voting conditional on attitudes to tax cuts and government spending (and to nationalisation). In both cases the changes in cell frequencies are derived from the nationalisation and death penalty time series, since as we have said these give the firmest estimate of the time trends.

Chapter 10

Ideological Change in the Parties

We saw in chapter 8 that a two-dimensional map of politics is required in order to understand the Alliance vote in 1983. And in chapter 9 we saw that the Alliance has benefitted from a movement of the electorate across the ideological map towards the north (representing liberalism) and east (representing free enterprise). This drift has brought the Alliance a small bonus in extra votes and a rather larger bonus of potential votes, and it corresponds in part with the changes in the class structure and the expansion of higher education, described in Part 1.

However, the movement of the electorate across our map is only one feature of the Alliance rise. A second, quite distinct, component is that the Alliance vote has become more coherent than before (even after making allowance for the changed distribution of voters on the map). As we shall show, the distinctive profile of Alliance voters described in chapter 8 is a relatively new phenomenon. It is also a quite separate phenomenon from the changes dealt with in chapter 9. In effect it means that the Alliance has created (or at least has acquired) a new ideological base or heartland that the Liberals alone did not have in the past. We then move to the question of whether this new coherence should be attributed to the movement of the Conservative and Labour parties away from the centre, or to the positive attraction of the newly-formed Social Democratic Party and its alliance with the Liberals. Has Alliance recruitment been more a matter of push or pull?

The Changing Character of the Liberal Vote

The conventional wisdom that Liberal voters were a rather amorphous collection of individuals, without any particular unifying beliefs, was probably not far from the truth in the 1960s when commentators first described it.

TABLE 10.1 Liberal Shares of the Vote in 1966

Percentage voting Liberal

5 (219)	9 (228)	11 (76)	spend more on services
4 (158)	10 (392)	8 (202)	cut taxes

nationalise private companies	no change	sell off nationalised industries

Figures in brackets give cell sizes

Table 10.1 represents the map for 1966, the earliest year for which we can construct one. For the east-west axis we have been able to use the standard question on nationalisation described in chapter 9. For the north-south axis we have used the question on tax cuts and government spending. (The question wording used in 1966 did not offer respondents the choice of the *status quo* on government spending and taxation, hence the asymmetrical form of the table.)[1] Table 10.1 shows that, for example, 158 of the voters in the 1966 survey were in favour *both* of further nationalisation *and* of tax cuts (the south-west corner of the map). Of these 158 respondents only 4 per cent voted Liberal.

We can see that even in 1966 Liberals were rare on the west of the map — among people who favoured further nationalisation. Liberals have always tended to the centre or to the right on the class axis, it would appear. But they were evenly distributed in other respects. There was no significant tendency for Liberal voters to prefer government spending to tax cuts or the *status quo* to privatisation.[2] Liberals were almost as common in the Conservative heartland of the south-east area of the map as they were in the north or north-east. The traditional view of Liberal voters was therefore more or less correct; apart from opposition to nationalisation, they lacked any discernible unifying set of beliefs.

A distinctive Liberal heartland on our map gradually emerged over the next twenty years. We do not have the data to construct a map for 1970, but the February 1974 contours are shown in table 10.2.[3]

As table 10.2 shows, a distinct heartland barely existed in February 1974, even when the Liberal vote was greatly expanded. Liberal voting increased in all areas of the map, rather than in particular territories, confirming the view that the Liberal surge in 1974 was more a protest against the Conservative and Labour parties than a positive endorsement of Liberal policies. As in 1966 Liberals in 1974 were, relatively speaking, less common on the west of the map than in the centre or east; there was also a slightly greater likelihood that they would now be found in the north (and centre) of our ideological map than in the south. The second axis was thus beginning to differentiate Liberals from nonLiberals, but only just. The differences do not reach statistical significance — at this stage they are merely straws in the wind.[4]

TABLE 10.2 Liberal Shares of the Vote in February 1974

Percentage voting Liberal

15 (236)	25 (218)	22 (78)	increase benefits
17 (147)	23 (318)	24 (128)	no change
15 (101)	18 (294)	16 (231)	cut benefits

nationalise private companies	no change	sell off nationalised industries

Figures in brackets give cell sizes

In 1979 the Liberal vote fell back once more, but it did not revert to the random distribution of 1966. Table 10.3 shows that a Liberal heartland was rather more clearly visible in 1979.[5] The Liberal party was now significantly more popular among people who favoured the *status quo* on nationalisation but preferred government services to tax cuts. The straws in the wind are now blowing more strongly in the same direction.[6]

TABLE 10.3 Liberal Shares of the Vote in 1979

Percentage voting Liberal

9 (155)	19 (436)	13 (342)	keep up services
7 (29)	21 (48)	13 (46)	doesn't matter
8 (36)	14 (133)	8 (190)	cut taxes

nationalise private companies	no change	sell off nationalised industries

Figures in brackets give cell sizes

In 1983, however, there was an even more marked change. The north-south axis becomes a clearer basis of Liberal (or rather Alliance) voting and their vote becomes much more coherent than before. The Alliance vote in different areas of the map in 1983 is given in table 10.4, and the contrast between that map and the one for February 1974 is striking. These two elections marked two 'surges' of Liberal voting, but we can see that the Liberal and Alliance gains since 1974 are wholly concentrated in the centre, north and north-east of the map. (The absolute figures of table 10.4 are rather different from those of table 8.7, since the question used for measuring the north-south axis is different, but the pattern of relative Alliance strength is much the same.)

TABLE 10.4 Alliance Shares of the Vote in 1983

Percentage voting Alliance

15 (301)	34 (570)	28 (417)		spend more on services
19 (115)	37 (400)	18 (510)		no change
14 (65)	19 (150)	15 (288)		cut taxes
nationalise private companies	no change	sell off nationalised industries		

Figures in brackets give cell sizes

In the Labour and Conservative heartlands of the north-west and south-east respectively there was no change in the Liberal share of the vote between 1974 and 1983. The Liberals achieved around 15 per cent of the vote in these areas in 1974, and the Alliance got almost exactly the same proportion there in 1983. Nor was there any significant change elsewhere along the west and south of the map. In all these alien areas for voters with Liberal or Social Democratic ideologies, the Alliance made no gains. Their most substantial gains were in the very centre of the map and, to a lesser degree, in the areas immediately adjacent to the north and north-east.[7] Thus in the very centre the Alliance gained 14 points (increasing from 23 to 37 per cent); in the north it gained 9 and in the north-east 6.

We must urge caution in the interpretation of these results, particularly of the absolute size of the changes, since the precise question wording on government spending changes from study to study. But we are confident that our account of the general direction of change is correct. The distinctive profile of Alliance voters — closer to Labour on the north-south axis and equidistant between Labour and Conservative on the east-west axis — is a relatively new phenomenon. There were glimmerings of it in 1974 and 1979, but in 1983 it shows a much stronger light.[8]

We can put this finding in a slightly different way. There has been the ideological movement that we saw in chapter 9 towards the north-east of our map giving the Alliance more *potential* voters. But in 1983 a greater number of these potential votes were converted into actual votes. To be sure, the Alliance parties are still much less successful than either Conservative or Labour in mobilising the potential vote in their respective heartlands. But it begins to make sense to talk about an Alliance heartland in 1983 in a way that it did not in, say, 1966 or even 1974.

Conservative and Labour Movements

Perhaps the most natural explanation for the increasing concentration of the Alliance vote in the centre and north of our map lies in the movements of the Conservative and Labour parties away from the centre. Here, in line with chapter 7, we would argue that it is the parties' overall character as institutions that counts rather more than their specific policies. Thus there are grounds for thinking that Labour actually moved to the left between 1970 and 1974, but that the electorate failed to notice, or perhaps believe, the shift. The Labour manifesto for the February 1974 election contained much more extensive proposals for public ownership than had those of 1964, 1966 or 1970. In the earlier years, the nationalisation of steel had been the only item on the agenda, but by February 1974 the manifesto promised that[9]

> "We shall not confine the extension of the public sector to the loss-making and subsidised industries. We shall also take over profitable sections of individual firms in those industries where a public holding is essential to enable the Government to control prices, stimulate investment, encourage exports, create employment, protect workers and consumers from the activities of irresponsible multi-national companies".

Despite these radical (but perhaps rather vague) proposals, the electorate contained similar proportions of people in 1970 and 1974 who thought that there was "a great deal of difference" between the parties. There was no clear perception that the parties had moved apart.[10]

This difference between 'objective' and 'subjective' accounts of Labour's position in 1974 should not, in our view, be put down simply to ignorance on the part of the electorate. To be sure, few people actually read election manifestos, but a more important point, we suggest, is that the party leadership had remained the same. Harold Wilson had led a skilfully pragmatic government in the 1960s; in 1974 his deputy leader was Edward Short, who was clearly on the right of the party; and other famous names — Healey, Jenkins and Williams — were all still in the Shadow Cabinet. Whatever the small print of the manifesto might have said, the Labour party as an institution could still reasonably be regarded as having a moderate rather than a radical character.

But by 1983 this seemed to have changed. There can be little doubt that many of the electorate saw the Labour party as a more radical institution than before. Half of our respondents believed that it had moved to the left since 1979 when Mr Callaghan was leader (Q46j). 82 per cent of the sample now believed that there was a great deal of difference between the Labour and Conservative parties compared with only 46 per cent even as recently as 1979. We have little doubt, although our data cannot prove it conclusively, that the changes in Labour's leadership were crucial to this perception. It is not just the package that counts. It is equally important who carries the package.

Another ingredient of this perceived gulf between the parties was almost certainly the changed character of the Conservative party. Its manifesto in 1983 was in most respects no more radical than its 1979 manifesto or indeed than Mr Heath's manifesto of 1970. What has become known as Thatcherism began life, or at any rate its most recent reincarnation, as Selsdon man, named after the Selsdon Park Hotel where Mr Heath's Shadow Cabinet drafted its manifesto in 1970. Mr Heath had long argued for the extension of market forces and the reduction of state interference in the economy. But when unemployment began to rise in 1972 the Heath government decided to change course from a noninterventionist policy to one of wage and price controls, along the lines of previous Labour policies.

By 1983 however Mrs Thatcher had demonstrated her unwillingness to change course as her predecessor had done. There were to be no reversals of policy from her government. The Falklands War established this reputation most powerfully. At the beginning of the war Enoch Powell said in the House of Commons[11]

"The Prime Minister, shortly after she came into office, received a soubriquet as the "Iron Lady". It arose in the context of remarks which she made about defence against the Soviet Union and its allies; but there was no reason to suppose that the Right Hon Lady did not welcome and, indeed, take pride in that description. In the next week or two this House, the nation and the right hon Lady herself will learn of what metal she is made".

He received his answer.

Perceptions of Movement

Just as issues alone do not determine how people vote, so the details of the manifestos do not determine perceptions of where the parties stand. Our suggestion is that people form a more synoptic view of the parties, a view based on perceptions of their leaders as well as of their ideologies. However, we must not exaggerate the uniformity of these perceptions. Half of the electorate in 1983 believed that the Labour party had moved to the left since Mr Callaghan had been leader, but this still leaves half who did not. And in the case of the Conservative party, only a quarter of our respondents thought it had moved to the right since Mr Heath had been leader.

Political sympathies naturally influence perceptions of these movements. Many of the people who thought Labour had moved to the left were staunch Conservatives, so *their* perceptions could hardly account for the rise of the Alliance at the expense of Labour. Of people who had actually voted Labour in 1979, less than a third believed the party had moved left. And of respondents who broadly agreed with Labour's fundamental principles (that is, those in the northwest corner of our map), only a quarter believed that Labour had moved to the left. What one sees depends on where one stands as well as what one looks at.

What one sees may also depend (for most people who are not activists) on what the mass media choose to present. A perennial complaint from the Labour party is that the mass media do not give them a fair deal. We cannot assess from our data whether a *general* 'bias' in the media contributed to Labour's poor result. But in any case our present concern is to explain why some people thought Labour had moved left (and the Conservative party had moved right) while others thought there had been no change. We can make some progress by seeing whether these perceptions varied according to the newspapers people read. The results are shown below.

TABLE 10.5 Newspaper Readership and Perceptions of the Parties

	Percentage believing Labour moved left	Percentage believing Conservatives moved right
Guardian (N = 153)	71	72
Times (N = 67)	82	55
Telegraph (N = 241)	64	34
Express (N = 265)	56	20
Mail (N = 297)	54	22
Sun (N = 339)	34	20
Mirror (N = 441)	37	24

The major finding is clearly that readers of the 'quality' press were more likely to believe that *both* parties had moved away from the centre. Guardian readers were particularly likely to believe that the Conservatives had moved right, and Times readers to believe that Labour had moved left, but even Telegraph readers (whom one might expect to have Conservative sympathies) were more likely to believe that the Conservative party had moved than were, say, readers of the Mirror. Clearly, the reader's prior sympathies and the political complexion of the newspaper are not the only ingredients.

The missing ingredient is education. By and large the readers of the Times, Guardian and Telegraph have higher educational qualifications than those of the Express, Mail, Sun and Mirror and, in a statistical sense, this is what accounts for the general difference between the top and bottom portions of table 10.5. Since, as we have seen in chapter 5, education also correlates with Alliance sympathies, this makes it rather difficult to sort out the causal processes involved. Do Alliance sympathisers read the Guardian and pay particular attention to articles on Conservative 'extremism'? Or does the Guardian specially alert its readers to evidence of Conservative extremism and help, unwittingly perhaps, to convert them into Alliance sympathisers? Our numbers are too small to draw any firm conclusions, but the safest bet is that both processes were at work.

Educational differences, on the other hand, do not wholly explain the differences in the perceptions of Mail and Express readers on the one hand from those of the Sun and Mirror on the other. Even among respondents who had no formal educational qualifications, Express and Mail readers were more likely to think that Labour had moved left than were Sun or Mirror readers.[12] However, the political biasses of the papers can hardly account for the difference since, on most people's reckoning, the Sun is now a right-wing paper. If political bias is the answer, Sun and Mirror readers should have very different perceptions of Labour movement. Our data suggest that they do not.

Our own interpretation, therefore, is that the tabloids simply fail to alert their readers to political change. The Sun may adopt strident right-wing views, but we see no evidence that this influenced its readers.[13] The mere expression of political opinions, however forcefully put, appears to do little to sway people's votes. Our hypothesis is that information, not opinion, is needed in order to change voters' attitudes towards the parties. The quality papers give most information and therefore are the most likely to persuade their readers that the parties have changed their character. The tabloids give least information and are therefore the least likely to succeed in any campaign of political persuasion.

We do not, then, rule out the possibility that papers influence their readership. But our interpretation is that they do so more by their selective presentation of information about the parties than by any overt political propaganda. The less information is presented, the less scope there is for successful persuasion.

Movements and Defections

Whatever the causes of people's perceptions, it is quite clear that people who believed that the Labour and Conservative parties had moved away from the centre were more likely to defect. This is shown in table 10.6.

TABLE 10.6 Party Movement and Voter Defections

Perception of party movement	Percentage defecting	
	Conservative voters in 1979	Labour voters in 1979
Labour moved left	16 (599)	47 (281)
Labour stayed put	14 (452)	25 (562)
Conservatives moved right	24 (209)	32 (344)
Conservatives stayed put	12 (801)	35 (564)

Figures in brackets give cell sizes

Here we have taken people who reported that they voted either Labour or Conservative in 1979 (thus excluding those who were too young to vote in 1979, or who had not voted); we then show the proportions who defected to another party in 1983. As previous studies have found, there is always a great deal of individual switching between elections, although most of these movements cancel each other out leaving a rather smaller net swing from one party to another. The fact that in every cell of the table more than 10 per cent defected is therefore not surprising.

However, it is also very clear that the level of defection is related to perceptions of movement by the parties. In the Labour case the defections are up by 22 per cent, and in the Conservative case by 12 per cent, among people who thought their *own* party had moved. In contrast whether they thought the *other* party had moved made virtually no difference.

There are, however, two ways of looking at the data of table 10.6 On the one hand we see that defection is related to perceived movement of the parties. On the other we also see that many people defected despite believing that Labour and Conservative had remained in the same ideological positions as before. Indeed half the defectors from Labour believed that Labour had *not* moved. It would therefore be quite wrong to maintain that Labour's newly perceived extremism was *the* cause of the 1983 debacle. It may have been one factor, but it should not shoulder all the blame.

Moreover, we must be cautious in drawing causal inferences even about the defectors who did believe that the Labour (or the Conservative) party had moved away from the centre. At the risk of being repetitious, we must once again emphasise that cross-sectional data of this kind cannot tell us about causation. The data give a snap-shot of the election and cannot, in their very nature, tell us about the direction of influence over time. It is perfectly consistent with the data of Table 10.6 to argue that defectors from Labour to the Alliance or the Conservatives merely rationalised their change of allegiance by claiming that it was Labour who had moved rather than themselves. This interpretation is by no means implausible. After all, the Social Democratic Party had been formed in 1981 mainly from Labour's ranks with the aim of attracting further defectors. Could it be 'pull' from the Alliance, rather than 'push' from Labour, which accounts for the defections?

'Push' and 'pull' are inextricably linked. After all, Labour's change in policy was the main reason given by the leaders of the Social Democratic Party for their breakaway, but the very breakaway gave the Labour party a different character from the one it had before. There is no sure way of answering the question how the Labour party would have been perceived, or how well would it have done, in the absence of the Social Democratic Party.

The Social Democratic Party and the Liberals

While we cannot prove that the formation of the Social Democratic Party 'made a difference', we can in good Popperian fashion attempt to disprove it. Thus, if there were no differences betwen Social Democratic and Liberal supporters in their attitudes, perceptions or source of recruitment, we could be fairly sure that the SDP had not exerted any distinct pull of its own. We would be more inclined to feel that defections to the Liberals would have occurred on much the same scale even if the Social Democratic Party had not broken away from Labour.

The deal struck between the Liberal and Social Democratic Party leaderships meant that (with few exceptions) there was only one Alliance candidate in each constituency. Many Liberal supporters therefore had to vote for a Social Democratic Party candidate, and *vice versa*. Since many people, even Alliance voters, had no idea whether the candidate in their constituency was a Liberal or a

TABLE 10.7 The Sources of Liberal and Social Democratic Party Support

Party supported in 1983	Vote in 1979					
	Conservative	Labour	Liberal	Others/ did not vote	Too young to vote in 1979	
Liberal Party	18	17	47	12	6	100% (N = 419)
Social Democratic Party	22	41	21	9	8	101% (N = 215)

Social Democrat, we cannot use voting behaviour to test whether the Social Democratic Party exerted any unique pull. However, we also asked Alliance voters whether they generally thought of themselves as 'Liberals' or 'Social Democrats'. By no means all would choose, but enough did to permit some analysis.

Table 10.7 shows that there were indeed differences in the sources of Social Democratic and Liberal recruitment. It is hardly surprising that Liberal supporters in 1983 were more likely to be people who had voted Liberal in 1979. More interesting is the fact that the Liberals obtained equal proportions of Labour and Conservative defectors whereas the Social Democratic Party obtained twice as many from the Labour party.

This difference in recruitment is reflected in the attitudes of the two sets of supporters. True, most of the attitudinal differences are small, and few reach statistical significance (although most are in the expected direction). The biggest differences occur on the two major class questions — nationalisation and trade union legislation — where the Social Democratic Party supporters were clearly to the left of the Liberals. On nationalisation the index of dissimilarity between the Social Democratic Party and Liberals was 16 and on trade unions it was 12. This does not make the Social Democratic Party a left-wing party; its supporters were more likely to favour privatisation than nationalisation. Rather, it means that the Social Democratic voters lay closer to the centre of the class dimension whereas the Liberal supporters were on the right.

We cannot, therefore, rule out the possibility that the formation of the Social Democratic Party 'made a difference' to the election result, taking votes from the Labour party that would not otherwise have gone to the Liberals. By the same token it is quite likely that the formation of the Social Democratic Party contributed to the greater coherence of the Alliance vote in 1983. As might be expected, the Labour voters who defected to the Social Democratic Party were of rather more centrist ideology than those who remained loyal.

However, we should not forget that the coherence of the Liberal and Alliance vote was not a wholly new phenomenon in 1983. There were clear signs of it in 1979, and we cannot therefore ascribe it solely to events, such as the formation of the Social Democratic Party and the perception of Labour's move to the left, which took place *after* 1979.[14] The Liberal party itself surely played some part in this process. Our interpretation is that the Liberal party has been gradually acquiring a more visible identity and has thus been exerting greater 'pull' on the electorate, particularly on those who inhabit the north-east area of our ideological map.[15] Doubtless, this increased pull was helped by the Alliance with the Social Democratic Party and the attendant media coverage, but it would also appear to antedate the Alliance.

These analyses do not suggest that the 'pull' hypothesis should be preferred to the 'push' one, or that the emphasis should be placed on Social Democratic Party pull rather than Liberal pull. It is, in our view, misguided to try to pinpoint a unique causal factor. It is in the nature of political events like these that they highlight and reinforce each other.

Notes

[1] The question used to measure the north-south axis in 1966 was as follows: "If the government has a choice between reducing taxes and spending more on social services, which should it do?" (1966, Q23).
We have checked the results using the death penalty question in place of that on taxes and social services. The results are as follows:

TABLE 10.8N Liberal Shares of the Vote in 1966: an Alternative View

Percentage voting Liberal

9 (100)	10 (99)	11 (35)	oppose death penalty
4 (276)	9 (528)	8 (257)	favour death penalty

nationalise private companies	no change	sell off nationalised industries

Figures in brackets give cell sizes

[2] To test significance we fitted the log-linear model NT,V and calculated the residuals (N representing the respondents' attitudes to nationalisation, T representing attitudes to tax cuts and V representing vote). The Liberal residuals are given below. It is customary to think of a residual of 2.0 as statistically significant.

TABLE 10.9N Relative Support for the Liberals in 1966

Liberal residuals

−1.6	0.3	0.7	increase services
−1.6	1.6	0.1	cut taxes

nationalise private companies	no change	sell off nationalised industries

[3] There is a problem with the government spending question in February 1974 since it does not offer respondents the choice between spending and tax cuts, as the questions in the other years did. The question was as follows:
"Which of these statements do you feel comes closest to your own views?
1 Social services and benefits have gone much too far and should be *cut back a lot.*

2 Social services and benefits have gone somewhat too far and should be *cut back a bit.*

3 Social services and benefits should *stay much as they are.*

4 *More* social services and benefits are needed." (February 1974, Q53). Unfortunately, no other suitable question, for example on the death penalty, was available in the 1974 surveys with which to check our results.

[4] The Liberal residuals for February 1974 are as follows:

TABLE 10.10N Relative Support for the Liberals in 1974

Liberal residuals

−1.5	1.9	0.4	increase benefits
−0.8	1.5	1.2	no change
−1.0	−0.6	−1.2	cut benefits

nationalise private companies	no change	sell off nationalised industries

[5] The question used to measure the north-south axis in 1979 was as follows:

"People have different views about whether it is more important to reduce taxes or keep up government services. Which of the statements A, B or C comes closest to your view? If you don't have an opinion on this, just say so.

A Taxes should be cut even if its means some reduction in government services such as health, education and welfare.

B It doesn't matter much either way.

C Government services such as health, education and welfare should be kept up even if it means that taxes cannot be reduced" (1979, Q23a).

The results are again confirmed when we use the death penalty question.

TABLE 10.11N Liberal Shares of the Vote in 1979

Percentage voting Liberal

13 (82)	19 (155)	14 (111)	oppose death penalty
6 (126)	16 (432)	12 (446)	favour death penalty

nationalise private companies	no change	sell off nationalised industries

Figures in brackets give cell sizes

[6] The Liberal residuals from the log-linear model NT,V in 1979 are as follows:

TABLE 10.12N Relative Support for the Liberals in 1979

Liberal residuals

−1.6	2.7	−0.2	keep up services
−1.0	1.3	−0.2	doesn't matter
−0.9	0.1	−2.0	cut taxes

nationalise private companies	no change	sell off nationalised industries

[7] The question used to measure the north-south axis in 1983 was Q31a. A somewhat similar pattern emerges if we compare 1979 with 1983 using the death penalty question. The 1983 Alliance vote, using the death penalty question, was as follows:

TABLE 10.13N Alliance Shares of the Vote in 1983: an Alternative View

Percentage voting Alliance

13 (220)	39 (414)	29 (372)	oppose death penalty
17 (237)	29 (607)	17 (740)	favour death penalty

nationalise private companies	no change	sell off nationalised industries

Figures in brackets give cell sizes

The comparison of tables 10.11N and 10.13N produces a rather puzzling Alliance increase in the south-west corner. However, we should note that the numbers who favour restoration of the death penalty are large and can be thought of as including *both* those who favour tax cuts *and* those who favoured the *status quo* on government spending.

[8] The picture is even clearer if we look at the residuals from the log-linear model NT,V. These were as follows in 1983 (although we should note the larger sample size in 1983 will also affect the size of the residuals):

TABLE 10.14N Relative Support for the Alliance in 1983

Alliance residuals

−3.6	4.7	1.3	spend more on services
−1.2	5.0	−3.3	no change
−1.7	−1.4	−3.5	cut taxes

nationalise private companies	no change	sell off nationalised industries

[9] See *The Times Guide to the House of Commons* (1974: 309).

[10] The proportions perceiving "a good deal of difference" between the parties were 46 per cent in 1964, 42 per cent in 1966, 32 per cent in 1970, 33 per cent in February 1974 and 39 per cent in October 1974. In the 1974 studies the wording was changed to "great deal".

[11] *Hansard*, 3 April 1983, column 644.

[12] Among respondents with no qualifications or qualifications below 'O' level, 49 per cent of Express readers (N = 131) thought that Labour had moved left, 45 per cent of Mail readers (N = 127), 28 per cent of Sun readers (N = 257) and 33 per cent of Mirror readers (N = 324).

[13] Among respondents who voted in 1983 and who reported voting Labour in 1979, 28 per cent of Mirror readers (N = 271) defected compared with 34 per cent of Sun readers (N = 153).

[14] A somewhat larger proportion of the electorate saw a "great deal of difference" between the parties in 1979 (46 per cent) than in 1974 (33 per cent in February, 39 per cent in October). It is possible therefore that the Labour and Conservative parties were believed by respondents to have moved apart and that this accounts for the greater concentration of the Liberal vote in 1979. However, the wording of the question had also been changed. In the 1974 studies the question was:

"Considering everything the parties stand for, would you say that there is a great deal of difference between them, some difference, or not much difference?" Oct 1974, Q8)

In the 1979 study the wording was:

"Considering everything the Conservative and Labour parties stand for, would you say that there is a great deal of difference between them, some difference or not much difference?" (1979, Q5).

[15] Evidence for a more distinctive Alliance identity is the increased proportion of respondents who saw it as inhabiting the north-east area of our map. In February 1974 24 per cent of respondents placed the Liberals in the north or north-east areas; this had increased to 33 per cent in 1983. The proportion who said they did not know where to place the Alliance had also fallen. (Unfortunately, questions about the Liberal position were not asked in 1979.)

Chapter 11

Competence and Fairness

We still have at best only a partial account of the Alliance rise at the expense of the other two parties. The perceived changes in the ideological stances of the Labour and Conservative parties are concentrated in the last ten years. Their movement away from the centre may help to explain why the Alliance did better in 1983 than the Liberals on their own had done in 1974, but it does not offer an explanation for the Liberal 'surge' in 1974. Nor does it wholly account for Labour's decline over the last decade. We need to look for other sources of political change as well.

Fluctuations in Political Popularity

The changing ideological positions of the parties and the electorate provide an explanation for the general tendency of the Conservative and Alliance shares of the vote to grow over time and for Labour's to decline. But there are large short-run swings around these long-run trends. This can be seen from Table 11.1 which plots the changing success of the Conservative and Labour parties in capturing the vote in their respective heartlands.

In order to secure reasonable comparability over time, we have (as in chapter 10) used the questions on nationalisation and on tax cuts and social services spending to identify the heartlands. The figures are thus constructed on the same basis as those of tables 10.1 to 10.4. They show, for example, that there were 219 voters in the 1966 sample who were in favour *both* of further nationalisation *and* of increased spending on social services. These 219 voters constituted the Labour heartland, and 89 per cent of them voted Labour.[1]

Unfortunately, we cannot construct proper estimates for 1964 and 1970, since the necessary questions were not asked in the election studies of those years. Nevertheless, such data as we have are quite illuminating. We see important variations in the Labour and Conservative parties' ability to capture their own heartlands in the four elections. Thus in 1966 Labour did extraordinarily well under Harold Wilson, capturing 89 per cent of the votes in its own heartland while Edward Heath's Conservatives could manage only 73 per cent in theirs. We may guess that in 1970 the picture would have been reversed, with Mr Heath faring much better.

TABLE 11.1 Changing Success in the Heartlands

	Percentage of the heartland vote			
	1966	Feb 1974	1979	1983
Labour	89 (219)	75 (236)	79 (155)	72 (301)
Conservative	73 (202)	71 (231)	87 (190)	81 (288)

Figures in brackets give cell sizes

Moving on to February 1974, the time of the first great Liberal surge, both Conservative and Labour fared rather badly in their respective heartlands. Yet they both recovered in 1979, Mrs Thatcher's Conservatives spectacularly so, almost matching the success that Mr Wilson's Labour party achieved in 1966. Finally, both parties slipped back, and by rather similar amounts, in 1983. It is particularly interesting that, on this criterion of success, Michael Foot's Labour party fared no worse than Mr Heath's Conservatives in 1974 — suggesting perhaps that a Labour revival under Mr Kinnock is no greater a task than the one that Mrs Thatcher faced, and achieved, when she took on the leadership of the Conservatives. This is not to underrate Mrs Thatcher's achievement, but it serves to put in perspective the task facing Labour. In 1983 Labour's relative 'failure' and the Conservatives' 'success' in their own heartlands were within the usual range of the ups and downs of politics.

A party's success in its own heartland seems to be a good barometer of its fortunes overall. The fluctuations in the heartlands shown in table 11.1 correspond closely with the fluctuations in the two parties' *overall* share of the vote in those elections. If a party 'fails' in its heartland it is likely to fail elsewhere too. Leaving on one side the increased concentration of the Alliance vote in recent elections, these fluctuations in support seem to be rather uniform ones, just as swings at general elections were once thought to be rather uniform in different areas of the country.

These fluctuations are, we believe, the major short-run sources of political change. The ideological shifts in the electorate described in chapter 9, and the shifts in party ideology described in chapter 10, define the character of the terrain on which each election is fought, but they do not, on their own, determine the outcome of the contest. Suppose, for example, that the terrain had been as it actually was in 1983 with few voters on the west of our ideological map and with the Alliance vote more concentrated in the centre and north-east than before.

Suppose too that Labour had managed to secure the 89 per cent of its heartland that it had under Mr Wilson in 1966 and that it had fared *pro rata* better in other areas of the map at the other parties' expense. Under these assumptions Labour would have secured many fewer votes than in 1966, reflecting the long-run changes since that time, but it would still have won a modest victory.[2]

The feature of these short-run fluctuations is that they are largely unconnected with ideological position. The Labour and Conservative parties may have lost some votes because they had moved away from the centre by 1983, but this cannot explain why Labour, for example, did so badly in its heartland. If ideological position were all that mattered, Labour should have done better in its heartland in 1983, not worse, than it did in 1979.

These short-run changes in support, independent of ideological position, decisively refute the conventional wisdom that elections are won and lost in the centre ground. They are won and lost in the heartlands as well. It would be quite wrong in our view to attribute Mr Wilson's victory in 1966 or Mr Foot's defeat in 1983 solely to the changes in party programme or to the shift of the electorate to the right over the intervening years. Whatever it was that caused these fluctuations in Labour's popularity, it affected those voters who remained in Labour's ideological heartland as well as those who had abandoned it.

Theories of Government Performance

The most natural explanation of these fluctuations is that they have to do with the electorate's evaluations of the government's record and the likely competence of the opposition. As Harold Wilson once put it, "All political history shows that the standing of a Government and its ability to hold the confidence of the electorate at a General Election depend on the success of its economic policy".[3]

Such theories of government performance have recently come into vogue. Some political scientists have argued for example that voters decide on the basis of all the accumulated past political experiences they have had with the parties. More distant political experiences have less weight than more recent ones, but of course are more stable and thus provide some degree of continuity in political preferences. More recent experiences, based on short-term political events, provide the main source of electoral change. The theory is thus a special case of the investment theory which, as we described in chapter 7, tries to account for voting behaviour in terms of the future benefits which the different parties might bring the voter. The current formulation, which we can term the 'performance theory', in essence asserts that past experiences are the best guide to the kind of future benefits that can be expected.[4]

At first sight the investment and performance theories have a great deal in their favour as explanations of the parties' electoral fortunes. We asked our respondents "Which party do you think would be the most likely to improve your standard of living over the next three or four years?" (Q33a). Answers to this question were strongly associated with the patterns of defection and recruitment between 1979 and 1983. People who switched vote usually did so to the party which they reported would be best at improving their standard of living.[5]

Even more encouragingly for the performance theory, judgements about the government's future performance were highly correlated with people's judgements of how well the government had handled Britain's economy over the last four years. An excellent 'predictor' of the prospective judgements was people's answer to the question "on the whole do you think the Conservative government over the last four years has handled the problem of unemployment very well, fairly well, not very well, or not at all well?" (Q29b).[6]

The difficulty with these questions however is that, like the question on 'best party' discussed in chapter 7, they invite circularity. If people are asked whether the party they voted for is a 'good' one, they are likely to answer yes. And if we ask whether it will also be 'good for them personally', we are still likely to get the answer yes. The answers tell us more about social definitions of what political parties are expected to be 'good for' than about the influences on voting behaviour. It is a safe bet that the better one's predictions in social science, the more likely they are to be trivial or tautological. The very success of the question "which party do you think would be the most likely to improve your standard of living" warns us to be sceptical about its meaning.

Our scepticism is reinforced by the fact that it was the government's *general* handling of unemployment rather than the respondent's own experience or fear of unemployment that turned out to be the better predictor.[7] According to the performance and investment theories, it should be the respondent's own well-being that is paramount. People may think that the government handled unemployment badly, yet if they are not themselves threatened by unemployment, their negative judgements of the government's performance should, in theory, become irrelevant. But we find that answers to the question "Which do you think threatens *you and your family* most — the threat of rising prices or the threat of unemployment?" (Q29c) were rather poor predictors of how one would vote.[8] Personal self-interest seems to play only a small part in voting behaviour.

We are, then, disposed to reject exaggerated claims for the performance theory and are sceptical of strong associations obtained through loaded questions. We doubt whether there is much truth in the claim that people vote *solely* according to their estimations of the contributions which the different parties will make to their personal standard of living. Nonetheless, there may still be scope for a more modest version of performance theory to explain short-run change. The distinction which we have referred to between consensus and dissensus issues is relevant here. The dissensus issues such as nationalisation and defence, on which the parties take fundamentally different stands, may be the sources of the long-run continuities of support. But the consensus issues, such as the management of the economy, may be the sources of short-run change. Even the inhabitants of the heartland who agree with their party's ideology may be disillusioned by evidence of incompetence.

The Conservative Record

At first sight the Conservative success in 1983 poses a serious problem for a performance theory. How did the Conservatives manage to do so well despite record levels of unemployment? In a classic article Goodhart and Bhansali, an economist and a statistician, once tried to show that the government's economic performance was an important cause of its popularity in the monthly opinion polls. Using sophisticated econometric techniques they were able to show to their satisfaction that the two key economic variables were the level of unemployment and the rate of price inflation. The fit was less good for the early post-war years "when political popularity was apparently much less sensitive to domestic economic conditions" but for the ten years after 1959 which their study covered these two economic indicators gave remarkably good predictions of Conservative and Labour popularity.

Unfortunately, all was not well with Goodhart and Bhansali's predictions. Their equations showed that "for every increase in unemployment of 10,000 the government loses nearly 1 per cent of its popular lead". And they concluded that, other things being equal, "a governing party which allows the level of unemployment to exceed 450,000 six months before the election is likely to lose" (Goodhart and Bhansali 1970: 64). If their conclusions had been sound, the Conservatives should have won no votes at all in 1983.

True, the Conservative vote was down slightly in 1983, and table 11.1 suggests a slightly bigger drop in the Conservatives' success in their heartland compared with 1979. But even so, table 11.1 also suggests that a share of 81 per cent in one's heartland was a better-than-average achievement. The conundrum about unemployment remains, therefore.

On the economic front the natural explanation of the Conservative success is that unemployment simply did not impinge greatly on potential Conservative voters. It has sometimes been argued (by Goodhart and Bhansali among others) that inflation is the greater threat to people on salaries and fixed incomes, and certainly the Conservative record on inflation was highly regarded by our respondents. 80 per cent thought that the Conservative government had handled the problem of inflation well over the previous four years.

We can use people's vote in 1979 as an index of whether they were potential Conservative voters or not. Table 11.2 shows how this related to people's reported experiences of unemployment and inflation.

TABLE 11.2 Experience of Inflation and Unemployment

Vote in 1979	Percentage agreeing that	
	Household's income fell behind prices	Self or spouse received unemployment benefit
Conservative (N = 1423)	38	10
Labour (N = 1246)	63	18
Liberal (N = 324)	51	14
Others (N = 60)	53	21

It is clear that former Conservative voters were much less likely to feel that their income had fallen behind prices or to have experienced unemployment. The costs and benefits of Conservative economic policy would seem to have been very unevenly distributed. These costs and benefits were also related, albeit modestly, to defections and recruitment. Of our respondents who voted Conservative in 1979, 85 per cent overall stayed loyal to the Conservatives in 1983 but only 74 per cent of the former Conservatives who had experienced unemployment did so.[9]

It is perhaps rather remarkable that only a quarter of former Conservatives who had suffered unemployment defected to one of the other parties. We believe that this is powerful testimony to the greater importance of values compared with personal well-being in shaping people's votes. The unemployed who stayed loyal were more likely to be people who inhabited the south-east of our ideological map — people who agreed with fundamental Conservative principles.[10]

However, our objective now is to explain the fluctuations in political support rather than the continuities. While the 11 point difference in loyalty of employed and unemployed former Conservatives is modest, it is nonetheless of the rough order of magnitude that we are looking for to explain the slight fall in the Conservative share of the vote between 1979 and 1983.

An alternative explanation for the Conservative success is of course the Falklands war. Did the war, not only at the time, but in the longer run too, deflect attention from the Conservatives' lack of success in reducing unemployment? By the time of the 1983 election few people believed that the war had actually affected their vote. Only 11 per cent of our respondents said that the government's handling of the war had been very important to them "when they were deciding about voting" (Q25c), but we can hardly use that as evidence. People may not have consciously weighed up the war in the balance against inflation or unemployment, but it may still have shaped their perceptions of, and confidence in, Mrs Thatcher and the Conservative party.

Of course, to some extent people's prior political sympathies will have determined their evaluation of the government's handling of the war, rather than the other way round. But approval, although greatest among Conservative loyalists, was more widespread than that. 75 per cent of our respondents more or less approved of the government's handling of the conflict (and most of them were more rather than less impressed). Approval and disapproval in turn were related, albeit modestly, to Conservative recruitment and defection. Such recruitment was rather more at Alliance expense than at Labour's. Of people who had voted Liberal in 1979 and who thought well of the government's handling of the war, 20 per cent defected to the Conservatives. The corresponding figure for former Labour voters was only 13 per cent.

Both figures are rather modest and they suggest that the 'Falklands factor' was of limited strength by 1983. This is hardly surprising. After all, the Conservative share of the vote, even in its own heartland, was not unusually high in 1983. The most that can be said for the Falklands is that the victory might have negated the usual political repercussions of rising unemployment. Perhaps so, but our evidence suggests that the protection of their potential voters' standard of living might have done the same job.

It is impossible to disentangle these various sources of defection and recruitment. Neither hypothesis can be rejected out of hand; both processes would seem to be quite modest in their impact.[11] Moreover, the two processes may not be quite so unrelated as our language has suggested. One evaluation will tend to colour another. People's judgements of whether their incomes have kept up with prices (particularly when asked in the context of an election survey) are bound to have a subjective component. People who have been favourably impressed with the government's handling of the war may be more inclined to take a charitable view of other matters for which the government might be held to blame.[12]

Labour Disunity

One of the most common explanations for Labour's poor result in 1983 was that people who agreed with its programme doubted its ability to put that programme into effect. As Butler and Kavanagh put it: "Surveys, and politicians' doorstep encounters with voters, uncovered 'a credibility gap' about the competence of the party and its ability to deliver on many of its promises" (Butler and Kavanagh, 1984: 296). In particular Labour's much-publicised internal divisions might have been expected to create doubts in the electorate's mind abouts its future competence. Similarly, Michael Foot's indecisive leadership was frequently blamed for the outcome.

Now there is no doubt that most of the electorate did notice Labour's divisions and did regard Mr Foot as a weak leader, although as usual there was also a measure of selective perception (or at least of selective reporting). Overall, 88 per cent of respondents thought that Labour was divided, and the 8 per cent who disagreed were overwhelmingly Labour supporters. Similarly Mr Foot received a much lower rating as a future Prime Minister than the other party leaders — only 29 per cent thought that he would be effective compared with 90 per cent for Mrs Thatcher, 78 per cent for Mr Steel and 48 per cent for Mr Jenkins. Again the people who believed Mr Foot would be effective were largely restricted to Labour supporters whereas the other leaders all gained support from a wider range of the electorate.

These judgements about the Labour party and its leadership correlate quite highly with judgements about which party would do most to improve one's standard of living in future, but again all this tells us is that one negative judgement about the Labour party will correlate highly with other negative judgements.[13] They do not prove a 'credibility gap'.

The more interesting question is whether people who had formed *positive* evaluations of Labour policy were led to doubt its ability to implement that policy by the evidence of disunity and division. If words like 'competence' or 'credibility' are to retain their proper meanings, rather than to become synonymous for 'good', this is the test we must ask the hypothesis to survive.

In order to compare like with like, we must take the two equally 'party-laden' questions "Which party's views on unemployment would you say come closest to your own views?" (Q20d) and "Which [party] would have been . . . the one most likely to reduce unemployment if it had been in government over the next five years?" (Q19b). Our hypothesis is that perceptions of Labour disunity and Mr Foot's weakness as leader would have led some people who preferred its policies to doubt its efficacy.

The hypothesis is almost certainly false. First of all, people who liked Labour's views on unemployment tended to think that the party would be effective too. As table 11.3 shows, 82 per cent of people who said the Labour party's views were closest to their own believed that the party would have been the most likely to reduce unemployment. Nor was this purely a matter of selective perception. The corresponding percentages for supporters of the other parties' views were much lower. Only 48 per cent of people who supported the Conservative view, and 49 per cent of people who supported the Alliance view, thought that their preferred party would also have been the most effective at reducing unemployment. Labour was quite clearly seen, even by many people who did not like its views, as the one most likely to do something effective about unemployment. If there was a credibility gap on unemployment it was more of a Conservative and Alliance gap than a Labour one.

TABLE 11.3 Party Competence on Unemployment

Party with preferred views on unemployment	Party most likely to reduce unemployment				
	Conservative	Labour	Alliance	None	
Conservative	48	26	4	22	100% (N = 1160)
Labour	4	82	6	8	100% (N = 1561)
Alliance	4	32	49	14	99% (N = 674)

Labour's disunity made no discernible difference to this. Among people who liked Labour's views, the great majority thought that the party was divided. 81 per cent of this majority thought that Labour would have been effective in reducing unemployment compared with 85 per cent of the minority who thought the party united — not a statistically significant difference.[14]

We asked similar questions about the control of inflation and the management of the welfare services. On the latter, perceptions of Labour disunity again had no significant relation with perceptions of Labour competence. But on inflation there was a stronger relationship between the two. Here only 66 per cent of people who liked Labour policy but thought the party was divided agreed that Labour was the most likely to keep prices down (compared with 86 per cent who thought the party united). But as table 11.4 shows, 66 per cent is almost as high as the overall Conservative figure and much higher than the Alliance figure.

TABLE 11.4 Party Competence on Inflation

Party with preferred views on inflation	Party most likely to keep prices down				
	Conservative	Labour	Alliance	None	
Conservative	72	11	6	11	100% (N = 2148)
Labour	13	71	7	9	100% (N = 815)
Alliance	28	14	45	13	100% (N = 471)

Again, then, we are sceptical about the existence of a Labour credibility gap. This is not to deny that disunity damaged Labour. We simply deny that it led people to doubt Labour's competence to achieve its specific objectives. Clearly people, even those who agreed with fundamental Labour principles, lacked confidence in the Labour party in 1983. But we must not equate confidence with competence. As we have seen, there is little hard evidence that potential supporters doubted whether Labour would put its policies into practice. Labour efficacy was not in question. If there was a credibility gap, it would seem to have been an Alliance one.

Alliance Fairness

While we do not pretend to have any full explanation of why parties gain and lose the confidence of the electorate, it seems to us that another ingredient, alongside competence and performance, may be fairness. The instrumental theories, of which the investment and performance theories are both variants, tend to take a narrow, selfish view of the voter's motivations. Voters are assumed to vote for the party that will best protect their own self-interests. This is, we think, a one-sided view. It may have been a useful corrective to the equally one-sided view of the expressive theory, but it neglects the role of moral judgements in political evaluation.

We suspect that an important part of a party's image is its 'fairness' as well as its competence, and one of the positive attractions of the Alliance may be its reputation for concern with all groups in society rather than a narrow sectarian concern for the interests of its own supporters alone. Conversely, Labour may have lost votes to the Alliance not because of doubts about its competence but because people disliked its sectionalism.

Certainly, there was general agreement among our respondents that the Alliance was "good for all classes" and that David Steel was the leader "with most concern for all groups in society". 66 per cent of our respondents agreed that the Alliance was good for all classes, but only 34 per cent thought that the Labour party was and 35 per cent that the Conservative party was. Moreover, these perceptions were almost as strongly related to recruitment and defection as were judgements about the party most likely to improve one standard of living. Thus, of people who had voted Conservative in 1979 but thought that the Conservative party was "good for one class" 31 per cent defected to the Alliance; among those who thought the Conservatives "good for all classes" only 4 per cent defected. The corresponding figures for Labour defections were 36 per cent and 14 per cent.

Attempts to demonstrate a causal connection are hindered by the same problem that confuses discussion of competence — the tendency of one positive evaluation to go with another. Rather than discovering the 'causes' of parties' rise and fall we could perhaps better be said to be discovering the character of political vocabulary.

However, it seems likely that these judgements about 'concern for all groups in society' are as central a part of the political vocabulary as those about competence or standards of living. In a general analysis of people's evaluations of the Conservative party, for example, their judgement of whether the party was good for one or good for all classes was the best single predictor of their vote.[15] It was substantially better than other equally 'party-laden' questions such as whether the Conservative government has been "successful or unsuccessful in improving your standard of living" (Q32b) or had "handled the problem of unemployment very well . . . or not at all well" (Q29b).

One positive judgement tends to go with another, but perhaps not surprisingly judgements of whether the Conservatives were good for one or good for all classes correlated most highly with evaluations of the government's handling of unemployment.[16] While unemployment can clearly be included as part of the government's record and performance, we should make a clearer distinction than is usually done between *personal* experience of unemployment and the *overall* level. We would suggest that a government's record is evaluated as much in terms of its fairness and social justice as in terms of its contribution to the individual voter's personal well-being. People's assessment of the overall unemployment figures may be one important component of their conclusions about the government's fairness.

Much the same holds for evaluations of the Labour party as well.[17] Labour party supporters, including those in its heartland, treat the expression 'good for one class' as a pejorative one. It is more plausible to ascribe Labour's decline in 1983 to doubts about its sectionalism than to doubts about its competence.

We do not, unfortunately, have the data from previous election surveys to determine whether perceptions of Labour and Conservative social divisiveness account for the rise of the Alliance in 1983.[18] We must end with a hypothesis rather than a conclusion. We suggest that the Liberals in 1974, and the Alliance in 1983, fared relatively well because of the electorate's anxieties about the other parties' perceived divisiveness. Class inequalities may be as great as ever; class interests may still be a basis of political allegiance; but that is not to say that people approve of class divisions or the rhetoric (or indeed the reality) of class struggle.

Notes

[1] As we have pointed out in previous chapters, the comparability over time of the questions on tax cuts and social services spending is not as great as would be desired. However, the time series of table 11.1 has the reassuring property that the sizes of the heartlands are very similar over time. They range from 15 per cent to 10 per cent of the total number of votes in each sample, and as can be seen the size of the respective Conservative and Labour heartlands is also very similar in each sample. We can thus be reasonably sure that we are comparing like with like.

We should note that the discrepancy between the results of table 11.1 for 1983 and those of table 8.7 can be explained partly be the sizes of the heartlands identified. Thus in table 8.7 the size of the Conservative heartland is over twice that of the Labour one (and twice that of the Conservative heartland in table 11.1), so it is hardly surprising that table 8.7 suggests a lower Conservative share of their own heartland than does table 11.1. We should also note that attitudes to defence were more strongly associated with vote in 1983 than were attitudes to government spending. This would tend, other things being equal, to increase the estimates of the two parties' shares in their respective heartlands.

[2] Such an exercise is necessarily rather speculative. Let us suppose that Labour had increased its vote by 15 points in the five cells running down the west side and along the south side of our ideological map (and containing 33 per cent of the voters in 1983). Let us also suppose that the Labour share had increased by only 10 points in the four remaining cells in the centre, north and east (reflecting the increased concentration of the Alliance vote in these areas since 1966). This would give an overall increase in the Labour share of 11.7 per cent, which would have brought it up to around 39 per cent of the vote — much less than in 1966 but almost certainly enough to win a victory since this increase would not have been just at the Alliance's expense.

[3] Quoted in Goodhart and Bhansali (1970: 45).

[4] This is a highly simplified account of Fiorina's theory of retrospective voting (Fiorina 1981). For other somewhat similar treatments see Hibbs (1982), Alt (1979, 1984).

[5] Thus, of people who reported voting Conservative both in 1979 and 1983 85 per cent thought the Conservative party would be the most likely to improve their standard of living. 75 per cent of recruits to the Conservative party in 1983 gave the same answer but only 27 per cent of defectors.

[6] Cramer's V for the association between Q33a and Q29b was .34. However, we should note that Cramer's V is even higher for the association between vote in 1979 and Q33a, namely .45.

[7] Cramer's V for the association between Q29c and Q33a was .12, and between Q29c and Q58j (whether respondent and spouse had received unemployment benefit) it was .14.

[8] Cramer's V for the association between Q29c and vote in 1983 was .14. This compares with .65 for the association between Q33a and vote in 1983.

[9] For the sake of simplicity we are using the term unemployed to cover people who answered yes to Q58j (that is, who reported that they or their spouses had received unemployment benefit). We have used this question in preference to that on current unemployment (Q52a) since the number involved is much larger (641 compared with 245). The general pattern of results is much the same with either question. Thus of people who reported voting Conservative in 1979, 83 per cent of those in paid work voted Conservative again in 1983 but 71 per cent did so of those (N = 34) who said they were currently unemployed.

[10] Of the unemployed who stayed loyal to the Conservatives in 1983 (N = 87), 43% occupied the Conservatives heartland of the south-east corner of our ideological map. Of the unemployed who defected (N = 30), 23% occupied the south-east corner.

[11] In a multiple regression of Conservative vote in 1983 on recall vote and evaluation of government performance, evaluations of government success both with the Falklands and with standards of living made significant improvements to variance explained (F being 1048 for 1979 Conservative vote, 101 for Q32b and 95 for Q25a). Q32b was used in preference to Q50b in order to have equally 'party-laden' questions in the analysis.

[12] For example, the correlation between Q32b and Q25a is .37, almost as high as that between either variable and Conservative vote (.39 and .41 respectively).

[13] Cramer's V for the association between Q18b2 (Labour unity) and Q33a was .18, and between Q15b (Mr Foot's likely effectiveness) and Q33a it was .39.

[14] There were slightly larger differences with respect to Mr Foot's leadership. Among people who liked Labour's views on unemployment, 86 per cent who thought Mr Foot would have been an effective Prime Minister, and 77 per cent who thought he would not, believed that Labour was the party most likely to reduce unemployment.

[15] We regressed Conservative vote on the following variables: Q18c1, Q29b, Q25a, Q18d1,Q18a1, Q29a,Q32b, Q18b1, Q32a. These are all equally party-laden questions and we are thus comparing like with like. The results were as follows:

TABLE 11.5N Multiple Regression of Conservative Vote on Evaluations

	Standardised regression coefficients	F
Good for one/all classes	−.35	387
Handling of unemployment	.20	116
Handling of Falklands	.08	27
Clear or vague policies	.07	22
Extreme or moderate	−.07	25
Handling of inflation	.06	13
Successful in improving own standard of living	.04	6
United or divided	.03	5
Successful in keeping taxes down	.02	1
R^2	.46	

We repeated the exercise controlling for Conservative vote in 1979, which may be taken to tap people's prior sympathies. This had the effect of reducing all the regression coefficients, but their order of importance remained the same.

[16] The correlation between Q18c1 and Q29b was .59.

[17] We did not ask people the hypothetical question how they thought the Labour party would have handled problems had it been in office. We therefore regressed Labour vote on evaluations of Conservative performance and of Labour character namely Q18c2, Q29b, Q18d2, Q18a2, Q25a, Q32b, Q29a, Q32a, Q18b2. The results were as follows:

(Notes continue on following page)

TABLE 11.6N Multiple Regression of Labour Vote on Evaluations

	Standardised regression coefficients	F
Labour good for one/all classes	−.16	99
Conservative handling of unemployment	−.15	61
Labour clear or vague policies	.15	87
Labour extreme or moderate	−.14	77
Conservative handling of Falklands	−.09	28
Conservative successful in improving own standard of living	−.09	24
Conservative handling of inflation	−.08	19
Conservative successful in keeping taxes down	−0.7	14
Labour united or divided	.05	10
R^2	.33	

[18] There are data from February 1974. These showed that the Conservative party was more likely to be seen as good for one class in 1974 than was the Labour party, whereas in 1983 the two parties were seen to be alike. Table 11.7N gives the details.

TABLE 11.7N Perceptions of Class Divisiveness

	Conservative party		Labour party	
	1974	1983	1974	1983
Good for one class	61	60	42	56
Neither	7	4	8	8
Good for all classes	32	36	50	36
	100%	100%	100%	100%
N =	2383	3837	2370	3786

Chapter 12

Conclusions

The implications that one draws from survey research depend in part upon one's theory. The facts never speak for themselves as there is always a problem of causal interpretation. The implications of council house sales, for example, depend on how one interprets the association between house purchase and Conservative voting. Does purchase lead to Conservatism or do Conservatives prefer to purchase? If one believes that housing influences how one votes, council house sales will be taken to help the Conservative party. If one believes that prior values (and resources) influence housing decisions, the spread of home-ownership would be regarded as neutral in its effects upon the parties' fortunes. Our evidence suggested the latter interpretation, but we cannot prove that our interpretation is correct. In the absence of proper, controlled experiments (which are rarely possible in social science) proof will remain elusive.

Two very different types of theory — the expressive and the instrumental — have dominated the recent study of electoral behaviour. They make different assumptions about causation and hence would lead to rather different interpretations of our findings. While we do not accept either in its entirety, it may be instructive to describe what we think their interpretations might be. They give interestingly different predictions about the future course of British politics. We shall conclude with our own rather different interpretation, although we shall not be so rash as to offer predictions.

The Expressive Interpretation

As we described in chapter 1, the expressive theory holds that party allegiance is determined by the norms and values of one's social group, particularly of primary groups such as the family. According to this theory one's attitudes towards the issues of the day are largely shaped by party loyalty. Labour loyalists for example will tend to support nationalisation and income redistribution because they are key elements of Labour philosophy. On this theory party allegiance determines attitudes, not the other way round.

In its most extreme version, this theory suggests that the parties are to a large extent prisoners of social structure and of the character and distribution of social groups in society. It will do the parties little good, or harm, if they modify their policies since policies do not determine vote. Rather the parties should work to build up their social bases, as for example the Conservatives have done with council house sales.

The major implication of such a view must be that the Labour party's recent electoral decline will continue. The contraction of the working class and the spread of home ownership mean that Labour's social base has shrunk and can be expected to continue to shrink. True, the extent of the reduction has been exaggerated by many commentators. Thus we saw that in 1964 20 per cent of the electorate were working-class council tenants while by 1983 this had fallen only to 13 per cent. Nevertheless the trend is likely to continue downwards. Conversely, salaried-class home owners have increased from 13 per cent to 23 per cent of the electorate and again the trend is likely to continue upwards. Despite the long period of economic stagnation, there is little sign that these trends have, or will, go into reverse.

As we saw in Part 1, these social trends cannot on their own account for the political trends. Labour's vote has fallen more than could be expected; the Conservative vote has failed to rise in the way expected. The interpretation of the expressive school of thought would be that class cohesion has weakened over and above the changes in size. On this view, class has become a less potent source of political loyalty.

We have raised serious doubts about this latter interpretation. There is no direct evidence that the classes have weakened in cohesion. The evidence is at best circumstantial. Our own interpretation is that there have been fluctuations in support for the parties around the underlying trend. Our analysis (in chapter 11) suggested that Labour's performance was rather better than expected in 1964 and 1966, was about average in 1979, and worse than expected in 1983. We would attribute these fluctuations to *political* not *social* influences. They reflect people's changing confidence in the parties. There is no need to introduce concepts like 'class dealignment' to explain them.

On this account Labour might be expected to fare slightly worse in 1987 or 1988 (when the next election is called) than it did in 1979, the difference being attributable to the continued contraction of its social base. In other words, Labour might be expected to recover to, say, 35 per cent of the vote if no other factors intervene.

Similar estimates could be made about the likely Conservative and Alliance shares of the vote. We have shown that the Alliance does indeed have a social base in the salariat particularly among its educated professional and technical wing. The Alliance vote is not, as previous interpretations have suggested, an amorphous protest vote drawn evenly from the different social classes. Its base, though small, is an expanding one and thus its share of the vote might be expected to have an underlying upward trend. Nonetheless, given its relatively high vote in

1983, the Alliance might still be expected to fare worse next time than in 1983. The social changes suggest 20 per cent of the vote for the Alliance in 1987. This would finally leave the Conservatives with around 45 per cent of the vote as their expected share.

These figures are based purely on extrapolations from the social trends of the last twenty years. They are not to be taken seriously as predictions. In the first place, political fluctuations are not going to stop. Chapter 11 suggested that these fluctuations might be of the order of plus or minus six or seven points around the 'expected' figure. If Mr Kinnock's Labour party fares as well *politically* as Mr Wilson's did, its share of the vote might exceed 40 per cent. Conversely, if the Conservatives fare as badly politically as they did under Mr Heath in October 1974, they might manage only, say, 38 or 39 per cent.

In the second place, talk of an underlying social trend is far too deterministic. It ignores the political sources of change dealt with in Part 2, such as the increasing concentration of the Liberal and Alliance vote and the changing ideological positions of the parties. It is these sources of change that have been the major concerns of the instrumental theories.

Instrumental Interpretations

The instrumental or rational choice theories assume that attitudes determine vote, rather than the other way round. Typically, the attitudes themselves are taken to be 'given' and their origins are taken to lie outside the scope of the theory. Rational choice theory explains how people behave *given* their views on the issues. It does not explain why the views are what they are.

A rational choice theorist would therefore see the major explicable sources of change as the options facing the voters, specifically the policies and performances of the parties. If a party fares badly it is assumed to be because it advocates the 'wrong' policies or has had a poor record in office. The implication is that the party should change its policies. Indeed, certain versions of the theory would go even further: they assume that the parties too are rational just like the voters, and not only *should* but actually *will* change their policies in order to maintain or increase their shares of the vote.

We have cast grave doubt on the versions of rational choice theory which suggest that voters weigh up the detailed policies of each party. But our evidence is certainly consistent with the interpretation that the overall ideological stance of a party will influence its vote. To that extent, we agree, the parties' character and behaviour must be treated as sources of electoral change.

This interpretation suggests that the underlying trends discussed above should be revised. If the Labour and Conservative parties have moved apart ideologically in the last decade, thus allowing more room in the centre for the Alliance to win votes, then (on the rational choice interpretation) the underlying Conservative growth will have been slowed down or even arrested while Labour's decline will have been further exacerbated. If we assume that in future the parties stay where they are now, then we might expect the underlying trends simply to have 'once and for all' kinks coinciding with the recent ideological movements.

A kink in the Conservative trend makes good sense. It reconciles our finding that the Conservatives did less well in 1983 than social change on its own predicted with the finding that they performed *above* average in their heartland. On this interpretation, the Conservative ideological shift to the right lost the party some centre votes that the structural change would otherwise have brought it.

However, will the parties retain their current ideological positions? On a rational choice interpretation this is unlikely to be the case. The rational choice theorist would predict that the parties will readjust their positions in the light of the 1983 result. Labour clearly might be expected to move back towards the centre, since it seems to have lost votes by moving away. More interestingly, we might expect the Alliance to move as well. The Alliance was seen by our respondents as lying in the centre on the class axis and slightly to the north on the liberal axis of our ideological map. But chapter 8 showed there were even more voters on the right of the map than in the centre (12 per cent in the centre cell of table 8.6 compared with 18 per cent in the cell immediately to the right). It might therefore be rational for the Alliance to move to the right (or east) on the class axis while staying slightly to the north on the liberal axis. The votes it might win from the Conservatives by so doing should more than make up for those it might lost to Labour.

Unfortunately for any predictions, the movements are unlikely to stop there. If the parties are rational, we must assume that they will all follow the same chain of reasoning. We might therefore expect the Conservatives to head off any Alliance attempt to capture their votes. Looking at table 8.6 we might guess that the Conservatives would choose to move north, that is to adopt a more liberal position on social welfare, defence, and the like.

Strict versions of the rational choice theory would predict that the parties would actually converge not at the centre of the map but at the 'centre of gravity' of the respondents, that is to say somewhere in the north east of our ideological map. In practice this is very implausible. In the first place, we doubt if the parties could convince the electorate that they really had moved. As we argued in chapter 7, it is not the detailed policy stances of the parties but their overall character which seems to be important. Without major changes in their respective leaderships, it is unlikely that the electorate could be persuaded that the Conservative and Labour parties had converged together again.

In the second place we suspect that the assumption that parties are rational vote-maximisers is no more satisfactory than the assumption that voters rationally pursue their individual self-interest. We have argued that ideological commitments are important in understanding voters' behaviour. We suspect that they are even more important in understanding political parties.

The major exception to this is likely to be the Social Democratic Party. As a new party it has a less clear public image and thus more freedom to create a new identity. Moreover, since its base is among the educated professionals, a position more visibly in the north-east corner of the ideological map would seem to be feasible as well as opportune. To this extent we would accept the prediction of rational choice theory and anticipate that the Social Democratic Party will move to the right on the class axis in an effort to capture Conservative dissidents.

The Interactionist Interpretation

Our own interpretation tries to combine the insights of both schools, but at the same time to develop them further. On the one hand, we do not hold that group membership or social background determines vote but that it provides a *potential*. Thus the changing shape of the class structure means that the number of potential recruits for a left-wing class identity has been declining — although we would emphasise that the working class is still the largest single class, and that, although the salariat has been growing its 'left-wing' of professional and technical workers does not have quite as much sympathy for free enterprise ideology as its 'right-wing' of managers has.

On the other hand, we also accept that a party's ideological stance will affect the level of support it can command. The perceived movements of the Conservative and Labour parties away from the centre almost certainly helped the Alliance increase their share of the vote, although as we have argued, it is the overall character of the party not the details of its manifesto that counts. To that extent we accept modified versions of the key elements of both theories.

However, we would wish also to add to the theory the idea that the parties themselves can help to shape and realize these potentials. The character of class *values*, for example, are the product of an interaction between class potential and party character. As we saw in chapter 9, the shift to the right on the class axis was greater in the petty bourgeoisie and the salariat than in the working class. Mrs Thatcher's espousal of free enterprise was able to make converts beyond those that social change on its own might have produced. But she was also able to make more converts where the potential was already there, as in the petty bourgoisie.

It would be wrong therefore simply to extrapolate from the previous social and political trends. Britain's political future depends on whether Labour or the Alliance in their turn can shape the social potentials. On the one hand, the working class is still the largest single class and, although not perhaps so disadvantaged in absolute terms as it once was, is still relatively disadvantaged not only in income terms but perhaps even more importantly in terms of job security, pension schemes, working conditions, and of course unemployment.

In principle, we would argue, these class inequalities provide a potential for class ideology. The conception of social class which reduces it to income differences and lifestyle suggests that Labour must shift its ground towards the affluent centre. Our conception, which emphasises the more enduring differences of interest suggests that Labour might be able to revive whilst remaining a class party. Just as the petty bourgeoisie was receptive to a free market ideology, so the working class might still be receptive to an egalitarian one. The Labour party does not have to take the existing distribution of values and attitudes as given. Nothing in our evidence indicates that the shift to the right on the class values was an inevitable or irreversible phenomenon. But we would suggest that the language of class struggle is unlikely to be successful in securing an ideological move back to the left. Class inequalities persist but the classes have not been polarised in their values at any time in the postwar period. We doubt if they will become so. An appeal to social justice rather than to class struggle has more hope of success.

For the Alliance, the potentials are of course rather different. As we have shown, their potential recruits are those who tend to the centre or right on the class axis but favour more liberal measures on defence, civil liberties and the welfare state. They have a 'heartland' just like Labour and Conservative, but they have not yet established themselves as the party of the professional and technical worker in the way that Labour and Conservative are *the* parties of the industrial worker and the entrepreneur respectively.

If the Alliance can establish its political identity more firmly, and thus perhaps break down its potential voters' traditional loyalties to the other two parties, it could in principle make the breakthrough in votes that it failed to achieve in 1983. If it secured the same proportion of its heartland as Labour and Conservative do in theirs, it could expect to win an extra 5 per cent to 10 per cent of the vote (largely at Conservative expense).

One of the striking features of the 1983 election was that the Alliance did succeed in establishing itself more securely as a political grouping with a distinctive appeal of its own. But it still falls far short of the other main parties in mobilising its potential supporters. To do so it will probably need to discover some distinctively Alliance principles or to politicise the 'second dimension' of our ideological map. (And perhaps the two will not be unconnected.) As long as the class axis is the primary one around which British politics is organised the Alliance vote will be particularly vulnerable to assaults from the Labour and Conservative parties. A centrist party is vulnerable on both flanks and can expect to have a more volatile vote but by developing an identity as an 'off-centre' party with a distinctive programme of its own, the Liberal (or Social Democratic) party could perhaps move still further from its recent role as a vehicle of protest rather than reform. Its difficulty in doing so is of course that many of the 'nonclass' issues — disarmament or the welfare state for example — have already been captured by the Labour party. International cooperation, the environment or local democracy and decentralisation might be better alternatives.

We do not intend this to be prescriptive; rather we wish to illustrate our points that social trends are not inexorable. Potentials exist for both Alliance and Labour but the future will depend on the success of the deliberate political initiatives that the parties can make to shape people's values and mobilise these potentials.

Doubtless potentials exist for the Conservatives too. We have tended to assume that their past success in converting people to the free enterprise ideology means that they have less scope for further advances. It is perhaps in the nature of conversion that initial enthusiasm will tend to wane. Moreover, the very success of the government in the Falklands war and in controlling inflation may bring its own reaction as the raised expectations of government success become harder to live up to. The cyclical nature of political trends suggests that at some point success will be followed by disillusion. But we would be foolish to predict when that point will come.

Appendix I

Technical Details of The Survey

The study was a joint project between investigators at Oxford University and Social and Community Planning Research, London. The project Directors were A F Heath, R M Jowell, J K Curtice and E J Field.

Sample Design

The survey was designed to yield a representative sample of eligible voters in Great Britain at the time of the 1983 general election. As with previous surveys in the series, electors in Northern Ireland and the Scottish Highlands and Islands were excluded from the sampling frame.

1 Selection of Parliamentary Constituencies

250 constituencies were selected with probability proportionate to size of electorate. Prior to selection the list of constituencies was stratified by percentage Labour vote in the 1979 general election, within three population density bands (10+, 3.1-9.9, and 3 or fewer persons per hectare), within Registrar General's standard regions (pre-1974 boundaries). In order to carry out fieldwork very soon after the election, sampling had to be carried out in the weeks before it. During that time, many electoral registration officers were still incorporating the constituency boundary changes (legislated for only in March 1983) into suitable voting lists. In view also of the extremely short period within which we had to mount the study, we decided to sample from the *old* constituency lists (which were already available in Social and Community Planning Research's computer file) and, at the data processing stage, to transfer the selected polling districts into their new constituencies. The computer tape therefore contains details of both the new and the old constituencies.

2 Selection of Polling Districts

Within each selected constituency one polling district was selected, again with probability proportionate to electorate. Polling districts within each constituency were ordered according to the register's ordering, and any polling district with fewer than 500 electors was combined with the one following it to form one potential selection unit.

3 Selection of Individuals

Within each selected polling district a systematic random sample of 24 electors was selected with equal probability. Any of the selected electors who turned out to be ineligible to vote in the general election (peers and 17 year-olds whose 18th birthday was later than 9 June) were deleted and replaced (using random number tables) by another name.

A sample of 6000 names was selected; this figure was considered to be viable in order to achieve around 4000 interviews. Since no substitution could be allowed, the issued sample had to be large enough to allow for losses through death or emigration, or movement to new addresses that could not be traced or followed up. It was estimated that around 85-90 per cent of the issued sample would still be resident at their registered addresses at the time of the fieldwork. Most of the remainder (except for those movers whom interviewers would be able to trace to their new addresses) would be out of the interviewers' scope. Then there would be further losses through refusals, temporary absences, noncontacts, illness or incapacity. The actual distribution of response is shown in Table I.1A below.

TABLE I.1A Statement of Response (Summary)

	N	Percentage of achieved sample
Addresses issued	6000	—
Out of scope (deceased, moved, untraceable, premises vacant, under age)	537	—
In scope	5463	100.0
Interview achieved	3955	72.4
Reason for nonresponse refused	1135	20.7
noncontact (after four or more calls) or away for survey period	211	3.9
other nonresponse (too ill or too old, no English, broke off interview)	162	3.0
Interview not achieved	1508	27.6

Fieldwork and Response

Having undertaken a small pretest of the questionnaire between 9 June (election day) and 16 June, fieldwork was carried out by 139 Social and Community Planning Research interviewers between 5 July and 5 October 1983. 73 per cent of the interviews were undertaken in the month of July, and 93 per cent were completed within 12 weeks of the election – a comparable proportion and period to those achieved in previous election studies.

Where it was felt that a further attempt to locate or persuade potential respondents to participate might be fruitful, their names were reissued to interviewers during the later phases of fieldwork. 1123 names were reissued, and 382 (34 per cent) were converted successfully, raising overall response by some 7 per cent to 72.4 per cent. The overall response summary is shown in Table I.1A.

Sample Characteristics and Weighting Adjustments

Selection biases in a sample may arise from three main sources.
1 *Nonrandom Selection.* Since each elector was given the same, known, nonzero probability of selection in the survey, potential bias from this source can effectively be ruled out.
2 *Sampling frame deficiencies,* in particular the omission or duplication of parts of the population. Since the electoral registers (by definition) include all those eligible to vote, no potential voter was omitted from the frame. The fact that some electors (very few) are included more than once in the registers is not of concern with a sample of this size and distribution.
3 *Differential response.* Some kinds of people may be more cooperative or available than others, leading them to be represented disproportionately in the achieved sample. If respondents differ from nonrespondents with respect to the survey variables, the estimates based on the achieved sample will be biased. Such potential bias needs to be investigated and, if appropriate, corrected.

Adjustments for nonresponse bias are appropriate if they are based on reliable data showing discrepancies between the characteristics of respondents and nonrespondents. Such information is often difficult to find.

The most direct way of finding out the characteristics of nonrespondents so as to compare them with those of respondents is through the sampling frame itself. Some frames attach details to the names they contain allowing basic characteristics of nonrespondents to be ascertained, but the electoral registers contain no such data. They do, however, contain geographical information which allows a reliable examination of response rates by area.

In common with most national surveys, this survey experienced considerable variation in response rate by region, ranging from 80 per cent in Scotland to 63 per cent in Greater London. The data were therefore weighted to correct the regional imbalances. The weights are shown in Table I.2A, and range from .905 in Scotland to 1.168 in Greater London.

These adjustments do not, of course, eliminate potential nonresponse bias. For that to happen, nonrespondents in each region would have to be a random subset

TABLE I.2A Regional Weighting Adjustments

Registrar General's Standard Regions	Issued		Achieved		Weight	Weighted sample	
	N	%	N	%		N	%
Scotland	552	9.2	402	10.2	.905	336.8	9.2
North	336	5.6	229	5.8	.967	221.4	5.6
North West	720	12.0	496	12.5	.957	474.7	12.0
Yorkshire and Humberside	552	9.2	408	10.3	.892	363.9	9.2
West Midlands	552	9.2	386	9.8	.943	364.0	9.2
East Midlands	408	6.8	268	6.8	1.004	269.1	6.8
East Anglia	216	3.6	141	3.6	1.010	142.4	3.6
South West	480	8.0	285	7.2	1.110	316.4	8.0
South East	1128	18.8	708	17.9	1.050	743.4	18.8
Greater London	744	12.4	420	10.6	1.168	490.6	12.4
Wales	312	5.2	212	5.4	.970	205.6	5.2
	6000	100.0	3955	100.1		3955	100.0

of the total sample in that region with respect to the survey variables — which is very unlikely. Nonetheless the regional adjustments help to mitigate potential biases.

A less direct way of redressing nonresponse bias is to compare the sample's characteristics with those of the population it seeks to represent. Thus a general population sample can usefully be compared with, say, 1981 Census data or the latest available General Household Survey data. Major discrepancies in sample composition can then be reduced by weighting.

In election surveys, however, the purpose is not to reflect the characteristics of the population as a whole but those of the electorate — a group about whom very little demographic information is directly available. The electoral registers explicitly exclude some people whom the Census includes, such as those who are ineligible to vote for one reason or another. But they also exclude people who are technically eligible but fail to register. Moreover, as Todd and Butcher (1983) have noted, underregistration is much more prevalent among some groups (such as ethnic minorities) than among others. So there are several important differences between the electorate and the population. Comparisons between our sample's characteristics and national characteristics may be instructive (some are shown in Table I.3A), but any conclusions to be drawn from them were always likely to be too tentative to encourage us to base weighting adjustments upon them. In the event, no further weighting (other than the regional weights) was undertaken.

Few discrepancies emerge from the figures in Table I.3A. There is an apparent slight tendency of the sample to overrepresent 25-44 year-olds and to underrepresent those over 60. But the age distributions are fairly close and actually conceal biases that our own supplementary data suggest may exist. Interviewers were asked to record, where possible, the sex and approximate age of certain categories of nonrespondents (principally 'refusers' with whom contact was made but no interview achieved). Around one in three of these nonrespondents were elderly, compared with around one in five respondents, which seems to be a very large discrepancy not reflected in the overall age profile.

The explanation appears to be that no recorded age estimates are available for untraceable movers, leading to their omission from the base on which the calculation above (one in three elderly nonrespondents) was made. Since movers are likely to be younger than nonmovers, as the age profile of traceable movers in the sample confirms, young people are underrepresented in these calculations.

It appears, therefore, that two compensating biases — refusals among the older age groups and noncontact among the younger age groups — have resulted in an age profile that is close to that of the 1981 Census.

Most importantly, the occupational profile of the three-quarters of our sample who were economically active or retired as defined by the census is very similar to that of the 1981 Census. There is at most a slight suggestion of an overrepresentation of those in nonmanual occupations (in particular socio-economic groups 1 and 5.1) at the expense of those in manual occupations (in particular socio-economic group 9).

As important for an election survey as demographic comparisons are political comparisons. As Table I.4A shows, the reported voting figures in our survey were close to the actual voting figures, with a slight tendency for our sample to report having voted Conservative at the expense of the Alliance.

TABLE I.3a Sample Characteristics — Sociological

	British General Election Study 1983			1981 Census
	N unweighted	N weighted	percentage	percentage
Gender (Q64b)				
Men	1871	1874	47	48
Women	2084	2081	53	52
Age group (Q56)				
18–19	166	164	4	4
20–24	395	394	10	10
25–34	742	744	19	19
35–44	717	717	18	16
45–54	632	634	16	15
55–59	303	302	8	8
60–64	293	292	7	7
65–74	442	442	11	12
75–79	142	143	4	4
80+	103	104	3	4
			100	99
			(0)	
Not answered	20	20		

Socio-economic Group (Q53a/b)

				Percentage economically active and retired
1 Employers/managers, large establishments	169	172	6	4
2 Employers/managers, small establishments	241	246	8	8
3 Professionals, self employed	25	26	1	1
4 Professionals, employees	85	86	3	3
5.1 Ancillary workers	319	321	11	9
5.2 Foremen & supervisors, nonmanual	57	58	2	1
6 Junior nonmanual	585	587	20	20
7 Personal service	192	192	6	5
8 Foremen & Supervisors, manual	108	108	4	3
9 Skilled manual	485	480	16	19
10 Semi-skilled manual	405	401	13	13
11 Unskilled manual	180	176	6	7
12 Own account	81	84	3	4
13 Farmers, employer/manager	12	12	0	1
14 Farmers, own account	9	9	0	1
15 Agricultural workers	26	26	1	1
16 Armed forces	7	7	0	1
	921	916	100	101
17 Inadequately described occupations	48	49	(1)	
Economically inactive/not answered	921	916	(23)	

TABLE I.4A Sample Characteristics — Political

	British General Election Study 1983 (percentage)	Official result (Great Britain) (percentage)
Conservative	45.2	43.5
Labour	28.7	28.3
Liberal/Social Democratic Party	24.8	26.0
Scottish National Party	0.9	1.1
Plaid Cymru	0.2	0.4
Others	0.2	0.7
	100.0	100.0
N unweighted	3203	
N weighted	3205	

The discrepancy between the reported vote of survey respondents and the official result may have been due, in part, to a tendency for respondents to claim to have voted for the winning side when they did not (particularly perhaps among those respondents who did not vote but claimed to have done so).

A more substantial discrepancy lies in reported turnout. 83.4 per cent of the sample reported having voted while the official turnout figure for the 1983 general election was 72.7 per cent. It is improbable, however, that this discrepancy simply reflects an overreport of turnout by respondents. Various other factors help to explain the difference between the sample's reported turnout and the official turnout.

First, as noted earlier, movers (and particularly nonlocal movers) are underrepresented in the sample and are also less likely to have voted. Second, abstainers are more likely than voters to have refused cooperation in an election survey, since as a group they may well be relatively apolitical, or at least resistant to being questioned about an event in which they did not actively participate. So abstainers, for one reason or another, are almost certainly underrepresented in the sample.

Moreover, the discrepancy between official turnout figures and those based on survey estimates is exacerbated by legitimate and illegitimate double-entries in the registers. For instance, people with two homes often appear twice, as do movers; in addition, the names of people who died may not have been removed from the registers.

We estimate tentatively that if turnout is recalculated allowing for the (calculable) factors we have referred to, overclaiming would be reduced to about 4 per cent.

Questionnaire

The questionnaire follows together with the scale card booklet that was used as a self-completion document at questions 24, 28, 31, 36, 41 and 46.

SOCIAL AND COMMUNITY PLANNING RESEARCH
and
THE UNIVERSITY OF OXFORD

Head Office
35 Northampton Square,
London, EC1V 0AX.
Telephone: 01-250 1866

BRITISH GENERAL ELECTION STUDY 1983

Serial number ☐☐☐☐   Area number ☐☐☐

Time interview started (24 hour clock) ☐☐ ☐☐

July 1983

Project Number 765   OFFICE USE: PA Constituency number ☐☐☐

(124 26)

QUESTIONNAIRE STRUCTURE

I. POLITICAL INTEREST

ASK ALL

1.a) Would you say you cared a good deal which Party won the
recent general election or that you didn't care very much   (127)
which party won?

Cared a good deal	1
Didn't care very much	2

---

2. During the election campaign:

	Yes	No	
a) Did you watch and listen to any Party election broadcasts on television or radio?	1	2	(128)
b) Did you read any newspaper articles about the election campaign?	1 →c)	2 →d)	(129)

IF YES (CODE 1)   (130-31)

c) Which daily newspaper did you read most?
PROBE IF NECESSARY: Which one did you rely on most?

	OFFICE USE
SPECIFY MAIN DAILY NEWSPAPER	

ASK ALL

	Yes	No	
d) Did you go to hear any candidate at a political meeting?	1	2	(132)
e) Did you do any canvassing or other work for a candidate?	1	2	(133)
f) Did you have any political Party's poster in a window? INCLUDE CAR WINDOW IF MENTIONED	1	2	(134)
g) Did a canvasser from any Party call at your home to talk to you during the election campaign?	1 ↓	2 →Q.3	(135)

IF YES (CODE 1 at g)

h) From which Party or Parties?
CODE ALL THAT APPLY
DO NOT PROMPT

	Conservative	1	(136)
	Labour	2	(137)
IF "ALL OF THEM", PROBE FOR WHICH.	(SDP/Lib) Alliance	3	(138)
IF CANNOT DISTINGUISH, CODE DK	Liberal	4	(139)
	Social Democratic	5	(140)
	(Scotland) Scottish National	6	(141)
	(Wales) Plaid Cymru	7	(142)

Other (SPECIFY) _____   1

Don't know/Can't remember any	2	(143-46)

OFFICE
USE

ASK ALL

3.a) Why do you think the Conservatives beat Labour
      in the general election?
      PROBE FULLY

(147-48)

(149-50)

(151-52)

(153-54)

(155-56)

b) And why do you think the SDP/Liberal Alliance
    did not do better than they did?
    PROBE FULLY

OFFICE
USE

(157-58)

(159-60)

(161-62)

(163-64)

(165-66)

4.   Do you know whether the Alliance candidate in   (167)
     your constituency was a Liberal or a Social Democrat?

                                          Yes, Liberal   1

                                              Yes, SDP   2

                                     Yes, one of each   3

                                    No, don't remember   4

ASK ALL

5.a) Which do you think would generally be better for Britain
nowadays ... (READ OUT)   (168)

    ... to have a government formed by one political party on its own,   1 →Q.6

    or to have a government formed by two political parties together -
in coalition?   2 →b)

    (Don't know)   8 →Q.6

IF TWO PARTIES/COALITION (CODE 2)

b) Which of these Party groupings do you think would   (169)
provide the best government for Britain ...
(READ OUT) ...

    ... Conservative and Alliance,   1 ⎫
    or - Labour and Alliance,   2 ⎬Q.6
    or - Conservative and Labour,   3 ⎭
    or - some other grouping?   4 →c)
    (Don't know)   8 →Q.6

IF OTHER GROUPING (CODE 4)

c) Which grouping is that?
WRITE IN

	OFFICE USE	
		(170-71)
		(172-73)
		(174-75)

ASK ALL

		a) Liberal	b) SDP
6.a) Generally speaking, do you think of the Liberal Party as being closer to the Conservative Party or closer to the Labour Party? RECORD IN COLUMN a)		(176)	(177)
	Closer to Conservatives	1	1
b) And the Social Democratic Party, would you say it was closer to the Conservative Party or closer to the Labour Party? RECORD IN COLUMN b)	Closer to Labour	2	2
	No difference/ neither	3	3
	Don't know	8	8

c) Considering everything the Liberal and Social
Democratic Parties stand for, would you say that   (178)
... (READ OUT)

    ... there is a great difference between them,   1
    some difference,   2
    or not much difference?   3
    (Don't know)   8

d) Now, considering everything the Conservative
and Labour Parties stand for, would you say   (179)
that ... (READ OUT)

    ... there is a great difference between them,   1
    some difference,   2
    or not much difference?   3
    (Don't know)   8

II. VOTING/PARTY PREFERENCE

Card 02

7.a) Talking to people about the general election, we have
found that a lot of people didn't manage to vote. How
about you? Did you manage to vote in the general
election?

(207)

	Yes, voted	1 →Q.8
	No	2

IF NO (CODE 2)

b) Why was that?
PROBE FULLY

OFFICE
USE

		(208-09)
		(210-11)
		(212-13)
		(214-15)

c) Suppose you <u>had</u> voted: which Party
would you have been most likely to
vote for? DO NOT PROMPT.
IF NONE/DON'T KNOW, PROBE BEFORE CODING:
Which Party would you most like to have won
in your constituency?

(216-17)

Conservative	01 ⎫
Labour	02
(SDP/Lib) Alliance	03
Liberal	04
Social Democratic	05 Q.11
Scottish National	06
Plaid Cymru	07

Other (SPECIFY) _____

None/Don't know (AFTER PROBE)	98 ⎭

---

(218)

8.a) How long ago did you decide that you would
definitely vote the way you did: was it ... (READ OUT)

	... a long time ago,	1 →Q.9
	sometime last year,	2
	sometime this year,	3
	or during the election campaign?	4
	(Don't know)	8 →Q.9

IF LAST YEAR, THIS YEAR OR DURING CAMPAIGN
(CODES 2, 3 OR 4)

b) Was there anything in particular that decided you?
What was that? PROBE FULLY

OFFICE
USE

		(219-20)
		(221-22)
		(223-24)
		(225-26)

9.a) Which Party did you vote for in the general election?
      DO NOT PROMPT (CODE IN COLUMN a) BELOW)

  b) Was there any time during the general election campaign
      when you seriously thought you might vote for another
      Party? IF YES: Which Party?
      DO NOT PROMPT - BUT SEE INSTRUCTION BOX. (ONE CODE IN COLUMN b) BELOW)
      IF MORE THAN ONE PARTY, RING CODE 96

  c) If the voting paper had required you to give two votes,
      in order of preference, which Party would you have put
      as your second choice?
      DO NOT PROMPT - BUT SEE INSTRUCTION BOX. (ONE CODE IN COLUMN c) BELOW)

> If respondent voted for Alliance,
> Liberal or SDP at a) (Codes 03, 04,
> 05), none of these codes should be
> ringed at b) or c). Explain if
> necessary: "they did not stand
> against each other; so is there any
> other Party (you seriously thought
> about/that you would put as
> second choice)"?

	a) Voted for (227-28)	b) Thought about (229-30)	c) 2nd Vote (231-32)
Conservative	01	01	01
Labour	02	02	02
(SDP/Lib) Alliance	03	03	03
Liberal	04	04	04
Social Democratic	05	05	05
Scottish National	06	06	06
Plaid Cymru	07	07	07
Other (SPECIFY)			
a) _____	97	-	-
b) _____	-	97	-
c) _____	-	-	97
Refused to disclose voting	95	-	-
More than one other Party thought about	-	96	-
No/none	-	00	00
Don't know	98	98	98

ASK ALL WHO VOTED - SHOW CARD A

10.a) Which one of the reasons on this card comes   (233)
closest to the main reason you voted for
the Party you chose?

I always vote that way	1
I thought it was the best Party	2 } Q.11
I really preferred another Party but it had no chance of winning in this constituency	3 →b)
Other (SPECIFY) _____	
_____	7
None of these/Don't know	8 } Q.11

IF CODE 3 AT a)

b) Which was the Party you really preferred?   [234-35]
DO NOT PROMPT

Conservative	01
Labour	02
(SDP/Lib) Alliance	03
Liberal	04
Social Democratic	05
Scottish National	06
Plaid Cymru	07
Other (SPECIFY) _____	97

ASK ALL

11. Now, thinking back to the last general election -   (236-37)
that is the one in 1979 - do you remember which
Party you voted for then - or perhaps you didn't
vote in that election? DO NOT PROMPT.
IF "Alliance" or "SDP" NAMED, EXPLAIN: "they did
not exist as such in 1979", BUT STILL DO NOT
PROMPT

Conservative	01
Labour	02
Liberal	04
Scottish National	06
Plaid Cymru	07
Other (SPECIFY) _____	97
Refused to disclose voting	95
Did not vote	00
Not eligible/ Too young to vote	94
Don't remember	98

12. Some people say that we should change the voting
system to allow smaller political parties to get
a fairer share of MPs. Others say that we should
keep the voting system as it is to produce effective   (238)
government. Which view comes closer to your own
... (READ OUT)

... that we should change the voting system,	1
or - keep it as it is?	2
(Don't know)	8

ASK ALL

13.a) Generally speaking, do you think of yourself as
Conservative, Labour, Liberal, Social Democrat,
(Nationalist/Plaid Cymru), or <u>what</u>?

IF "ALLIANCE" PROBE: Liberal or Social Democrat?

ONE CODE IN COLUMN a)

IF NONE/DON'T KNOW (CODE 00 OR 98)

b) Do you generally think of yourself as
a little closer to one of the Parties
than the others? IF YES, Which
Party?

IF "ALLIANCE" PROBE: Liberal
or Social Democrat?

ONE CODE IN COLUMN b)

(239-40) (241-42)

	a)	b)
Conservative	01	01
Labour	02	02
Liberal	04	04
Social Democrat	05	05
Scottish Nationalist	06	06
Plaid Cymru	07	07
Other (SPECIFY) a) ___	97	-
b) ___	-	97
Alliance (AFTER PROBE)	03	03
None/No	00	00
Don't know	98	98

c) }   Q.14   b)

IF PARTY CODED AT a)

(243)

c) Would you call yourself very strong
... (QUOTE PARTY AT a), fairly strong,
or not very strong?

Very strong	1
Fairly strong	2
Not very strong	3
Don't know	8

ASK ALL - SHOW CARD B

FIRST MARK 'X' AGAINST PARTY NAMED AT Q.13a) OR b) ABOVE.
DO NOT ASK THIS QUESTION ABOUT <u>THAT</u> PARTY. ASK ABOUT ALL OTHERS.

14. Now I want to ask you about some Parties you don't support. Looking at
the card, would you say you are very strongly against, somewhat against,
or not really against ... (READ OUT)

	'X'	Very strongly against	some- what against	Not really against	(Don't know)	
a) ... the Conservative Party?	___	1	2	3	8	(244)
b) ... the Labour Party?	___	1	2	3	8	(245)
c) ... the Liberal Party?	___	1	2	3	8	(246)
d) ... the Social Democratic Party?	___	1	2	3	8	(247)
e) ... (IF SCOTLAND) - the Scottish National Party?	___	1	2	3	8	(248)
f) ... (IF WALES) - Plaid Cymru?	___	1	2	3	8	(249)
g) ... the British Communist Party?	___	1	2	3	8	(250)
h) ... the National Front?	___	1	2	3	8	(251)

III. LEADERSHIP & PARTY IMAGES

ASK ALL - SHOW CARD C

		Very effective	Fairly effective	Fairly ineffective	Very ineffective	Don't know	
15.a)	Looking at this card, on the whole how effective or ineffective do you think Mrs Thatcher is as a prime minister?..............	1	2	3	4	8	(252)
b)	And on the whole how effective or ineffective do you think Mr Foot would have been as a prime minister?	1	2	3	4	8	(253)
c)	How about Mr Jenkins?	1	2	3	4	8	(254)
d)	And Mr Steel?	1	2	3	4	8	(255)

SHOW CARD D

		Mrs Thatcher	Mr Foot	Mr Jenkins	Mr Steel	None/ Don't know	
16.	Still thinking of these four Party leaders: at the time of the general election, which one do you think would have been ... (READ OUT)						
a)	... the prime minister most able to unite the nation?	1	2	3	4	8	(256)
b)	... the prime minister most likely to get things done?	1	2	3	4	8	(257)
c)	... the one most likely to improve Britain's standing abroad?	1	2	3	4	8	(258)
d)	... the one with most concern for all groups in society?	1	2	3	4	8	(259)
e)	... the one who would get the most out of a team?	1	2	3	4	8	(260)
f)	... the one most in touch with ordinary people's problems?	1	2	3	4	8	(261)

SHOW CARD E

		a) Mrs Thatcher		b) Mr Foot		c) Mr Jenkins		d) Mr Steel	
17.a)	Which of the qualities on this card would you say Mrs Thatcher has: choose as many as you think apply?								
	Caring	1	(262)	1	(271)	1	(307)	1	(316)
	Determined	2	(263)	2	(272)	2	(308)	2	(317)
	Shrewd	3	(264)	3	(273)	3	(309)	3	(318)
b)-d) REPEAT FOR OTHER THREE LEADERS IN TURN	Likeable as a person	4	(265)	4	(274)	4	(310)	4	(319)
	Tough	5	(266)	5	(275)	5	(311)	5	(320)
	Listens to reason	6	(267)	6	(276)	6	(312)	6	(321)
	Decisive	1	(268)	1	(277)	1	(313)	1	(322)
	Sticks to principles	2	(269)	2	(278)	2	(314)	2	(323)
	NONE OF THESE	0	(270)	0	(279)	0	(315)	0	(324)
	Don't know	8		8		8		8	

Card 03

ASK ALL

18. Moving now from the Party leaders to
     the Parties themselves

			Conservative	Labour	Alliance
a)	i)	On the whole, would you describe the Conservative Party as ... (READ OUT)	(325)	(326)	(327)
		... extreme,	1	1	1
	ii)	And the Labour Party nowadays, is it ...	2	2	2
		or moderate?			
		(READ OUT) (Neither or both)	3	3	3
		(Don't know)	8	8	8
	iii)	And the SDP/Liberal Alliance, is it ... (READ OUT)			
b)	i)	And would you describe the Conservative Party nowadays as ... (READ OUT)	(328)	(329)	(330)
		... united,	1	1	1
	ii)	And the Labour Party nowadays, is it ... (READ OUT) or divided?	2	2	2
		(Neither or both)	3	3	3
	iii)	And the Alliance, is it ... (READ OUT) (Don't know)	8	8	8
c)	i)	On the whole, would you describe the Conservative Party as ... (READ OUT)	(331)	(332)	(333)
		... good for one class,	1	1	1
	ii)	And the Labour Party, is it ... or good for all classes?	2	2	2
		(READ OUT) (Neither or both)	3	3	3
	iii)	And the Alliance, is it ... (READ OUT) (Don't know)	8	8	8
d)	i)	Do you think the Conservative Party has ... (READ OUT)	(334)	(335)	(336)
		... clear policies,	1	1	1
	ii)	And the Labour Party, does it have ... or vague policies?	2	2	2
		(READ OUT) (Neither or both)	3	3	3
		(Don't know)	8	8	8
	iii)	And the Alliance, does it have ... (READ OUT)			

		Conservative	Labour	Alliance	None/ Don't know	
19.a)	Still thinking only of the Conservatives, Labour and the Alliance: which one of them would have been the most likely to keep prices down if it had been in government over the next five years?					
	Keep prices down	1	2	3	8	(337)
b)	And the one most likely to reduce unemployment?	1	2	3	8	(338)
c)	And to prevent strikes?	1	2	3	8	(339)
d)	And to look after the health and social services?	1	2	3	8	(340)

IV.   CAMPAIGN ISSUES & IDEOLOGY

ASK ALL - SHOW CARD F (FOR WHOLE PAGE)

20.a) Here is a list of six issues that were discussed during the election.
When you were deciding about voting, how important was each of these
issues to you? First defence: was it extremely important, quite
important or not very important to you in <u>deciding about voting</u>?
REPEAT FOR ISSUES ii) - vi)

	i) Defence (341)	ii) Unem- ployment (342)	iii) Inflation (343)	iv) The health & social services (344)	v) National- isation (345)	vi) Law and order (346)
Extremely important	1	1	1	1	1	1
Quite important	2	2	2	2	2	2
Not very important	3	3	3	3	3	3

b) Which <u>one</u> of the six
issues on the card
would you say was
<u>most important</u> to
you in deciding
about voting?

              (347-48)   Can't
choose

    1   2   3   4   5   6 8 → d)

c) And which <u>next</u>?
    1   2   3   4   5   6 8

d)i)Which Party's views
on defence would you
say <u>come closest</u> to
to your own views?
DO NOT PROMPT

	i) Defence (349-50)	ii) Unem- ployment (351-52)	iii) Inflation (353-54)	iv) The health & social services (355-56)	v) National- isation (357-58)	vi) Law and order (359-60)
Conservative	01	01	01	01	01	01
ii)-vi) Labour	02	02	02	02	02	02
REPEAT FOR OTHER Alliance	03	03	03	03	03	03
ISSUES Liberal	04	04	04	04	04	04
Social Democratic	05	05	05	05	05	05
Scottish National	06	06	06	06	06	06
Plaid Cymru	07	07	07	07	07	07
Other (SPECIFY) →						
None	00	00	00	00	00	00
Don't know	98	98	98	98	98	98

e) Besides the six issues on the card, are there any other
things that were at least as important as these were to
you in deciding about voting?

                                  (361)
                                  Yes   1

                                  No   2 → Q.21

IF YES (CODE 1 <u>at</u> e)

f) Which? Any others?

OFFICE USE		
		(362-63)
		(364-65)
		(366-67)
		(368-69)

ASK ALL

21.a) Some people say that British governments nowadays –
of whichever Party – can actually do very little to
change things. Others say they can do quite a bit.
Do you think that British governments nowadays can
do very little or quite a bit ... (READ OUT)

	Very little	Quite a bit	Don't know	
... to keep prices down?	1	2	8	(370)
b) And can British governments nowadays do very little or quite a bit to reduce unemployment?	1	2	8	(371)
c) And to reduce taxes?	1	2	8	(372)
d) To improve the general standard of living?	1	2	8	(373)
e) To improve the health and social services?	1	2	8	(374)
f) To control wage and salary increases?	1	2	8	(375)
g) To reduce crime?	1	2	8	(376)
h) To prevent strikes?	1	2	8	(377)

SHOW CARD G

22. If you had to choose from among the items on
this card, which are the two that seem most
desirable to you? RING ONE CODE IN EACH COLUMN

	(378) 1st	(379) 2nd
Maintaining order in the nation	1	1
Giving people more say in important political decisions	2	2
Fighting rising prices	3	3
Protecting freedom of speech	4	4
Don't know at all	8 ↓	-
No second choice	-	8

23. There are some people whose views are considered
extreme by the majority.

Card 04

a) Consider people who wish to overthrow the system
of government in Britain by revolution. Do you
think such people should be allowed to ... (READ OUT)

		a)	b)	
i) ... hold public meetings to express their views?	Yes	1	1	
CODE IN COLUMN a)	No	2	2	(407-08)
	Don't know	8	8	
ii) And to teach in schools?	Yes	1	1	
CODE IN COLUMN a)	No	2	2	(409-10)
	Don't know	8	8	

b) Now consider people who say that all blacks and Asians should be
forced to leave Britain. Do you think such people should be
allowed to ... (REPEAT i) AND ii) ABOVE AND CODE IN COLUMN b)

Defence

ASK ALL

24.   One of the election issues was whether the government should keep or
get rid of nuclear weapons in Britain.

SHOW SCALE CARD 1 AND GIVE PENCIL

> Please look at this card. People who are convinced that we should get
> rid of all nuclear weapons in Britain without delay will put a
> tick in the last box on the left (Letter P) - POINT TO BOX P AND
> STATEMENT - while those who are convinced that we should increase
> nuclear weapons in Britain without delay will put a tick in the
> last box on the right (Letter J) - POINT TO BOX J AND STATEMENT.
> So, as you can see, people who hold views that come somewhere
> between those two positions will tick a box somewhere along here -
> POINT TO BOXES FROM LEFT TO CENTRE - or somewhere along here - POINT
> TO BOXES FROM RIGHT TO CENTRE.   RE-EXPLAIN IF NECESSARY

a) First, would you tick the box anywhere along the scale that comes
closest to your own views about nuclear weapons in Britain.

ASK WHICH BOX, REFER TO   (411-13)

LETTER KEY AND ENTER CODE NO. OF LETTER   [| |]

IF DON'T KNOW, ENTER 098

Now where do you think the Conservative and
Labour Parties stand?

b) First, the Conservative Party. In the next
row of boxes, put a tick in the box that you
think comes closest to the views of the
Conservative Party?

ASK WHICH BOX, REFER TO   (414-16)

LETTER KEY AND ENTER CODE NO. OF LETTER   [| |]

IF DON'T KNOW, ENTER 098

c) Now, in the next row, please put a tick in the
box that you think comes closest to the views
of the Labour Party?

ASK WHICH BOX, REFER TO   (417-19)

LETTER KEY AND ENTER CODE NO. OF LETTER   [| |]

IF DON'T KNOW, ENTER 098

d) And, finally, please tick the box in the last
row that you think comes closest to the views
of the SDP/Liberal Alliance?

ASK WHICH BOX, REFER TO   (420-22)

LETTER KEY AND ENTER CODE NO. OF LETTER   [| |]

IF DON'T KNOW, ENTER 098

INTERVIEWER NOTE: Throughout this question you may change a code
already entered if, on reflection, a respondent wants to change
his or her mind. Please ensure that your final entry is clear
and corresponds to respondent's version. If respondent asks, you
may confirm that Letter Q is the central position on the scale.

LETTER KEY
B = 001
C = X08
D = X01
E = 005
F = X04
G = 009
H = 008
J = 010
K = 002
L = 006
M = X07
N = X05
P = X10
Q = 000
R = X03
S = X06
T = 003
U = 007
V = X02
W = X09
Y = 004
LEFT OF P = X97
RIGHT OF J = 097

OFFICE USE

Get rid   Increase

X10	X09	X08	X07	X06	X05	X04	X03	X02	X01	000	001	002	003	004	005	006	007	008	009	010
P	W	C	M	S	N	F	R	V	D	Q	B	K	T	Y	E	L	U	H	G	J

ASK ALL

25.a) On the whole, do you think the Conservative   (423)
government handled the Falklands dispute
... (READ OUT)

... very well,	1
fairly well,	2
not very well,	3
or not at all well?	4

(Other answer - SPECIFY) _____ 7

(Don't know)   8

b) If the Labour Party had been in government at
the time, do you think they would have handled   (424)
the Falklands dispute better than the Conservatives,
worse, or much the same?

Better	1
Worse	2
Same	3
Mixed views	4
Don't know	8

c) When you were deciding about voting, was the   (425)
government's handling of the Falklands dispute
... (READ OUT)

... extremely important to you,	1
quite important,	2
or not very important?	3

26.a) Do you think that the siting of
American nuclear missiles in Britain
makes Britain a safer or a less safe
place to live?
CODE IN COLUMN a)

b) And do you think that having our own
nuclear missiles makes Britain a
safer or a less safe place to live?
CODE IN COLUMN b)

	a) American nuclear missiles	b) Own nuclear missiles
	(426)	(427)
Safer	1	1
Less safe	2	2
Don't know	3	3

27. Do you think the government should
or should not do each of the following
things, or doesn't it matter either way
... (READ OUT)

	Should	Should not	Doesn't matter	Don't know	
a) ... Pull British troops out of Northern Ireland immediately?	1	3	2	8	(428)
b) ... Negotiate with Argentina over the future of the Falklands?	1	3	2	8	(429)
c) ... Spend less on defence?	1	3	2	8	(430)

Unemployment & Inflation

ASK ALL

28.   Another election issue was whether inflation or unemployment is the more urgent issue to tackle.

SHOW SCALE CARD 2

> Please look at this card.   People who are convinced that getting people back to work should be the government's top priority will put a tick in the last box on the left (Letter P) - POINT TO BOX P AND STATEMENT - while those who are convinced that keeping prices down should be the government's top priority will put a tick in the last box on the right (Letter J) - POINT TO BOX J AND STATEMENT. So, just as before, people who hold views that come somewhere between those two positions will tick a box somewhere along here - POINT TO BOXES FROM LEFT TO CENTRE - or somewhere along here - POINT TO BOXES FROM RIGHT TO CENTRE.

a)   First, would you tick the box anywhere along the scale that comes closest to your own views about unemployment and inflation.

	LETTER KEY
ASK WHICH BOX, REFER TO (431-33)	
LETTER KEY AND ENTER CODE NO. OF LETTER [ ][ ][ ]	B = 001
IF DON'T KNOW, ENTER 098	C = X08

Now where do you think the Conservative and Labour Parties stand?

D = X01

b)   First, the Conservative Party.   In the next row of boxes, put a tick in the box that you think comes closest to the views of the Conservative Party?

E = 005
F = X04

ASK WHICH BOX, REFER TO (434-36)

G = 009

LETTER KEY AND ENTER CODE NO. OF LETTER [ ][ ][ ]

H = 008

IF DON'T KNOW, ENTER 098

J = 010

c)   Now, in the next row, please put a tick in the box that you think comes closest to the views of the Labour Party?

K = 002

ASK WHICH BOX, REFER TO (437-39)

L = 006
M = X07

LETTER KEY AND ENTER CODE NO. OF LETTER [ ][ ][ ]

N = X05

IF DON'T KNOW, ENTER 098

P = X10

d)   And, finally, please tick the box in the last row that you think comes closest to the views of the SDP/Liberal Alliance?

Q = 000
R = X03
S = X06

ASK WHICH BOX, REFER TO (440-42)

T = 003

LETTER KEY AND ENTER CODE NO. OF LETTER [ ][ ][ ]

U = 007

IF DON'T KNOW, ENTER 098

V = X02
W = X09

> INTERVIEWER NOTE: Throughout this question you may change a code already entered if, on reflection, a respondent wants to change his or her mind.   Please ensure that your final entry is clear and corresponds to respondent's version.   If respondent asks, you may confirm that Letter Q is the central position on the scale.

Y = 004.
LEFT OF P = X97
RIGHT OF J = 097

Back to work   OFFICE USE   Prices down

X10	X09	X08	X07	X06	X05	X04	X03	X02	X01	000	001	002	003	004	005	006	007	008	009	010
P	W	C	M	S	N	F	R	V	D	Q	B	K	T	Y	E	L	U	H	G	J

ASK ALL

29.a) On the whole, do you think the Conservative government over the last four years has handled the problem of inflation ... (READ OUT)   (443)

... very well,	1
fairly well,	2
not very well,	3
or not at all well?	4
(Don't know)	8

b) And unemployment: on the whole do you think the Conservative government over the last four years has handled the problem of unemployment ... (READ OUT)   (444)

... very well,	1
fairly well,	2
not very well,	3
or not at all well?	4
(Don't know)	8

c) Which do you think threatens you and your family most ... (READ OUT)   (445)

... the threat of rising prices,	1
or - the threat of unemployment?	2
(Don't know)	8

---

30. Please say whether you agree or disagree with each of these statements, or say if you are not sure either way ... (READ OUT)

		Agree	Disagree	Not sure	
a)	... When someone is unemployed it's usually his or her own fault?	1	3	2	(446)
b)	... The government should set firm guidelines for wages and salaries?	1	3	2	(447)
c)	... The high level of unemployment in Britain is mainly the British Government's fault?	1	3	2	(448)
d)	... The government should spend more money to create jobs?	1	3	2	(449)
e)	... Much of our unemployment has been caused by trade union leaders?	1	3	2	(450)
f)	... The rise in unemployment has helped Britain's products to be more competitive?	1	3	2	(451)

Taxation and government services

ASK ALL

31.   Another election issue was to do with taxes and government spending.
SHOW SCALE CARD 3

> Please look at this card. People who are convinced that we should put
> up taxes a lot and spend much more on health and social services will put a
> tick in the last box on the left (Letter P) - POINT TO BOX P AND
> STATEMENT - while those who are convinced that we should cut taxes a lot
> and spend much less on health and social services will put a tick in the
> last box on the right (Letter J) - POINT TO BOX J AND STATEMENT.
> So, just as before, people who hold views that come somewhere
> between those two positions will tick a box somewhere along here -
> POINT TO BOXES FROM LEFT TO CENTRE - or somewhere along here - POINT
> TO BOXES FROM RIGHT TO CENTRE.

a)   First, would you tick the box anywhere along the scale that comes
closest to your own views about taxes and government spending.

ASK WHICH BOX, REFER TO   (452-54)

LETTER KEY AND ENTER CODE NO. OF LETTER [| |]

IF DON'T KNOW, ENTER 098

LETTER KEY
B = 001
C = X08
D = X01
E = 005
F = X04
G = 009
H = 008
J = 010
K = 002
L = 006
M = X07
N = X05
P = X10
Q = 000
R = X03
S = X06
T = 003
U = 007
V = X02
W = X09
Y = 004
LEFT OF P = X97
RIGHT OF J = 097

Now where do you think the Conservative and
Labour Parties stand?

b)   First, the Conservative Party. In the next
row of boxes, put a tick in the box that you
think comes closest to the views of the
Conservative Party?

ASK WHICH BOX, REFER TO   (455-57)

LETTER KEY AND ENTER CODE NO. OF LETTER [| |]

IF DON'T KNOW, ENTER 098

c)   Now, in the next row, please put a tick in the
box that you think comes closest to the views
of the Labour Party?

ASK WHICH BOX, REFER TO   (458-60)

LETTER KEY AND ENTER CODE NO. OF LETTER [| |]

IF DON'T KNOW, ENTER 098

d)   And, finally, please tick the box in the last
row that you think comes closest to the views
of the SDP/Liberal Alliance?

ASK WHICH BOX, REFER TO   (461-63)

LETTER KEY AND ENTER CODE NO. OF LETTER [| |]

IF DON'T KNOW, ENTER 098

> INTERVIEWER NOTE: Throughout this question you may change a code
> already entered if, on reflection, a respondent wants to change
> his or her mind. Please ensure that your final entry is clear
> and corresponds to respondent's version. If respondent asks, you
> may confirm that Letter Q is the central position on the scale.

OFFICE USE

Services up   Taxes down

X10	X09	X08	X07	X06	X05	X04	X03	X02	X01	000	001	002	003	004	005	006	007	008	009	010
P	W	C	M	S	N	F	R	V	D	Q	B	K	T	Y	E	L	U	H	G	J

ASK ALL

32.a) On the whole, do you think the Conservative government over the last four years was successful or unsuccessful in keeping taxes down generally? PROBE: Very or fairly? CODE IN COLUMN a)

b) And was it successful or unsuccessful in improving your standard of living? PROBE: Very or fairly? CODE IN COLUMN b)

	a) Taxes (464)	b) Standard of living (465)
Very successful	1	1
Fairly successful	2	2
Fairly unsuccessful	3	3
Very unsuccessful	4	4
Don't know	8	8

33.a) Which Party do you think would be the most likely to improve your standard of living over the next three or four years?

DO NOT PROMPT
CODE IN COLUMN a)

b) And over the next ten years or so?
DO NOT PROMPT
CODE IN COLUMN b)

	a) 3-4 years (466-67)	b) 10 years (468-69)
Conservative	01	01
Labour	02	02
(SDP/Lib) Alliance	03	03
Liberal	04	04
Social Democratic	05	05
Scottish National	06	06
Plaid Cymru	07	07
Other (SPECIFY)		
a) _____	97	-
b) _____	-	97
NONE	00	00
Don't know	98	98

34. Please say whether you agree or disagree with each of these statements, or say if you are not sure either way ... (READ OUT)

	Agree	Disagree	Not sure	
a) ... High income tax makes people less willing to work hard?	1	3	2	(470)
b)... Income and wealth should be redistributed towards ordinary working people?	1	3	2	(471)
c) ... Too many people these days like to rely on government handouts?	1	3	2	(472)

35. Do you think the government should or should not do each of the following things, or doesn't it matter either way ... (READ OUT)

	Should	Should not	Doesn't matter	Don't know	
a) ... get rid of private education in Britain?	1	3	2	8	(473)
b) ... spend more money to get rid of poverty?	1	3	2	8	(474)
c) ... increase the standard of living of pensioners?	1	3	2	8	(475)
d)... encourage the growth of private medicine?	1	3	2	8	(476)
e) ... put more money into the National Health Service?	1	3	2	8	(477)

Nationalisation

ASK ALL

36.   There was a lot of discussion during the election about nationalisation.

SHOW SCALE CARD 4   Card 05

> Please look at this card. People who are convinced that we should
> nationalise many more private companies will put a
> tick in the last box on the left (Letter P) - POINT TO BOX P AND
> STATEMENT - while those who are convinced that we should sell
> off many more nationalised industries will put a tick in the
> last box on the right (Letter J) - POINT TO BOX J AND STATEMENT.
> So, just as before , people who hold views that come somewhere
> between those two positions will tick a box somewhere along here -
> POINT TO BOXES FROM LEFT TO CENTRE - or somewhere along here - POINT
> TO BOXES FROM RIGHT TO CENTRE.

a) First, would you tick the box anywhere along the scale that comes
    closest to your own views about nationalisation.

	LETTER KEY
	B = 001
	C = X08
	D = X01
	E = 005
	F = X04
	G = 009
	H = 008
	J = 010
	K = 002
	L = 006
	M = X07
	N = X05
	P = X10
	Q = 000
	R = X03
	S = X06
	T = 003
	U = 007
	V = X02
	W = X09
	Y = 004
	LEFT OF P = X97
	RIGHT OF J = 097

ASK WHICH BOX, REFER TO   (507-09)
LETTER KEY AND ENTER CODE NO. OF LETTER   [| |]
IF DON'T KNOW, ENTER 098

Now where do you think the Conservative and
Labour Parties stand?

b) First, the Conservative Party. In the next
    row of boxes, put a tick in the box that you
    think comes closest to the views of the
    Conservative Party?
                    ASK WHICH BOX, REFER TO   (510-12)
    LETTER KEY AND ENTER CODE NO. OF LETTER   [| |]
                    IF DON'T KNOW, ENTER 098

c) Now, in the next row, please put a tick in the
    box that you think comes closest to the views
    of the Labour Party?
                    ASK WHICH BOX, REFER TO   (513-15)
    LETTER KEY AND ENTER CODE NO. OF LETTER   [| |]
                    IF DON'T KNOW, ENTER 098

d) And, finally, please tick the box in the last
    row that you think comes closest to the views
    of the SDP/Liberal Alliance?
                    ASK WHICH BOX, REFER TO   (516-18)
    LETTER KEY AND ENTER CODE NO. OF LETTER   [| |]
                    IF DON'T KNOW, ENTER 098

> INTERVIEWER NOTE: Throughout this question you may change a code
> already entered if, on reflection, a respondent wants to change
> his or her mind. Please ensure that your final entry is clear
> and corresponds to respondent's version. If respondent asks, you
> may confirm that Letter Q is the central position on the scale.

OFFICE USE

Nationalise   Privatise

X10	X09	X08	X07	X06	X05	X04	X03	X02	X01	000	001	002	003	004	005	006	007	008	009	010
P	W	C	M	S	N	F	R	V	D	Q	B	K	T	Y	E	L	U	H	G	J

ASK ALL - SHOW CARD H

37.   Just to clarify your views on nationalisation, please tell me from this
card which of the four statements comes closest to what you think should
be done, or say if you can't choose any?   (519)

A lot more industries should be nationalised   1

Only a few more industries should be nationalised   2

No more industries should be nationalised, but
industries that are now nationalised should stay nationalised   3

Some of the industries that are now nationalised
should become private companies   4

Can't choose/Don't know   8

---

38.   Thinking now of trade unions and big business in this country:

a)   First do you think that trade unions ... (READ OUT)   (520)

have too much power,   1

or not?   2

(Don't know)   8

b)   Do you think that big business in this country ...(READ OUT)   (521)

has too much power,   1

or not?   2

(Don't know)   8

---

39.   Do you think the Conservative government over the last four   (522)
years has generally handled the problem of strikes ... (READ OUT)

... very well,   1

fairly well,   2

not very well,   3

or not at all well?   4

(Don't know)   8

---

40.   Do you think the government should or should not do each of
the following things, or doesn't it matter either way... (READ OUT)

	Should	Should not	Doesn't matter	Don't know	
a)... Introduce stricter laws to regulate the activities of trade unions?	1	3	2	8	(523)
b)... Give workers more say in running the places where they work?	1	3	2	8	(524)
c)... Allow private industry to keep more of its profits?	1	3	2	8	(525)
d)... Do more to help the economy of the area in which you live?	1	3	2	8	(526)

Law and order

ASK ALL

41.   This card is about the importance of controlling crime on the one hand,
or protecting people's rights against the authorities, on the other.

SHOW SCALE CARD 5

> Please look at this card. People who are convinced that <u>protecting
> civil rights is more important than cutting crime</u> will put a
> tick in the last box on the left (Letter P) - POINT TO BOX P AND
> STATEMENT - while those who are convinced that <u>cutting crime is more
> important than protecting civil rights</u> will put a tick in the
> last box on the right (Letter J) - POINT TO BOX J AND STATEMENT.
> So, just as before, people who hold views that come somewhere
> between those two positions will tick a box somewhere along here -
> POINT TO BOXES FROM LEFT TO CENTRE - or somewhere along here - POINT
> TO BOXES FROM RIGHT TO CENTRE.

a) First, would you tick the box anywhere along the scale that comes
closest to <u>your own</u> views about law and order.

ASK WHICH BOX, REFER TO   (527-29)

LETTER KEY AND ENTER CODE NO. OF LETTER [| |]

IF DON'T KNOW, ENTER 098

Now where do you think the Conservative and
Labour Parties stand?

b) First, the <u>Conservative Party</u>. In the next
row of boxes, put a tick in the box that you
think comes closest to the views of the
<u>Conservative Party</u>?

ASK WHICH BOX, REFER TO   (530-32)

LETTER KEY AND ENTER CODE NO. OF LETTER [| |]

IF DON'T KNOW, ENTER 098

c) Now, in the next row, please put a tick in the
box that you think comes closest to the views
of the <u>Labour Party</u>?

ASK WHICH BOX, REFER TO   (533-35)

LETTER KEY AND ENTER CODE NO. OF LETTER [| |]

IF DON'T KNOW, ENTER 098

d) And, finally, please tick the box in the last
row that you think comes closest to the views
of the <u>SDP/Liberal Alliance</u>?

ASK WHICH BOX, REFER TO   (536-38)

LETTER KEY AND ENTER CODE NO. OF LETTER [| |]

IF DON'T KNOW, ENTER 098

LETTER KEY	
B	= 001
C	= X08
D	= X01
E	= 005
F	= X04
G	= 009
H	= 008
J	= 010
K	= 002
L	= 006
M	= X07
N	= X05
P	= X10
Q	= 000
R	= X03
S	= X06
T	= 003
U	= 007
V	= X02
W	= X09
Y	= 004
LEFT OF P	= X97
RIGHT OF J	= 097

> INTERVIEWER NOTE: Throughout this question you may change a code
> already entered if, on reflection, a respondent wants to change
> his or her mind. Please ensure that your final entry is clear
> and corresponds to respondent's version. If respondent asks, you
> may confirm that Letter Q is the central position on the scale.

OFFICE USE

Protect rights   Cut crime

X10	X09	X08	X07	X06	X05	X04	X03	X02	X01	000	001	002	003	004	005	006	007	008	009	010
P	W	C	M	S	N	F	R	V	D	Q	B	K	T	Y	E	L	U	H	G	J

ASK ALL

42. Please say whether you agree or disagree with each of these statements, or say if you are not sure either way ... (READ OUT)

	Agree	Disagree	Not sure	
a) ... If you want to cut crime, cut unemployment?	1	3	2	(539)
b) ... The police should be given more power?	1	3	2	(540)
c) ... Britain should bring back the death penalty?	1	3	2	(541)
d) ... The aim of prisons should be to reform criminals rather than punish them?	1	3	2	(542)
e) ... People who break the law should be given stiffer sentences?	1	3	2	(543)

Other issues

43.a) When you were deciding about voting, how important was the issue of the Common Market - was it ... (READ OUT)   (544)

... extremely important to you,   1

quite important,   2

or not very important?   3

SHOW CARD J

b) Which of the three statements on this card comes closest to your own views on the Common Market?   (545)

Britain should leave the Common Market without further ado   1

Britain should stay in the Common Market provided we can get better terms   2

Britain should stay in the Common Market anyway   3

Don't know   8

SCOTLAND/WALES ONLY

44. An issue (in Scotland/in Wales) is the question of an elected Assembly - a special parliament for (Scotland/Wales) dealing with (Scottish/Welsh) affairs. Which of these statements comes closest to your view ...(READ OUT)   (546)

... (Scotland/Wales) should become completely independent,   1

or - there should be an elected assembly for (Scotland/Wales),   2

or - some other way should be found to make sure the needs of (Scotland/Wales) are better understood by the government in London   3

or - keep the governing of (Scotland/Wales) much as it has been?   4

(Other - SPECIFY) _____

_____   7

(Don't know)   8

(Spare) (547)

208   HOW BRITAIN VOTES

ASK ALL - SHOW CARD K

45. Finally on election <u>issues</u>, I want to ask about some changes that have
     been happening in Britain over the years.   For each one I read out can
     you say whether you think it has gone too far, not gone far enough, or is
     it about right.

		Gone too far	About right	Not gone far enough	Don't know	
a)	Thinking first about the <u>welfare</u> benefits that are available to people today. Would you say they have gone too far, are they about right or have they not gone far enough?	1	2	3	8	(548)
b)	How about attempts to give equal opportunities to women in Britain?	1	2	3	8	(549)
c)	The right to show nudity and sex in films and magazines?	1	2	3	8	(550)
d)	Government spending on education?	1	2	3	8	(551)
e)	The building of nuclear power stations?	1	2	3	8	(552)
f)	The right to have protest marches and demonstrations?	1	2	3	8	(553)
g)	Attempts to give equal opportunities to black people and Asians in Britain?	1	2	3	8	(554)
h)	Allowing the sale of council houses to tenants?	1	2	3	8	(555)
i)	The movement towards comprehensive schooling?	1	2	3	8	(556)
j)	Cutting immigration from the Commonwealth?	1	2	3	8	(557)
k)	Government support for public transport?	1	2	3	8	(558)
l)	The availability of abortion on the National Health Service?	1	2	3	8	(559)

ASK ALL - SHOW SCALE CARD 6

46.

> On the last of these cards, the British Communist Party would place itself on the extreme left (Letter P) - POINT TO BOX P - while the National Front would place itself on the extreme right (Letter J) - POINT TO BOX J. The other main Parties would probably place themselves somewhere between these two positions, somewhere along here - POINT TO BOXES FROM LEFT TO CENTRE - or somewhere along here - POINT TO BOXES FROM RIGHT TO CENTRE.

Now, this time I want to ask you first where you think the Conservative and Labour Parties are on the scale.

a) First the Conservative Party: tick the box the comes closest to where you think the Conservative Party is on the scale? (560-62)
   ASK WHICH BOX, REFER TO LETTER KEY AND ENTER CODE NO.
   IF DON'T KNOW, ENTER 098

b) Now the Labour Party: tick the box in the next row that comes closest to where you think it is. (563-65)   ENTER CODE NO.
   IF DON'T KNOW, ENTER 098

c) Now the Liberal Party and the Social Democrats separately. First the Liberal Party: tick the box in the next row that comes closest to where you think it is. (566-68)
   ENTER CODE NO.
   IF DON'T KNOW, ENTER 098

d) Now the Social Democratic Party: tick the box in the next row that comes closest to where you think it is. (569-71)
   ENTER CODE NO.
   IF DON'T KNOW, ENTER 098

IF SCOTLAND
e) Now tick the box in the next row that comes closest to where you think the Scottish National Party is. (572-74)
   ENTER CODE NO.
   IF DON'T KNOW, ENTER 098

IF WALES
f) Now tick the box in the next row that comes closest to where you think Plaid Cymru is. (575-77)   ENTER CODE NO.
   IF DON'T KNOW, ENTER 098

ASK ALL
g) Now tick the box in the last row that comes closest to where you are on the scale. (578-80)   ENTER CODE NO.
   ------------------------------ IF DON'T KNOW, ENTER 098 -----------
   UNLESS 098 AT g)   Card 06
h) Would you have been in the same box about four years ago - at the time of the last general election?
                          IF YES, ENTER 100
                          IF DK, ENTER 098   (607-09)
   IF NO: Which box were you in then? →   ENTER CODE NO.

UNLESS 098 AT a) ABOVE
i) Now looking at the top row, where you put the Conservative Party: would it have been in the same box when Mr Heath was its leader?   IF YES, ENTER 100
                          IF DK, ENTER 098   (610-12)
   IF NO: Which box was it in then? →   ENTER CODE NO.

UNLESS 098 AT b) ABOVE
j) Finally, looking at the second row, where you put the Labour Party: would it have been in the same box when Mr Callaghan was its leader?   IF YES, ENTER 100
                          IF DK, ENTER 098   (613-15)
   IF NO: Which box was it in then? →   ENTER CODE NO.

LETTER KEY	
B	= 001
C	= X08
D	= X01
E	= 005
F	= X04
G	= 009
H	= 008
J	= 010
K	= 002
L	= 006
M	= X07
N	= X05
P	= X10
Q	= 000
R	= X03
S	= X06
T	= 003
U	= 007
V	= X02
W	= X09
Y	= 004
LEFT OF P	= X97
RIGHT OF J	= 097

INTERVIEWER NOTES FROM PREVIOUS SCALE QUESTIONS APPLY AT THIS QUESTION TOO.

CP										Office Use									NF
X10	X09	X08	X07	X06	X05	X04	X03	X02	X01	000	001	002	003	004	005	006	007	008	009	010
P	W	C	M	S	N	F	R	V	D	Q	B	K	T	Y	E	L	U	H	G	J

V. BACKGROUND & CLASSIFICATION

<u>ASK ALL</u>

Now some questions about yourself and your background.

47.a) Do you remember which Party your <u>father</u> usually voted for when you were growing up? <u>ONE CODE IN COLUMN a)</u>

b) And your <u>mother</u>?
<u>ONE CODE IN COLUMN b)</u>   DO NOT PROMPT

	a) Father (616-17)	b) Mother (618-19)
Conservative	01	01
Labour	02	02
Liberal	04	04
Scottish National	06	06
Plaid Cymru	07	07
<u>Other</u> (SPECIFY) a)_____	97	-
b)_____	-	97
Varied	96	96
Not applicable/Not brought up in Britain	94	94
Refused to disclose voting	95	95
Did not vote	00	00
Can't remember/Don't know	98	98

48. Thinking back to when you were aged about 14,
what job did your father have then? <u>OBTAIN AS MUCH DETAIL AS POSSIBLE.</u>

<u>IF NO DETAILS CAN BE OBTAINED, GIVE REASON BELOW AND RING CODE</u>

No details of father's job 1 →Q.49   (620)

OFFICE USE

Reason:_____   (621-25)

a) What was the name or title of his job? _____   (626-27)

_____   (628-29)

b) What kind of work did he do in that job? IF RELEVANT: What were
the materials made of? _____   (630-31)

_____   (632-34)

_____   (635)

c) Did he have any training or qualifications that were needed
for that job? Which? _____   (636-38)

_____   (639-40)

_____   (641-42)

d) Did he supervise or was he responsible for the work of
any other people? <u>IF YES</u> About how many?   Yes (number)   (643-46)

No (ring) 0000

e) Was he ... (READ OUT)   ... an employee, 1   (647)

or self employed? 2

f) What did his employer (or, if self-employed,
he) make or do? _____   (648)

SPARE

g) Roughly how many people were employed at the
place where he worked: Was it ... (READ OUT)   ... fewer than 10, 1   (649)

10-24, 2

or 24+? 3

ASK ALL

49.a) <u>Do you</u> ever think of yourself as belonging to any particular class?   (650)
    <u>IF YES</u> Which class is that?

Yes, middle class	1	} Q.50
Yes, working class	2	

    Yes, other (SPECIFY IN FULL) _____ 3

No	4
Don't know	8

<u>IF OTHER, OR NO, OR DON'T KNOW (CODES 3, 4 OR 8)</u>
b) <u>Most</u> people say they belong either to the middle
   class or the working class. If you had to make a   (651)
   choice, would you call yourself ... <u>(READ OUT)</u>

... middle class	1
or working class?	2
(Refused)	0
(Don't know)	8

ASK ALL   (652)

50.a) Compared with British families in general, would you
   say your household's income is ..(READ OUT)

... far below average,	1
below average,	2
average,	3
above average,	4
or far above average?	5
(Don't know)	8

b) Looking back over the <u>last year</u> or so, would you   (653)
   say your household's <u>income has</u>...(READ OUT)

... fallen behind prices,	1
kept up with prices,	2
or gone up by more than prices?	3
(Don't know)	8

c) And looking forward to the <u>year ahead</u>, do you   (654)
   expect your household's <u>income will</u>...(READ OUT)

... fall behind prices,	1
keep up with prices,	2
or go up by more than prices?	3
(Don't know)	8

51.a) Do you, or does anyone in your household, own or   (655)
   have the use of a car or a van?

Yes - one	1
Yes - two or more	2
No	3

   IF YES: <u>PROBE</u>: One car/van or more than one?

b) Are you, or is anyone in your household, covered
   by a private health insurance scheme that allows   (656)
   you to get private medical treatment?
   IF YES: <u>PROBE</u>: Through a group (e.g. employer/
                 trade union) or as an individual?

Yes - through group	1
Yes - individually	2
No	3
Don't know	8

SHOW CARD L

52.a) Which of these descriptions applies to what you were doing last week,
that is in the seven days ending last Sunday? PROBE: Any others?
CODE ALL THAT APPLY IN COLUMN I

IF ONLY ONE CODE AT I, TRANSFER IT TO COLUMN II

IF MORE THAN ONE AT I, TRANSFER HIGHEST ON LIST TO II   I   II
(657-58)

		I	II
In full-time education (not paid for by employer, including on vacation)	A	01 → Q.54
On government training/employment scheme (e.g. Community Programme, YOP, WEEP, YTS, etc.)	B	02 → b)
In paid work (or away temporarily) for at least 10 hours in the week	C	03 ⎫ c)
Waiting to take up paid work already accepted	D	04 ⎭
Unemployed and registered at a Jobcentre/ employment office	E	05
Unemployed, not registered, but actively looking for a job	F	06
Unemployed, wanting a job (of at least 10 hrs per week), but not actively looking for a job	G	07
Permanently sick or disabled	H	08 b)
Wholly retired from work	J	09
Looking after the home	K	10
Doing something else	L	11

IF CODE 02, or 05 - 11

b) How long ago did you last have a paid job (other than
the government scheme you mentioned) of at least 10   (659)
hours a week, excluding Saturday or holiday jobs?

Within past 12 months	1 ⎫
Over 1-5 years ago	2 ⎪
Over 5-10 years ago	3 ⎬ c)
Over 10-20 years ago	4 ⎪
Over 20 years ago	5 ⎭
Never had paid job of 10+ hrs a week	6 → Q.54

IF CODE 03-04 AT a) OR CODE 1-5 AT b)   (660)

c) Are you now, or have you ever been, a member of a trade union?

Yes - now	1 ⎫
Yes - used to be	2 ⎬ Q.53
No	3 ⎭

ASK ALL WHO ARE IN WORK (CODE 03 AT Q.52a) OPPOSITE,
OR WHO ARE WAITING FOR A JOB (CODE 04 AT Q.52a) OPPOSITE,
OR WHO HAVE EVER HAD A JOB (CODES 1-5 AT Q.52b) OPPOSITE.

OFFICE USE	

(661-65)
(666-67)
(668-69)
(670-71)
(672-74)
(675)

53.   Now I want to ask you about your (present/future/last) job?
CHANGE TENSES FOR (BRACKETED) WORDS AS APPROPRIATE THROUGHOUT

a) What (is) the name or title of that job? _____

_____

b) What kind of work (do) you do most of the time? IF RELEVANT:
What (are) the materials made of? _____

_____

CARD 07

(707-09)
(710-11)
(712-13)
(714-17)

c) What training or qualifications (do) you have that (are) needed
for that job? _____

_____

d) (Do) you supervise or (are) you responsible for the work of any
other people? IF YES How many?

Yes (number)

No (ring) | 0000 |

(718)

e) (Are) you ... (READ OUT)

... an employee,   1

or self-employed?   2 → g)

IF EMPLOYEE (CODE 1)

f) (Is) the organisation you (work) for ... (READ OUT)   (719)

... a private firm,   1

a nationalised industry,   2

a local or central government organisation,   3

a charity,   4
or what?

(SPECIFY OTHER) _____   7

(ALL)

g) What (does) the employer (or, if self-employed, you) make or do
at the place where you usually (work)? IF FARM, GIVE NO. OF ACRES

_____

_____

_____

h) Including yourself, how many people (are) employed at the place   (720)
you usually (work) [from]?

Under 10   1

10-24   2

25-99   3

100-499   4

500 or more   5

i) (Is) the job ... (READ OUT)   (721)

... full-time, (30 hrs +)   1

or part-time? (10-29 hrs)   2

ASK ALL   (722)

54.a) At present are you ... (READ OUT) ... married (or living as married), 1 →b)

                                                          widowed, 2 ⎫
                                                                        ⎬
                                         divorced or separated, 3 ⎬ Q.56
                                                                        ⎬
                                               or single? 4 ⎭

IF MARRIED OR LIVING AS MARRIED (CODE 1) - SHOW CARD L AGAIN
b) Which of these descriptions applies to what your (husband/
    wife) was doing last week, that is in the seven days
    ending last Sunday? PROBE: Any others? CODE ALL THAT APPLY IN
                                    IN COLUMN I

    IF ONLY ONE CODE AT I, TRANSFER TO COLUMN II

    IF MORE THAN ONE AT I, TRANSFER HIGHEST ON LIST TO II   I   II
                                                                      (723-24)
                      In full-time education (not paid for by employer,
                                 including on vacation) A   01 →Q.56

              On government training/employment scheme (e.g. Community
                          Programme, YOP, WEEP, YTS, etc.) B   02 →c)

                           In paid work (or away temporarily)
                             for at least 10 hours in the week C   03 ⎫
                                                                        ⎬d)
                    Waiting to take up paid work already accepted D   04 ⎭

                          Unemployed and registered at a Jobcentre/
                                          employment office E   05 ⎫
                                                                        ⎬
        Unemployed, not registered, but actively looking for a job F   06 ⎬
                                                                        ⎬
        Unemployed, wanting a job (of at least 10 hrs per week),   ⎬
                       but not actively looking for a job G   07 ⎬
                                                                        ⎬c)
                           Permanently sick or disabled H   08 ⎬
                                                                        ⎬
                              Wholly retired from work J   09 ⎬
                                                                        ⎬
                              Looking after the home K   10 ⎬
                                                                        ⎬
                              Doing something else L   11 ⎭

IF CODE 02, OR 05 - 11

c) How long ago did your (husband/wife) have a paid job
    (other than the government scheme you mentioned) of   (725)
    at least 10 hours a week, excluding Saturday or
    holiday jobs?
                                   Within past 12 months   1 ⎫
                                      Over 1-5 years ago   2 ⎬
                                     Over 5-10 years ago   3 ⎬d)
                                    Over 10-20 years ago   4 ⎬
                                     Over 20 years ago   5 ⎭
                        Never had paid job of 10+ hrs a week   6 →Q.56

IF CODE 03-04 AT a) OR CODE 1-5 AT b)   (726)

d) Is your (husband/wife) now, or has (he/she)
    ever been, a member of a trade union?   Yes - now   1 ⎫
                                          Yes - used to be   2 ⎬
                                                      No   3 ⎬ Q.55
                                              Don't know   4 ⎭

ASK ALL WHOSE SPOUSE IS IN WORK (CODE 03 AT Q.54b) OPPOSITE,
OR WHOSE SPOUSE IS WAITING FOR A JOB (CODE 04 AT Q.54b) OPPOSITE.
OR WHOSE SPOUSE HAS EVER HAD A JOB (CODES 1-5 AT Q.54c) OPPOSITE.

55.   Now I want to ask you about your (husband's/wife's)

OFFICE USE

(727-31)
(732-33)
(734-35)

a)   What (is) the name or title of that job? _____   (736-37)

_____

b)   What kind of work (does)(he) do most of the most of the time?   (738-40)
      IF RELEVANT: What (are) the materials made of?   _____   (741)

_____

_____   (742-44)

c)   What training or qualifications (does) (he) have that (are)   (745-46)
      needed for that job? _____

_____   (747-48)

d)   (Does) (he) supervise or (is) (he) responsible for the work
      of any other people? IF YES How many?
                                        Yes (number) | | | | | (749-52)
                                         No (ring) | 0000 |
                                                        (753)
e)   (Is) (he) ... (READ OUT)
                                         ... an employee   1
                                      or self-employed?   2 →g)
      IF EMPLOYEE (CODE 1)   (754)
      f) (Is) the organisation (he) (works) for ... (READ OUT)
                                       ... a private firm,   1
                               a nationalised industry,   2
              a local or central government organisation,   3
                                           a charity,   4
                                           or what? ↓

      (SPECIFY OTHER) _____   7

      (ALL)
g)   What (does) the employer (or, if self-employed, (he) make
      or do at the place where (he) usually (works)?
      IF FARM, GIVE NO. OF ACRES _____

_____

_____   (755)

h)   Including (himself), roughly how many people (are) employed
      at the place where (he) usually (works) [from]?   Under 10   1
                                                    10-24   2
                                                    25-99   3
                                                   100-499   4
                                              500 or more   5
i)   (Is) the job (READ OUT) ...   (756)
                                      ... full-time, (30 hrs +)   1
                                      or part-time? (10-29 hrs)   2

<u>ASK ALL</u>

56. What was your age last birthday?

ENTER [ ] (757-58)

IF RESPONDENT IS MALE AGED 70+ OR FEMALE AGED 65+ }
OR IF RESPONDENT IS IN FULL-TIME EDUCATION (Q.52a) CODE 01) } <u>SKIP TO Q.58 BELOW</u>
FOR ALL OTHERS, ASK Q.57

57.a) May I check: during the last <u>five years</u>, that is since   (759)
the middle of 1978, have you been unemployed and looking
for a job- for a period lasting 13 weeks or longer?   Yes   A

<u>IF YES (Code A)</u>   No   0 → Q.58

   b) Was this just once, or for two or more separate
periods in the last five years?   Once   1
2 or more times   2

   c) For how many months in <u>total</u> during the last five
years have you been unemployed and looking for a job?

<u>ENTER</u>: Months [|] (760-61)
OR   Years   [   ]

<u>ASK ALL - SHOW CARD M</u>

58. Have you (or your husband/wife) been in receipt of
any of the benefits on this card during the last
five years?

   IF YES: Which ones?   Child benefit (family allowance)   1   (762)

   <u>CODE ALL THAT APPLY</u>   Maternity benefit or allowance   2   (763)
One-parent benefit   3   (764)
Family Income Supplement   4   (765)
State retirement or widow's pension   5   (766)
Supplementary pension   6   (767)
Invalidity or disabled pension or benefit   1   (768)
Attendance/Invalid care/Mobility allowance   2   (769)
Sickness or injury benefit   3   (770)
Unemployment benefit   4   (771)
Supplementary benefit   5   (772)
Rate or rent rebate or allowance   6   (773)
Other benefit(s) volunteered(SPECIFY) _____   7   (774)

_____

_____

NO, NONE   0   (775-78)
[| | |]

ASK ALL

59.a) How old were you when you left school (or 6th form college)?   (807-08)

ENTER AGE [ ]

UNLESS NO SCHOOLING CODE 00   Had no schooling at all   00 →Q.61

b) Where did you go to school, that is the last   (809)
school you attended, was it ... (READ OUT)   ... in the U.K.   1

or not?   2 →Q.61

ASK ALL WHOSE LAST SCHOOL WAS IN U.K.(CODE 1)

60.a) What kind of school was your last school: for instance,
was it an elementary school, grammar school, comprehensive,
or what?

PROBE FOR FULL DESCRIPTION.   IF UNSURE OF CODE, DESCRIBE AT OTHER   (810-11)

Primary/elementary	01	→c)
Secondary modern	02	
Technical	03	
Grammar	04	
Comprehensive	05	
Direct grant	06	
Grant or voluntary aided	07	
Independent fee-paying (e.g. private or 'public')	08	
Junior secondary/Higher elementary	09	
Senior secondary	10	
Convent/church school (PROBE FOR TYPE)+	11	

Special school   12 → c)

Other (GIVE DETAILS)+   97

UNLESS PRIMARY ONLY (CODE 01) OR SPECIAL SCHOOL (CODE 12)   (812)

b) Did you have to pass any kind of exam to
get into that school, or not?   Yes   1

No   2

Don't know/Don't remember   3

(ALL U.K.)

c) Did you go to any school where your parents or
guardian had to pay tuition fees?   (813)
IF YES: At primary level, secondary level, or both?

Yes - primary level   1

Yes - secondary level   2

Yes - both   3

No - neither   4

Don't know/Don't remember   8

ASK ALL

61.a) Have you had (or are you now in) any full-time
higher or further education at any kind of college,
university or polytechnic after leaving school or   (814)
later? IF YES PROBE: At a university or polytechnic,
or at another kind of college?   No, never   1

RING ONE CODE   Yes - in past - at university/polytechnic   2

                          Yes - in past - at other college   3

                    Yes - now - at university/polytechnic   4 ⎫
                                                               ⎬ Q.62
                        Yes - now - at other college   5 ⎬ Q.62
                                                               ⎪
                                    Still at school   6 ⎭

IF CODES 1, 2, OR 3

b) Have you ever sent - or are you considering   (815)
    sending - any children in your care to a
    fee-paying school?   Yes - in past   1

                                                      Yes - now   2

                                              Yes - considering   3

                                                            No   4

                                            Never had children   5

ASK ALL - SHOW CARD N   ⌷⌷⌷⌷⌷⌷ SPARE   (816-21)

62. Have you passed any exams or got any of the
    qualifications on this card? PROBE: Any others?   No, none   0   (822)

    BRITISH QUALIFICATIONS   CSE Grades 2-5   1   (823)

        CSE Grade 1, GCE 'O' level, Scottish (SCE) lower, School Certificate   2   (824)

                          GCE 'A' level, Scottish (SCE) higher   3   (825)

                                                        Degree   4   (826)

                RSA or similar clerical or commercial qualification   5   (827)

                          City & Guilds - craft/ordinary level   6   (828)

                          City & Guilds - advanced/final level   7   (829)

                           City & Guilds - full technological   8   (830)

                      ONC, OND, BEC or TEC ordinary/general   1   (831)

                        HNC, HND, BEC or TEC higher level   2   (832)

                          Full apprenticeship qualification   3   (833)

                            Teachers training qualification   4   (834)

                                   Nursing qualification   5   (835)

    Other professional qualification (SPECIFY) _____

                                                                6   (836)

    Other diploma/certificate (SPECIFY) _____

                                                                7   (837)

    OVERSEAS EXAMS/QUALIFICATIONS   Any school leaving exam/certificate   1   (838)

                                                        Degree   2   (839)

    Other (post-school) exam/qualification (SPECIFY) _____   3   (840)

ASK ALL

63.a) Do you regard yourself as belonging to any particular religion?   (841-42)

IF YES: Which one?

PROBE FOR DENOMINATION

	No religion	00	→Q.64
Christian:	No denomination	01	
	Roman Catholic	02	
	Church of England/Wales, Anglican, Episcopal	03	
	Church of Scotland	04	
	Methodist	05	
	Baptist	06	
	United Reform Church (UCR), Congregational	07	
Other Christian (SPECIFY) _____		08	
Non-Christian:	Jew	12	
	Hindu	13	
	Islam/Moslem	14	
	Sikh	15	
	Buddhist	16	
Other Non-Christian (SPECIFY) _____		97	

IF RELIGION CODED (01-97)

b) Apart from special occasions, such as weddings,
    funerals, baptisms and so on, how often nowadays   (843)
    do you attend services or meetings connected with
    your religion?

Once a week or more	1
Several times a month	2
Less often but at least once a month	3
Several times a year	4
At least once a year	5
Less often than once a year	6
Varies/Don't know	7
Never/practically never	0

ALL RESPONDENTS

64. CODE FROM OBSERVATION   (844)

i) Ethnic origin:	White/European	1
	Indian/E. African Asian/Pakistani/Bangladeshi/Sri Lankan	2
	Black/African/West Indian	3
	Other (including Chinese)	4
		(845)
ii) Sex:	Male	1
	Female	2

ALL   (846-47)

65.a) <u>CODE WHETHER ACCOMMODATION IS</u> ...   Private household,   A →b)

or Institution (SPECIFY TYPE) _____   01 →Q.66

IF PRIVATE HOUSEHOLD (CODE A)

b) Do you - your household - own or rent this
    (house/flat/accommodation)?   OWNS   House   02 ⎱
                                          or   ⎬ c)
    <u>INCLUDE MORTGAGES AS OWNERSHIP</u>   CO-OWNS   Flat/maisonette 03 ⎰

    IF RENTED: From whom?   <u>RENTS FROM</u>   Local Authority - house   04 ⎱
                                   Local Authority - flat/maisonette 05 ⎰ e)

                                            Housing Association   06 ⎱
                                      Private company/landlord   07 ⎬ f)
              OTHER (SPECIFY) _____   97 ⎰

<u>IF OWNS (CODE 02 OR 03 AT b))</u>   (848)

c) Have you ever been a local authority tenant?   Yes   1

<u>IF YES (CODE 1)</u>   No   2 → f)

d) Were you a local authority tenant in this
    (house/flat/accommodation) before your household   (849)
    purchased it?   Yes   1 ⎱
                                                                    ⎬ f)
                                                         No   2 ⎰

<u>IF RENTS FROM LOCAL AUTHORITY (CODE 04 OR 05 AT b))</u>

e) How likely is it that your household will try to   (850)
    buy this house/flat from the local council in the
    next 5 years or so; would you say ... (READ OUT) ... very likely,   1

                                           quite likely,   2

                                            not likely,   3

                                      or definitely not?   4

                        (Negotiations already started)   5

                                        (Don't know)   8

<u>ALL (IN PRIVATE HOUSEHOLDS)</u>

f) Including yourself, how many people live here
    with you as members of your household?
                                        ENTER NO. [   ]   (851-52)

g) And how many of these are aged 15 or under? ENTER NO. [ ]   (853)

h) In whose name is this (house/flat/accommodation)
    owned or rented?   (854)
                            Respondent and/or spouse only   1

                            Parent or parent-in-law   2

            Other (SPECIFY IN FULL) _____   7

                    _____

(856-57)

ASK ALL

66.a) Are you a member of a political Party?   No   00

    IF YES: <u>PROBE</u> Which one? <u>DO NOT PROMPT</u>   Yes - Conservative   01 → Q.67

    <u>INCLUDE PEOPLE WHO HAVE TEMPORARILY</u>   - Labour   02 → b)

    <u>NOT PAID SUBS BUT INTEND TO.</u>   - Liberal   04

        - Social Democratic   05

        - Scottish National   06 } Q.67

        - Plaid Cymru   07

        Other (SPECIFY) _____   97

IF 'LABOUR' (CODE 02)

(858)

  b) Are you a member of the Labour Party through a trade
    union or did you join as an individual member?   Individual   1
        IF 'BOTH', RING CODE 1 ONLY   Through TU   2

67.a) Just in case we need to clarify anything you've told   (859)
    us, I'd like to know whether there is a telephone in
    (your part of) this accommodation?   Yes   1 → c)

    IF NO AT a) (CODE A)   No   A

  b) Do you have easy access to a 'phone in this
    building, where you can receive incoming calls?
    <u>DO NOT ASK ABOUT WORK ACCESS</u>   Yes - in building   2

    Yes - at work (<u>VOLUNTEERED</u>)   3

    No   4 → Q.68

    IF YES AT a) OR b) (CODES 1, 2 OR 3)

  c) What is your telephone number? <u>ADD IF NECESSARY:</u>
    I should say it is very unlikely that anyone will   (860)
    'phone you. <u>DO NOT RECORD NUMBER HERE BUT ON</u>
    <u>ARF ADDRESS SLIP ONLY.</u>   Number given   1

    Number refused   2

ASK ALL

68. When the next general election comes round - which is
    likely to be in 4 or 5 years time - there may be   (861)
    another survey like this one. Would you be willing
    to take part in it again?   Yes, willing   1

    No, not willing   2

(862-64)

TIME INTERVIEW COMPLETED [ ][ ] [ ][ ]   DURATION (Minutes) [ ][ ]

(865-66)   (867-68)

DATE OF INTERVIEW ———————————→ DAY [ ][ ]   MONTH [ ][ ]

SIGNATURE _____   INTERVIEWER NUMBER [ ][ ][ ][ ]

SOCIAL AND COMMUNITY PLANNING RESEARCH
and
THE UNIVERSITY OF OXFORD

BRITISH GENERAL ELECTION STUDY 1983

SCALE CARDS I – 6

Serial Number

P.765, July 1983

Get rid of all nuclear weapons in Britain without delay

Tick the box you think comes closest to **your own** views

P W C M S N F R V D Q B K T Y E L U H G J

Increase nuclear weapons in Britain without delay

Get rid of all nuclear weapons in Britain without delay

Tick the box you think comes closest to the **Conservative Party's** views

P W C M S N F R V D Q B K T Y E L U H G J

Increase nuclear weapons in Britain without delay

Get rid of all nuclear weapons in Britain without delay

Tick the box you think comes closest to the **Labour Party's** views

P W C M S N F R V D Q B K T Y E L U H G J

Increase nuclear weapons in Britain without delay

Get rid of all nuclear weapons in Britain without delay

Tick the box you think comes closest to the **SDP/Liberal Alliance's** views

P W C M S N F R V D Q B K T Y E L U H G J

Increase nuclear weapons in Britain without delay

Scale 1

Tick the box you think comes closest to **your own** views

Getting people back to work should be the Government's top priority

Keeping prices down should be the Government's top priority

P W C M S N F R V D Q B K T Y E L U H G J

Tick the box you think comes closest to the **Conservative Party's** views

Getting people back to work should be the Government's top priority

Keeping prices down should be the Government's top priority

P W C M S N F R V D Q B K T Y E L U H G J

Tick the box you think comes closest to the **Labour Party's** views

Getting people back to work should be the Government's top priority

Keeping prices down should be the Government's top priority

P W C M S N F R V D Q B K T Y E L U H G J

Tick the box you think comes closest to the **SDP/Liberal Alliance's** views

Getting people back to work should be the Government's top priority

Keeping prices down should be the Government's top priority

P W C M S N F R V D Q B K T Y E L U H G J

Scale 2

Cut taxes a lot and spend much less on health & social services

Tick the box you think comes closest to **your own** views

P W C M S N F R V D Q B K T Y E L U H G J

Put up taxes a lot and spend much more on health & social services

Cut taxes a lot and spend much less on health & social services

Tick the box you think comes closest to the **Conservative Party's** views

P W C M S N F R V D Q B K T Y E L U H G J

Put up taxes a lot and spend much more on health & social services

Cut taxes a lot and spend much less on health & social services

Tick the box you think comes closest to the **Labour Party's** views

P W C M S N F R V D Q B K T Y E L U H G J

Put up taxes a lot and spend much more on health & social services

Cut taxes a lot and spend much less on health & social services

Tick the box you think comes closest to the **SDP/Liberal Alliance's** views

P W C M S N F R V D Q B K T Y E L U H G J

Put up taxes a lot and spend much more on health & social services

Scale 3

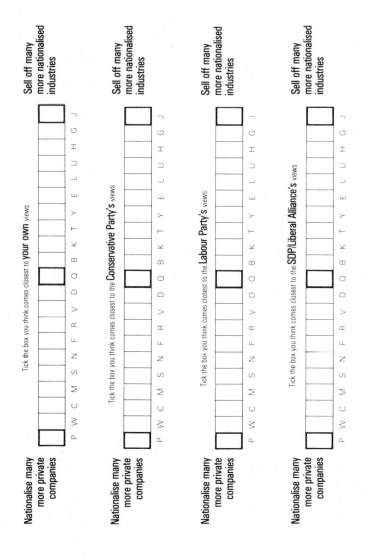

Nationalise many more private companies — Tick the box you think comes closest to **your own** views — Sell off many more nationalised industries

P W C M S N F R V D Q B K T Y E L U H G J

Nationalise many more private companies — Tick the box you think comes closest to the **Conservative Party's** views — Sell off many more nationalised industries

P W C M S N F R V D Q B K T Y E L U H G J

Nationalise many more private companies — Tick the box you think comes closest to the **Labour Party's** views — Sell off many more nationalised industries

P W C M S N F R V D Q B K T Y E L U H G J

Nationalise many more private conpanies — Tick the box you think comes closest to the **SDP/Liberal Alliance's** views — Sell off many more nationalised industries

P W C M S N F R V D Q B K T Y E L U H G J

Scale 4

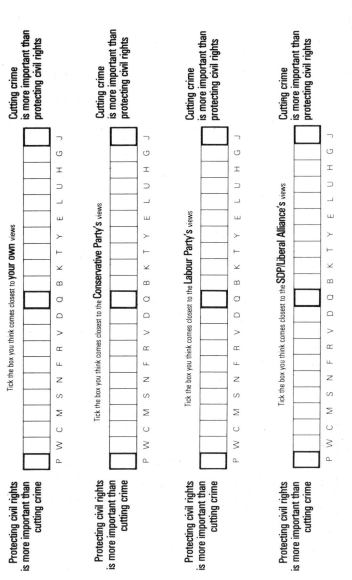

Scale 5

Scale 6

British Communist Party — Tick the box you think comes closest to where the **Conservative Party** is — **The National Front**

P W C M S N F R V D Q B K T Y E L U H G J

British Communist Party — Tick the box you think comes closest to where the **Labour Party** is — **The National Front**

P W C M S N F R V D Q B K T Y E L U H G J

British Communist Party — Tick the box you think comes closest to where the **Liberal Party** is — **The National Front**

P W C M S N F R V D Q B K T Y E L U H G J

British Communist Party — Tick the box you think comes closest to where the **Social Democratic Party** is — **The National Front**

P W C M S N F R V D Q B K T Y E L U H G J

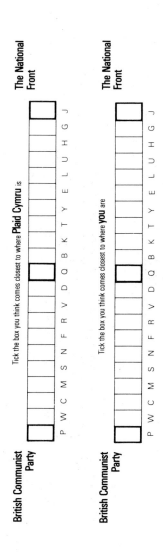

British Communist Party

Tick the box you think comes closest to where **Plaid Cymru** is

P W C M S N F R V D Q B K T Y E L U H G J

The National Front

British Communist Party

Tick the box you think comes closest to where **you** are

P W C M S N F R V D Q B K T Y E L U H G J

The National Front

Appendix II

The British Election Surveys 1963-1983

The British Election Surveys constitute the longest academic series of nationally representative probability sample surveys in this country.[1] They have taken place immediately after every general election since 1964, giving a total of seven so far. There have also been two nonelection year surveys, in 1963 and 1969, a postal referendum study in 1975, additional Scottish studies in 1974 and 1979, and an additional Welsh study in 1979.[2]

The series was originated by David Butler (Nuffield College, Oxford) and Donald Stokes (University of Michigan), who continued to direct the studies until 1970. The series then passed on to Ivor Crewe, Bo Sarlvik and James Alt at the University of Essex (later joined by David Robertson) who organised the two 1974 surveys and the 1979 one. The 1983 study has been directed by Anthony Heath (Jesus College, Oxford), Roger Jowell (Social and Community Planning Research), Julia Field (Social and Community Planning Research) and John Curtice (University of Liverpool).

Nuffield College found the bulk of the funds for the initial fieldwork of the Butler and Stokes' surveys. The Economic and Social Research Council (previously the Social Science Research Council) then became the major funding agency, wholly supporting the Essex surveys. The Heath, Jowell and Curtice study has been jointly funded by the Economic and Social Research Council, Pergamon Press and Jesus College, Oxford.

Broadly speaking, the aim of the Election Studies series has been to explore the changing determinants of electoral behaviour in contemporary Britain. Initially it was modelled on the work of the Michigan school of political science in the USA (of which Donald Stokes was a member) and shared the Michigan interest in socialisation and partisan identification as major and stable influences on electoral behaviour. Since then, other interests have come to the fore reflecting developments in academic political science (such as the rise of the 'consumer' theory of political choice) and changes in the political context.

Despite the different interests of the three research groups, there has been substantial continuity and a common core of questions has been asked in each of the surveys. Thus there have almost always been questions, first, on electoral behaviour itself (turnout, party choice, and timing of the vote decision); second, on political perceptions and identification (perceived difference between the parties, political interest and party identification); third, on social and political attitudes (towards trade unions and big business, the death penalty, nationalisation, taxes and social services spending); fourth, on subjective social class and political antecedents; and fifth on objective biographical data (education, housing tenure, trade union membership, occupation, religion, age, sex and marital status). There is broad agreement from the political science community that this common core of questions is an essential component of the past series of Election Studies and of any future ones.

Taken in conjunction with the sets of questions unique to each of the individual surveys (most notably those concerning topical political issues), this common core makes the Election Studies a particularly rich series of data sets, valuable both for cross-sectional and time-series analyses. It is particularly outstanding for the details of the occupational information. This usually covers the respondent's spouse and father, as well as the respondent him/herself, and is coded both into the market research social grade scheme[3] and the Office of Population Censuses and Surveys system of occupational groups (from which can be derived social class, socio-economic group and other classifications). The Election Studies are unique in having such detailed data going back in a continuous series to 1963.

The sample sizes of the cross-section Election Surveys have varied from just over 1000 to nearly 4000. They have been designed to yield representative cross-sections of the electorate in England, Wales and Scotland (south of the Caledonian canal). Northern Ireland has always been excluded. Many of the surveys have also included a substantial panel element composed of respondents who had been interviewed in one or more previous surveys.

The series began in 1963 with a stratified random sample of 2009 respondents drawn from the current electoral registers of 80 constituencies in Britain.[4] In 1964 such respondents as could be traced and contacted from the 1963 list were reinterviewed yielding 1481 completed panel interviews. Ageing, death and migration necessarily made these surviving panel members unrepresentative of the electorate, so new names were also drawn from the new registers in the same 80 constituencies. When appropriately weighted, these two elements give a representative cross-section of the electorate in 1964. (Note, however, that panel members who had moved from their original addresses were excluded from the cross-section, producing a sample size smaller than the total number of interviews conducted.)

This pattern, with variations, was followed up to and including 1979. Diagram II.1A and table II.2A describe the structure of the panels and cross-sections in detail.[5] Table II.3A gives the response rates. It will be seen that the 1983 sample consists of a cross-section only. It had been planned to conduct a postal panel survey in addition to, rather than as a component of, the 1983 electorate sample. Timing and lack of finance, however, ruled this option out.

Although a panel structure has advantages, and its inclusion as a component of the cross-section reduces the cost, there are also drawbacks. There is a high rate of attrition of panel members. For example, of the original 2009 respondents interviewed in 1963, only 36 per cent remained in 1970; and of the 2462 new respondents drawn in February 1974, only 31 per cent remained in 1979. Furthermore, this attrition does not seem to be a consequence solely of death and migration. It can be seen from table II.3A that response rates (after eliminating names 'out of scope' due to death or migration) were lower in surveys with a panel component than in the pure cross-section samples. In general, surveys with a large panel component (for example, 1964, 1970 and 1979) have response rates around 10 per cent lower than in pure cross-sections interviewed around the same time (for example, 1963, 1969 and 1983). This suggests of course that response in the panel element itself is lower still.

DIAGRAM II.1A Election Study Interviews

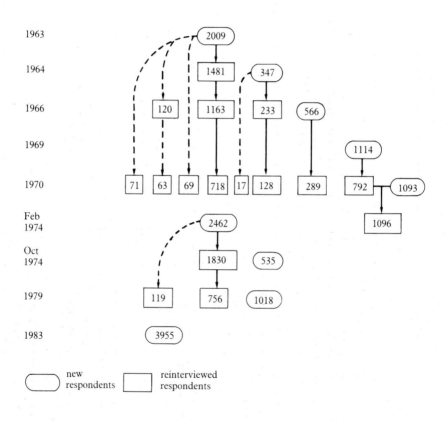

TABLE II.2A Sample Size

		Electorate sample
1963	Electorate: new respondents 2009	2009
1964	Electorate: new respondents 347; from 1963 electorate 1422	1769
	1963–64 panel 1481 (59 no longer at sample address and therefore not included in 1964 electorate sample)	
1966	Electorate: new respondents 566; from 1963 and 1964 electorates 1308	1874
	1963–64–66 panel 1163 (165 no longer at sample address; part of panel but not 1966 electorate sample)	
	1963–66 panel 1283 (166 no longer at sample address; part of panel but not 1966 electorate sample)	
	1964–66 panel 1360 (192 no longer at sample address; part of panel but not 1966 electorate sample)	
1969	Electorate: new respondents 1114	1114
1970	Electorate: new respondents 1093; from 1969 electorate 750	1843
	1963–64–66–70 panel 718	
	1963–64–70 panel 787	
	1963–66–70 panel 781	
	1963–70 panel 921 not included in 1970 electorate sample	
	1964–66–70 panel 831	
	1964–70 panel 915	
	1966–70 panel 1107	
	1969–70 panel 792 (42 no longer at sample address and therefore not included in 1970 electorate sample)	
Feb 1974	Electorate: new respondents 2462	2462
	1969–70–Feb 1974 panel 1096 (not included in Feb 1974 electorate sample)	
Oct 1974	Electorate: new respondents 535; from Feb 1974 electorate 1830	2365
1979	Electorate: new respondents 1018; from Feb 1974 electorate 875	1893
	Feb 1974–79 panel 866	
	Oct 1974–79 panel 765	
	Feb 1974–Oct 1974–79 panel 756	
1983	Electorate: new respondents 3955	3955

TABLE II.3A Response Rates in Cross-Section Surveys 1963–1983

	1963	1964	1966	1969	1970	Feb 1974	Oct 1974	1979	1983
Percentage response rate	79.4	68.3	69.9	78.2	69.7	75.8	73.7	60.9	72.4

Notes

[1] Social and Community Planning Research's Social Attitudes Study which began in 1983 will become a second series of representative probability sample surveys. For details see Jowell and Airey (1984).

[2] On the Scottish study see Miller (1981), on the Welsh study see Balsom et al (1983), and see Economic and Social Research Council *Data Archive Bulletin*, No 21, p4.

[3] There are in fact some differences between the market research scheme and that used in the Election Studies. Strictly speaking, the market research scheme is coded by interviewers and some of the criteria employed relate to the household rather than the individual. See Monk (1978).

[4] The names drawn from the electoral register were used to obtain a sample of households rather than individuals. The aim was to secure a sampling frame closer to the register on which the 1964 election would be fought rather than the already out of date 1963 register.

[5] Sources for diagram II.1A and tables II.2A and II.3A are as follows: for the 1963-1970 surveys they are *Study of Political Change in Britain 1963-1970*, Volume I: Introduction and Codebook, Volume II: Questionnaire and Notes; *Political Change in Britain 1969-1970:* codebooks and questionnaire; and Butler and Stokes (1974). (The codebooks and questionnaries were made available by the Inter-University Consortium for Political and Social Research, Ann Arbor, Michigan.) For the 1974-1979 surveys they are *British Election Study at the University of Essex Technical Paper 1980: 1* and the codebooks for the British Election Study 1969-February 1974 Panel Sample, the February 1974 Cross-section, and the October 1974 Cross-section. (These codebooks were made available by the Economic and Social Research Council Data Archive at the University of Essex.)

Figures for the 1970 electorate sample and 1969-1970 panel sample are taken from the relevant codebook. Butler and Stokes (1974), Appendix A, provides slightly different figures. The 1969-February 1974 panel sample figure is taken from section 1 of Crewe, Sarlvik and Alt codebook for the British Election Study 1969-1970-February 1974 Panel Sample. A sample size of 1113 will be found in Table 1 of the codebook. Figures for the October 1974 cross-section sample are taken from the codebook for the British Election Study October 1974 Cross-section Sample. A sample size of 2376 will be found from Tables 2 and 3 of the codebook.

Appendix III[1]

Sampling Errors

No sample reflects precisely the characteristics of the population it represents because of both sampling and non-sampling errors. As far as *sampling error* is concerned, if a sample were designed as a *simple random sample* — ie if each elector had an equal and independent chance of inclusion in the sample – then we could calculate the sampling error of any percentage, p, using the formula

$$\text{s.e. } (p) = \sqrt{\frac{p(100-p)}{n}}$$

here n is the number of electors on which the percentage is based. Once the sampling error has been obtained, it would be a straightforward exercise to calculate a confidence interval for the true population percentage. For example a 95 per cent confidence interval would be given by the formula

$$p \pm 1.96 \times \text{s.e. } (p)$$

This means that the probability that the true percentage in the population lies in this interval is 0.95. Clearly, for a simple random sample (srs), the sampling error depends only on the values of p and n. However, simple random sampling is almost never used in practice because of its inefficiency in terms of time and cost.

As noted in Appendix I, the 1983 British General Election sample, like most large scale surveys, was selected according to a stratified multistage design. With a complex design like this, the sampling error of a percentage is not simply a function of the number of electors in the sample and the size of the percentage, but also depends on how the characteristic is spread within and between polling districts. The complex design may be assessed relative to simple random sampling by calculating some of the *design factors*, DEFTS, associated with it where

$$\text{DEFT} = \sqrt{\frac{\text{Variance of estimator with complex design, sample size n}}{\text{Variance of estimator with srs design, sample size n}}}$$

and represents the multiplying factor to be applied to the simple random sampling error to produce its complex equivalent. A design factor of 1 means that the complex sample has achieved the same precision as a simple random sample of the same size. A design factor greater than one means the complex sample is less precise than its simple random sample equivalent. If the DEFT for a particular characteristic is known, a 95 per cent confidence interval for a percentage may be calculated using the formula

$$p \pm 1.96 \times \text{complex sampling error (p)}$$

$$= p \pm 1.96 \times \text{DEFT} \times \sqrt{\frac{p(100-p)}{n}}$$

In order to assess the impact of clustering the British General Election Study sample in 250 polling districts, sampling error computations were carried out for a range of variables which were expected to exhibit very different degrees of clustering: these included some classification variables, some behavioural variables and some attitudinal variables. The computations were carried out for the sample as a whole and also for the sample broken down into various subgroups defined by age, sex, region, social class and party identification.

Findings

The design factors calculated range from 0.79 – 2.35. The vast majority lie in the interval 1.0 – 1.5. There are a handful below one and a few above 1.5. Table III.1A contains a subset of the findings.

The *classification* variables have DEFTs in the range 1.0 – 1.4 with one important exception: housing tenure. The high values of 2.14, 2.35 and 1.61 recorded for, respectively, owner occupiers, Local Authority tenants and private tenants are consistent with previous findings for the variable tenure which is known to be strongly related to area. The design factors for behavioural variables lie in the range 1.3 – 1.6. The attitudinal characteristics exhibit consistently low design factors in the range 1.0 – 1.2. For values of DEFT less than 1, the safest assumption is to take DEFT = 1. This is because the calculation of the numerator in formula 3 is itself an estimate and therefore subject to a variance. The most likely (although not the only) explanation of a design factor smaller than 1 is that the estimate of variance is inaccurate.

We have taken note of these DEFTS in reporting our findings. In the case of attitudinal characteristics, the fact that the DEFTS are close to 1.0 means that the

TABLE III.1A Design Factors in the British General Election Study 1983

Characteristic	Category	% (p)	Base	Complex s.e. of p	DEFT
Ocupational status	In full-time education	1.6	3951	0.2	1.17
	In paid work	56.2		0.9	1.17
	Unemployed	6.1		0.4	1.14
	Permanently sick	2.1		0.2	1.06
	Wholly retired	15.2		0.7	1.16
	Looking after home	18.1		0.7	1.12
Housing tenure	Lives in institution	0.5	3952	0.1	1.13
	Owns/co-owns house/flat	65.4		1.6	2.14
	Rents house/flat from local authority	25.6		1.6	2.35
	Rents privately	8.2		0.7	1.61
Socio-economic Group[2]	1	15.5	3785	0.6	1.08
	2	10.8		0.7	1.30
	3	27.5		0.7	0.95
	4	6.5		0.5	1.22
	5	6.0		0.4	0.96
	6	12.5		0.6	1.21
	7	19.3		0.9	1.33
Party voted for in 1983	Conservative	43.9	3295	1.2	1.38
	Labour	27.9		1.3	1.60
	SDP/Liberal Alliance	24.1		0.9	1.17
	Other	1.3		0.3	1.39
	Refused/don't know	2.8		0.3	1.14
Party identification	Conservative	36.1	3953	1.1	1.46
	Labour	30.7		1.2	1.59
	SDP/Liberal Alliance	16.8		0.6	1.05
	Other	2.0		0.2	1.00
	Refused/don't know	13.7		0.6	1.16
Police should be given more power	Should	45.6	3933	0.9	1.14
	Should not	45.8		0.9	1.11
	Doesn't matter	8.6		0.5	1.11
Views on nationalisation	A lot more industries should be nationalised	6.1	3937	0.4	1.16
	A few more industries should be nationalised	9.4		0.5	1.05
	No more industries should be nationalised	34.9		0.8	1.06
	Some industries now nationalised should become private companies	38.1		0.9	1.21
	Can't choose/don't know	11.5		—	—

use of standard statistical tests of significance (based on the assumption of simple random sampling) is unlikely to be seriously misleading. In the case of the classification variables, by contrast, more care needs to be taken in the interpretation of test statistics and estimated parameter values.

Notes

[1] We are grateful to Denise Lievesley and Jennifer Waterton for their help with this appendix.

[2] This is a collapsed version of the Office of Population Censuses and Surveys' socio-economic group classification (1970). The SEGs have been collapsed as follows:

SEG 1.1, 1.2, 3, 4 = 1
SEG 2.2, 5 = 2
SEG 6, 7 = 3
SEG 2.1, 12, 13, 14 = 4
SEG 8 = 5
SEG 9, 16 = 6
SEG 10, 11, 15 = 7.

This collapsed version gives a reasonable approximation to Goldthorpe's seven-fold class scheme described in chapter 2, footnote 7. All tables in the text use Goldthorpe's actual scheme, but the details of this were not available at the time when the Design Factors were calculated; hence our use of the socio-economic group approximation in this appendix.

Bibliography

Abrams, M, Rose, R, and Hinden, R, (1960) *Must Labour Lose?*, Harmondsworth, Middx: Penguin

Alford, R R, (1963) *Party and Society: Anglo-American Democracies*, Chicago: Rand McNally

Alt, J, (1979) *The Politics of Economic Decline: Economic Management and Political Behaviour in Britain since 1964*, Cambridge: Cambridge University Press

Alt, J, (1984) Dealignment and the Dynamics of Partisanship in Britain, P Dalton, S Flanagan and P Beck, (eds), *Electoral Change in Advanced Industrial Democracies*, Princeton, N J: Princeton University Press

Alt, J, Crewe, I, and Sarlvik, B, (1977) Angels in Plastic: the Liberal Surge in 1974, *Political Studies*, **25**, 343-68

Alt, J, Sarlvik, B, and Crewe, I, (1976) Partisanship and Policy Choice: Issue Preferences in the British Electorate, February 1974, *British Journal of Political Science*, **6**, 273-90

Alt, J, and Turner, J, (1982) The Case of the Silk-stocking Socialists and the Calculating Children of the Middle Class, *British Journal of Political Science*, **12**, 239-48

Balsom, D, Madgwick, P J, and Van Mechelen, D, (1983) The Red and the Green: Patterns of Partisan Choice in Wales, *British Journal of Political Science*, **13**, 299-325

Barry, B, (1970) *Sociologists, Economists and Democracy*, London: Collier Macmillan

Bealey, F, Blondel, J, and McCann, W P, (1965) *Constituency Politics*, London: Faber and Faber

Bell, D, (1960) *The End of Ideology*, Illinois: The Free Press of Glencoe

Benney, M, Gray, A P, and Pear, R H, (1956) *How People Vote*, London: Routledge and Kegan Paul

Bishop, Y M M, Fienberg, S E, and Holland, P W, (1975) *Discrete Multivariate Analysis*, Cambridge, Mass: MIT Press

Bodman, A R, (1983) The Neighbourhood Effect: a Test of the Butler-Stokes Model, *British Journal of Political Science*, **13**, 243-249

Bonham, J, (1954) *The Middle Class Vote*, London: Faber and Faber

Bradley, I, (1981) *Breaking the Mould?*, Oxford: Martin Robertson

Braverman, H, (1974) *Labour and Monopoly Capital*, New York: Monthly Review Press

Britten, N, and Heath, A F, (1983) Women, Men and Social Class, *Gender, Class and Work*, E Gamarnikow, D Morgan, J Purvis and D Taylorson, (eds), London: Heinemann

Butler, D, and Kavanagh, D, (1984) *The British General Election of 1983*, London: Macmillan

Butler, D, and Rose, R, (1960) *The British General Election of 1959*, London: Macmillan

Butler, D, and Stokes, D, (1974) *Political Change in Britain*, second edition, London: Macmillan

Butt Phillip, A, (1983) The Liberals and Europe, *Liberal Party Politics*, V Bogdanor, (ed), London: Oxford University Press

Campbell, A, Converse, P E, Miller, W E, and Stokes, D E, (1964) *The American Voter*, New York: John Wiley

Carchedi, G, (1977) *On the Economic Identification of Social Classes*, London: Routledge and Kegan Paul

Castells, M, (1977) *The Urban Question*, London: Arnold

Castells, M, (1978) *City, Class and Power*, London: Macmillan

Central Statistical Office, (1971) *Annual Abstract of Statistics*, **108**, London: HMSO

Central Statistical Office, (1976) *Regional Statistics*, **XII**, London: HMSO

Central Statistical Office, (1982) *Annual Abstract of Statistics 1982 Edition 118*, London: HMSO

Central Statistical Office, (1983) *Regional Trends: 1983 edition*, London: HMSO

Central Statistical Office, (1984) *Social Trends: 1984 edition*, London: HMSO

Central Statistical Office, (1985) *Annual Abstract of Statistics 1985 Edition 121*, London: HMSO

Charlot, M, (1975) The Ideological Distance between the Two Major Parties in Britain, *European Journal of Political Research*, **3**, 173-180

Craig, F W S, (1980) *Britain Votes 2: British Parliamentary Election Results 1974-1979*, Chichester: Parliamentary Research Services

Craig, F W S, (1981) *British Electoral Facts 1832-1980*, Chichester: Parliamentary Research Services

Craig, F W S, (1984) *Britain Votes 3: British Parlimentary Election Results 1983*, Chichester: Parliamentary Research Services

Crewe, I, (1973) The Politics of "Affluent" and "Traditional" Workers in Britain, *British Journal of Political Science*, **3**, 29-52

Crewe, I, (1974) Do Butler and Stokes Really Explain Political Change in Britain?, *European Journal of Political Research*, **2**, 47-92

Crewe. I, (1981) Why the Conservatives Won, *Britain at the Polls*, H R Penniman, (ed) Washington DC: American Enterprise Institute

Crewe, I, (1982a) The Labour Party and the Electorate, *The Politics of the Labour Party*, D Kavanagh, (ed), London: George Allen and Unwin

Crewe, I, (1982b) Is Britain's Two-Party System Really About to Crumble? The Social-Democratic-Liberal Alliance and the Proposals for Realignment, *Electoral Studies*, 1, No 3, 275-313

Crewe, I, (1983a) How Labour was trounced all round, *The Guardian*, 14 June

Crewe, I, (1983b) Reply, *Electoral Studies*, 2, 85

Crewe, I, (1984) The Electorate: Partisan Dealignment Ten Years On, *Change in British Politics*, H Berrington, (ed), London: Frank Cross

Crewe, I, (forthcoming) How to Win a Landslide Without Really Trying: Why the Conservatives Won in 1983, *Britain at the Polls 1983*, A Ranney, (ed), Durham, North Carolina: Duke University Press

Crewe, I, and Payne, C, (1976), Another Game with Nature, an Ecological Regression Model of the British Two-party Vote Ratio in 1970, *British Journal of Political Science*, 6, 43-81

Crewe, I, Sarlvik, B, and Alt, J, (1977) Partisan Dealignment in Britain 1964-1974, *British Journal of Political Science*, 7, 129-90

Crewe, I, Alt, J, and Fox, A, (1977) Non-voting in British General Elections 1966-October 1974, *British Political Sociology Yearbook Vol III (Political Participation)*, C Crouch, (ed), London: Croom Helm

Criddle, B, (1984) Candidates, *The British General Election of 1983*, D Butler and D Kavanagh, London: Macmillan

Curtice, J K, (1983) Liberal Voters and the Alliance: Realignment or Protest?, *Liberal Party Politics*, Bogdanor, V, (ed), Oxford: Clarendon Press

Curtice, J K, and Steed, M, (1982) Electoral Choice and the Production of Government: The Changing Operation of the Electoral System in the United Kingdom since 1955, *British Journal of Political Science*, 12, 249-98

Curtice, J K, and Steed, M, (1984a) Appendix 2: an Analysis of the Voting, *The British General Election of 1983*, D Butler and D Kavanagh, London: Macmillan

Curtice, J K, and Steed, M, (1984b) The End of the Cube Law (Paper presented at the Annual Session of the European Consortium for Political Research, University of Salzburg, 1984)

Daniel, W W, and Millward, N, (1983) *Workplace Industrial Relations in Britain*, London: Heinemann

Downs, A, (1957) *An Economic Theory of Democracy*, New York: Harper and Row

Dunleavy, P, (1979) The Urban Basis of Political Alignment: Social Class, Domestic Property Ownership, and State Intervention in Consumption Processes, *British Journal of Political Science*, 9, 409-43

Dunleavy, P, (1980) The Political Implications of Sectoral Cleavages and the Growth of State Employment, *Political Studies*, 28, 364-383 and 527-549

Dunleavy, P, (1982) How to Decide that Voters Decide, *Politics*, 2, 24-29

Ellis, A, and Heath, A F, (1983) Positional Competition, or an Offer You Can't Refuse?, *Dilemmas of Liberal Democracies. Studies in Fred Hirsch's 'Social Limits to Growth'*, A Ellis and K Kumar, (eds), London: Tavistock

Erikson, R, (1984) Social Class of Men, Women and Families, *Sociology*, 18, 500-514

Ferejohn, J A, and Fiorina, M P, (1974) The Paradox of Not Voting, *American Political Science Review*, **68**, 525-536

Fiorina, M P, (1981) *Retrospective Voting in American National Elections*, New Haven: Yale University Press

Flanagan, S C, (1982) Changing Values in Advanced Industrial Societies: Inglehart's 'Silent Revolution' from the Perspective of Japanese Findings, *Comparative Political Studies*, **14**, 403-444

Francis, J G, and Payne, C, (1977) The Use of Logistic Linear Models in Political Science: the British Elections, 1964-70, *Political Methodology*, **4**, 233-70

Franklin, M N, (1982) Demographic Components in the Decline of British Class Voting 1964-79, *Electoral Studies*, **1**, 195-220

Franklin, M N, (1983) The Rise of Issue Voting in British Elections, *Strathclyde Papers on Government and Politics*, No 3 (second edition)

Franklin, M N, (1984) How the Decline of Class Voting Opened the Way to Radical Change in British Politics, *British Journal of Political Science*, **14**, 483-508

Franklin, M N, and Mughan, A, (1978) The Decline of Class Voting in Britain: Problems of Analysis and Interpretation, *The American Political Science Review*, **72**, 523-534

Garnsey, E, (1978) Women's Work and Theories of Class and Stratification, *Sociology*, **12**, 223-243

Garrahan, P, (1977) Housing, The Class Milieu and Middle-class Conservatism, *British Journal of Political Science*, **7**, 125-6

General Registrar Office London and Edinburgh, (1969) *Sample Census 1966: Great Britain: Economic Activity Tables: Part III*, London: HMSO

Gilbert, G N, (1981) *Modelling Society*, London: Allen and Unwin

Goldthorpe, J H, (1980) *Social Mobility and Class Structure in Modern Britain*, Oxford: Clarendon Press

Goldthorpe, J H, (1982) On the Service Class: its Formation and Future, *Social Class and the Division of Labour*, A Giddens and G Mackenzie, (eds), Cambridge: Cambridge University Press

Goldthorpe, J H, (1983) Women and Class Analysis: in Defence of the Conventional View, *Sociology*, **17**, 465-488

Goldthorpe, J H, and Hope, K, (1974) *The Social Grading of Occupations: A New Approach and Scale*, Oxford: Clarendon Press

Goldthorpe, J H, Lockwood, D, Bechhofer, F, and Platt, J, (1968) *The Affluent Worker: Political Attitudes and Behaviour*, Cambridge: Cambridge University Press

Goodhart, C A E, and Bhansali, R J, (1970) Political Economy, *Political Studies*, **28**, 43-106

Haddon, R, (1970) A Minority in a Welfare State, *New Atlantis*, **2**, 80-133

Halsey, A H, Heath, A F, and Ridge, J M, (1980) *Origins and Destinations: Family, Class and Education in Modern Britain*, Oxford: Clarendon Press

Hamnett, C, (1976) Social Change and Social Segregation in Inner London, 1961-1971, *Urban Studies*, **13**, 261-271

Hamnett, C, (1984) Housing the Two Nations: Socio-tenurial Polarisation in England and Wales, 1961-1981, *Urban Studies*, **21**, 389-405

Harris, R, and Seldon, A, (1979) *Over-ruled on Welfare*, London: Institute of Economic Affairs

Heath, A F, (1976) *Rational Choice and Social Exchange*, Cambridge: Cambridge University Press

Heath, A F, and Britten, N, (1984) Women's Jobs, *Sociology*, **18**, 475-490

Hibbs, D A, Jnr, (1982) Economic Outcomes and Political Support for British Governments among Occupational Classes: a Dynamic Analysis, *American Political Science Review*, **76**, 259-79

Himmelweit, H, Jaegar, M, and Stockdale, T, (1978) Memory for Past Vote: Implications of a Bias in Recall, *British Journal of Political Science*, **8**, 365-84

Himmelweit, H, Humphreys, P, Jaegar, M, and Katz, M, (1981) *How Voters Decide*, London: Academic Press

Hirsch, F, (1977) *Social Limits to Growth*, London: Routledge and Kegan Paul

Hobsbawm, E, (1981) The Forward March of Labour Halted?, *The Forward March of Labour Halted?*, M Jacques and F Mulhern, (eds), London: NLB; first published in *Marxism Today*, September 1978

Hyman, R, and Price, R, (eds) (1983) *The New Working Class? White Collar Workers and their Organisations*, London: Macmillan

Imber, V, and Todd, P, (1983) Public Expenditure: Definitions and Trends, *Economic Trends*, No 361, 138-151

Inglehart, R, (1971) The Silent Revolution in Europe: Intergenerational Change in Post-industrial Societies, *American Political Science Review*, **65**, 991-1017

Inglehart, R, (1977) *The Silent Revolution: Changing Values and Political Styles among Western Publics*, Princeton: Princeton University Press

Inglehart, R, (1981) Post-Materialism in an Environment of Insecurity, *American Political Science Review*, **75**, 880-900

Inglehart, R, (1982) Changing Values in Japan and the West, *Comparative Political Studies*, **14**, 445-479

Johnston, R J, (1983a) Class Location, Consumption Location, and the Geography of Voting in England, *Social Science Research*, **12**, 215-235

Johnston, R J, (1983b) The Neighbourhood Effect Won't Go Away: Observations on the Electoral Geography of England in the Light of Dunleavy's Critique, *Geoforum*, **14**, 161-168.

Joint Industry Working Party, (1981) *An Evaluation of Social Grade Validity*, London: The Market Research Society

Jowell, R, and Airey, C, (eds) (1984) *British Social Attitudes: the 1984 Report*, Aldershot: Gower

Kahan, M J, Butler, D E, and Stokes, D E, (1966) On the Analytical Division of Social Class, *British Journal of Sociology*, **17**, 123-130

Kelley, J, McAllister, I, and Mughan, A, (1982) The Changing Electoral Salience of Class: England, 1964-79, *Working Papers in Sociology*, Canberra: Australian National University, Institute of Advanced Studies

Kelley, J, McAllister, I, and Mughan, A, (1984) The Decline of Class Revisited:

Class and Party in England, 1964-1979 (Paper presented to the Annual Meetings of the American Sociological Association, San Antonio, 1984)

Kogan, D, and Kogan, M, (1983) *The Battle for the Labour Party, Second edition*, London: Fontana

Laver, M, (1984) On Party Policy, Polarisation and the Breaking of Moulds: the 1983 British Party Manifestos in Context, *Parliamentary Affairs*, **37**, 33-39

Lemieux, P, (1977) Political Issues and Liberal Support in the February 1974, British General Election, *Political Studies*, **25**, 323-342

Lipset, S M, (1960) *Political Man*, Garden City, N.Y: Doubleday

Lipset, S M, and Rokkan, S, (1967) Cleavage Structures, Party Systems and Voter Alignments: An Introduction, *Party Systems and Voter Alignments*, S M Lipset and S Rokkan, (eds), New York: Free Press

Mallet, S, (1963) *The New Working Class, Paris: Editions du Seuil*

Maslow, A H, (1954) *Motivation and Personality*, New York: Harper

McAllister, I, (1984) Housing, Tenure and Party Choice in Australia, Britain and the United States, *British Journal of Political Science*, **14**, 509-522

McKibbin, R, (1974) *The Evolution of the Labour Party*, London: Oxford University Press

Miller, W L, (1977) *Electoral Dynamics*, London: Macmillan

Miller, W L, (1978) Social Class and Party Choice in England: a New Analysis, *British Journal of Political Science*, **8**, 257-84

Miller, W L, (1981) *The End of British Politics?*, Oxford: Clarendon Press

Miller, W L, (1983) *The Social Survey Method in the Social and Political Sciences*, London: Francis Pinter

Miller, W L, (1984) There Was No Alternative: The British General Election of 1983, *Parliamentary Affairs*, **37**, 364-384

Monk, D, (1978) *Social Grading on the National Readership Survey*, fourth edition, London: Joint Industry Committee for National Readership Surveys

Morton-Williams, J, (1977) The Use of Verbal Interaction Coding for Evaluating a Questionnaire, *Social and Community Planning Research Methodological Working Paper No 6*

Musgrove, F, (1979) *School and the Social Order*, Chichester: John Wiley

Nicholson, R J, (1967) The Distribution of Personal Income, *Wealth, Income and Inequality*, A B Atkinson, (ed), Harmondsworth, Middx: Penguin

Office of Population Censuses and Surveys, (1970) *Classification of Occupations 1970*, London: HMSO

Office of Population Censuses and Surveys, (1980) *Classification of Occupations 1980*, London: HMSO

Office of Population Censuses and Surveys, (1981) *Census 1981: Definitions: Great Britain*, London: HMSO

Office of Population Censuses and Surveys/Registrar General Scotland, (1983) *Census 1981: National Report: Great Britain: Part 2*, London: HMSO

Parkin, F, (1968) *Middle Class Radicalism*, Manchester: Manchester University Press

Parkin, F, (1967) Working Class Conservatives: A Theory of Political Deviance, *British Journal of Sociology*, **18**, 278-290

Rallings, C S, (1975) Two Types of Middle-class Labour Voter?, *British Journal of Political Science*, **5**, 107-128

Reid, I, (1981) *Social Class Differences in Britain*, second edition, London: Grant McIntyre

Rex, J, and Moore, R, (1967) *Race, Community and Conflict*, London: Oxford University Press

Riker, W, and Ordeshook, P A, (1968) A Theory of the Calculus of Voting, *American Political Science Review*, **62**, 25-42

Roberts, K, Cook, F G, Clark, S C, and Semenoff, E, (1977) *The Fragmentary Class Structure*, London: Heinemann

Robertson, D, (1976) *A Theory of Party Competition*, London: John Wiley

Robertson, D, (1984) *Class and the British Electorate*, Oxford: Basil Blackwell

Rokeach, M, (1973) *The Nature of Human Values*, New York: The Free Press

Rose, R, (ed), (1976) *Studies in British Politics*, third edition, London: Macmillan

Rose, R, (1980) Class Does Not Equal Party: the Decline of a Model of British Voting, *Studies in Public Policy*, No 74, Glasgow: University of Strathclyde

Rose, R, (forthcoming) *Politics in England*, fourth edition, London: Faber

Routh, G, (1980) *Occupation and Pay in Great Britain 1906-79*, second edition, London: Macmillan

Sarlvik, B, and Crewe, I, (1983) *Decade of Dealignment – The Conservative Victory of 1979 and Electoral Trends in the 1970s*, Cambridge: Cambridge University Press

Saunders, P, (1978) Domestic Property and Social Class, *International Journal of Urban and Regional Research*, **2**, 233-251

Steed, M, (1974) The Results Analysed, *The British General Election of February 1974*, D Butler and D Kavanagh, London: Macmillan

Steed, M, (1978) The National Front Vote, *Parliamentary Affairs*, **31**, 282-293

Steed, M, (1979) The Liberal Party, *Multi-party Britain*, H M Drucker, (ed), Oxford: Martin Robertson

Stephenson, H, (1982) *Claret and Chips*, London: Michael Joseph

Taylor, P J, and Johnston, R J, (1979) *Geography of Elections*, London: Penguin

Taylor-Gooby, P, (1983) Legitimation Deficit, Public Opinion and the Welfare State, *Sociology*, **17**, 165-184

Taylor-Gooby, P, (1984) The Politics of Welfare: Public Attitudes and Behaviour (Paper presented at the Economic and Social Research Council, University of Bath, 1984)

The Times Guide to the House of Commons, (1974), London: Times Newspapers Limited

Todd, J, and Butcher, B, (1982) *Electoral Registration in 1981*, London: Office of Population Censuses and Surveys

Watson, W, (1964) Social Mobility and Social Class in Industrial Communities, *Closed Systems and Open Minds*, M Gluckman, and E Devons, (eds), London: Oliver and Boyd
Worcester, R M, (1983) Comment, *Electoral Studies*, **2**, 84
Wright, E O, (1979) *Class Structure and Income Determination*, New York: Academic Press

Index